WITTENBERG, REVISITED

A Polymorphous Critique
of Religion and Theology

Howard P. Kainz

UNIVERSITY
PRESS OF
AMERICA

BX
1751.2
.K28
1981

Library of Congress Catalog Card Number: **81-40729**

ACKNOWLEDGEMENTS

I began this book twenty years ago, and have drawn upon the help and wisdom of a number of people in the writing of it. I would like to thank in particular Tom Michaud, Louise Kirby and Ken Perszyk for their expert assistance in proofreading the manuscript; Brooke Barker and Laureen Panek for their assistance in preparing the final camera-ready printed version of the book; and Ken Hagen, Bert Thelen, S.J. and William Kelly, S.J. for reading and critiquing the book from a theological perspective and offering their suggestions (which were frequently incorporated).

"What I tell you in darkness, speak in the light. What you hear in private, proclaim from the housetops."

-- Matt. X, 27

TABLE OF CONTENTS

INTRODUCTION. 1

CHAPTER I: AN ECUMENICAL DISCUSSION WITH MARTIN LUTHER. 4

CHAPTER II: FORTY-ONE THESES ON THE CHURCH AND RELIGION
        IN GENERAL. 12
    A. Catholicism
        1A. Confession of sins should be replaced by
        reform. 14
        1B. But reform is often impossible without
        confession. 15
        2. The Church can transcend all times only by
        taking on current temporal political structures . . 16
        3. To have an effect on morals, the Church must
        withdraw from the sphere of morals. 18
        4. Protestantism's split with Catholicism
        necessitated Catholicism's emphasis on tradition
        over Scripture and authority over individual
        freedom. 20
        5. The church that is "one" is the church that
        unifies. 22
        6A. The way to create more saints is to abrogate
        the institution of sainthood. 23
        6B. A church that can't produce its own saints
        should import them. 25
        7A. "Communion" can be a hindrance to union with
        God. 27
        7B. Union with God may be impossible without
        communion (in the Catholic sense). 28
        8. The music and rituals of the Church must become
        both foreign and familiar. 29
        9. The most orthodox form of Thomism is non-Thomism. 31
        10. The claim of infallibility increases
        fallibility; the admission of fallibility creates
        relative infallibility. 32
    B. Christianity
        11. It is better not to proclaim the Gospel than to
        proclaim it outside of one's personal
        revelation. 36
        12. The split of Christianity and Judaism had the
        effect of making the Jews worldly and the Christians
        escapist. 37
        13. The ultimate goals of Communism can be
        attained only through Christianity; and vice-
        versa. 39
        14A. Private charity is at a maximum only when
        it is completely organized. 41
        14B. Organized charity can be effective only

to the extent that it is personalized and
non-systematic. 42
15. We can perceive the "true Christ" only if we come
to doubt that Jesus (historically) is the
Christ. 44
16. "Universal love" can only become a reality when
the enmity in the world is complete. 46
17. The final objective of the Church is to do
away with itself. 48
18A. Sin is the unconsciousness of sin. 50
18B. The consciousness of "sin" has no efficacy
without the consciousness of particular sins. 50
19. Sin in some sense was necessary to establish man
as an independent being. 51
C. Religion in General
20. One can convert others only by being converted. .54
21. "Natural religions" are the result of inner
revelation; revealed religions can be effective only
through correspondence to natural needs and insights.55
22. The supernatural is the truly natural. 57
23. Angels can approach us now only after some
wing-trimming. 58
24. Spiritual alienation can be dissipated only
if social alenation is overcome, and vice-versa. . . 60
25A. Laws in religion are in a certain sense
superfluous (or counterproductive) because
spontaneity is of the essence of religion. 62
25B. Laws are necessary in religion to inculcate
spontaneity of spirit. 63
26. Marxism is an alienated form of religion. 65
27. Belief in the afterlife is most effective
if it is vague. 66
28. Religious "self-surrender" and secular
"self-determination" are identical in essence. . . . 68
29. The most complete miracle would require the
complete perfection of science. 69
30. Religious toleration is at present the greatest
nemesis of religious unity. 71
D. God
31A. The logical conclusion of theism is atheism. . .74
31B. But the culmination of reflective atheism is
a return of theism. 74
32. God can only be our absolute "other" insofar
as he is our absolute self-identity. 76
33. God can only become present through His absence .77
34. God is a projection of the future of man; but
He must be present now, in order to be projected. .79
35. God is neither transcendent nor immanent but
a limiting case for both transcendence and

       immanence. 80
  E. Faith, Knowledge and Revelation
      36. Faith emerges only in the absence of knowledge. .82
      37. Faith can only exist in a "credibility gap". . . 84
      38. The dissolution of faith leads to the dissolution
      of knowledge. 86
      39. One who insists on seeing before believing will
      end up neither seeing nor believing. 87
      40. The primary "object" of faith is faith
      itself--that is, the belief in faith. 89
      41A. We can only understand the Scriptures by
      disregarding the literal meanings. 91
      41B. But the revelations of the Scriptures can become
      clear only through emphasis on the written word. . 91

CHAPTER III. PRIVATE INTERPRETATION OF THE SCRIPTURES. 93
  A. Greatness
      1. Matt. XXIII, 8 96
      2. Matt. XX, 26 97
      3. Gal. II, 11 99
      4. Matt. XXXIII, 4. 100
      5. John, XIV, 12. 101
      6.1 Cor. XII. 102
  B. Sex and Marriage
      1. 1 Tim. II, 12. 105
      2. Matt. XIX,6. 106
      3. Eph. V, 28. 107
      4. 1 Cor. VII, 9. 108
      5. Matt. V, 32. 110
      6. Matt. V, 28. 110
  C. God
      1. Acts XVII, 23ff 112
      2. Revelations IV, 8. 113
  D. Faith
      1. Luke XVI, 31. 114
      2. Rom. XIV, 23. 115
      3. James II, 26. 116
      4. Matt XVII, 20. 116
      5. Mark XI, 23. 118
  E. Prayer
      1. Matt. VII, 11 119
      2. Matt. XVIII, 20 120
  F. Suffering
      1. Matt. XI, 29-30 121
      2. Peter, 10 122
      3. Luke XIII, 4 123
  G. The Christian's Way of Life
      1. Rom. XII, 20 125
      2. 1 Cor. VI, 7 126
      3. 1 John II, 15 127

        4. Matt. V, 44 128
        5. The Epistle of Paul to Philemon 129
  H. Evangelization
        1. Acts II, 4-6 132
        2. Luke IX, 5 133
        3. 1 Cor. IX, 18 134
        4. 2 John, 10 136
        5. Luke XXII, 35 137
        6. 1 Tim. V, 17 139
  I. Mystical Body
        1. Luke II, 35 141
        2. 1 Cor. XII, 26-27 142
  J. End of the World
        1. Mark XIII, 32 144
        2. James V, 7-8 145

CHAPTER IV: THE REVOLUTION VERSUS THE AFTERLIFE: A CHRISTIAN
REVOLUTIONARY BUTTONHOLES A REVOLUTIONARY THEORETICIAN 147

CHAPTER V: AN ECCLESIASTICAL COMEDY 164
    Introduction 164
  A. Via purgativa
        1. The ex-priest 169
        2. The missionary 173
        3. The theologian 176
  B. Via illuminativa
        4. The journalist 182
        5. The revolutionary 186
        6. The saint 190
  C. Via unitiva
        7. The last Pope, 1999 A.D. 196
        8. Sister Superior in the new dispensation 201
        9. The Pentecostalist holdout 204
  D. The great ecumenical demonstration 208

NOTES 213

INTRODUCTION

The town of Wittenberg might be a Mecca for pilgrimage and true Protestant piety in our day, if it were not situated at some distance on the other side of the Iron Curtain. The East German government still allows some tourism to those who have the proper visas, and it is still possible to view the church door on which Martin Luther was supposed to have posted his 95 theses[1], and thus taken the decisive step that ultimately led to what we call the "Protestant Reformation." However, the atmosphere is obviously lacking for dramatic, colorful outpourings or enthusiastic celebrations of the historical and spiritual importance of the happenings on All Saints' Eve at the castle church in Wittenberg in 1517.

It might be worthwhile to reflect on the significance of this landmark of Western Christendom now situated in the heart of an anti-Christian communist state:

To the Roman Catholic, it will no doubt seem ironical that what became a symbol of the Protestant resistance to "Roman" ecclesiastical authority should now be situated at the center of a heightened secular authority-- the same secular authority that in another form in bygone days helped to give the necessary boost at the proper time to Luther, saving him from execution as a heretic, fostering and defending his "new religion" as it began to gather momentum.

The Catholic may find it equally ironic that a leading landmark in the evolution of the importance of "individual conscience" in the Western world, should now be set in the context of a repressive atmosphere in which a few individuals maintain ideological supervision of, and sanctions against, the consciences of many.

To the Protestant, the symbolism would not appear ironical. There is no irony in the fact that Christian witness finds itself in bondage. This was predicted in a clear and straightforward way in the Gospels, and the bondage of the Church in the time of Jesus was simply repeated, with certain variations, in the time of Paul, the Roman Empire, and Luther. Other variations are taking place in our own time.

To the Marxist, it may seem quite fitting that Luther's enterprise of demythologizing ecclesiastical authority in order to restore Scripture as the source

of religious autnority, should eventually be followed
by the further demythologization of the religious
beliefs in Scripture, so that, emancipated from
religious illusion, we may give our full and undivided
attention to the alienated condition of man (the
alienation which had given rise to the mythical
religious projections of an afterlife and heavenly
salvation, for the oppressed masses for whom this
present life was miserable and unfulfilling).

To the non-Christian Proponent of Western
Democracy, it may appear merely unfortunate that the
Lutheran shrine should now find itself in such
inauspicious surroundings. For, after all, Martin
Luther was a pathfinder in the religious sphere, and
his rejection of arbitrary ecclesiastical authority did
help lead ideologically to the political emancipation,
beginning with the English (Whig) Revolution, of men
from arbitrary and tyrannical governments.

*   *   *   *

The following chapters are not concerned
exclusively with the stand taken by Martin
Luther--whether at Wittenberg, Augsburg, or the Diet of
Worms. (The spirit of Luther is not recaptured merely
by applying Lutheran tenets to modern circumstances;
just as the spirit of Thomas Aquinas cannot be
recaptured by applying and updating the principles of
Thomism. See Thesis #9 infra.) Rather, Wittenberg and
its aftermath is taken as a world-historical exemplar
of religious reform/revolution, a starting point from
which we may derive some stimulation, some inspiration
for extending the horizons of religious
reform/revolution in our day. Accordingly, while the
first chapter is devoted to a direct exploration of
some of the far-reaching effects of the events which
took place at Wittenberg, succeeding chapters are
devoted to suggesting some directions which religious
and theological reform may take now, in our
world--sometimes using themes or motifs from the
Lutheran prototypes.

A word about methodology: Religious positions and
religious conclusions are hardly ever the result of
straightforward dispassionate logical reasoning based
on facts. So I have had my doubts as to whether that
straightforward prose style which is eminently logical
and seems eminently suited to the discussion of
Newtonian scientific realities, is as serviceable for
the discussion and critique of religious truths. On

the supposition that there may be some validity in
McLuhan's well-known maxim that "the medium is the
message," I have decided to revive some well-known
classical methodologies for the critique of religion:
Plato's use of philosophical dialogue to explore the
meaning of religion, e.g. in his _Euthyphro_ (compare
Chapters One and Four below); Dante's excursus on
infernal and supernal hierarchies in the _Divine Comedy_,
which, of course, was not just fiction, but a critique
of the religiously-charged socio-political atmosphere
of mediaeval man (cp. Chapter Five below); Luther's 95
"theses," a group of deliberately provocative
statements intended to jar men into rethinking some
basic religious truths (cp. Chapter Two below); and
Calvin's commentaries on Scripture used as a Protestant
instrument for criticizing prevailing religious mores
and doctrines and the conventional "Romanist"
interpretation of the Gospel (cp. Chapter Three below).

CHAPTER I

AN ECUMENICAL DISCUSSION WITH MARTIN LUTHER

Time: the 1530's

FRATER ORTHODOXUS: After much time and many battles, your separation from the Roman Church is now complete. "Lutheranism" has attained a great following in your own country, and is beginning to have an effect on other countries also. Have you ever had any second thoughts about approving such a complete rupture with the Church of Rome?

LUTHER: You make it sound as if we revolted against the papists. We never revolted against them. It was the other way around! Long before we had blown our trumpets, they had revolted against Christ. It was quite in keeping with their peevish and supercilious arrogance that they should react the way they did when we made some initial efforts to reestablish the authority of Christ.

FRATER ORTHODOXUS: You have been accused of trying to establish your own authority in place of that of the Pope.

LUTHER: Anyone who tries to establish the Word of God will get reactions like that from the Philistines. Isaiah and Jeremiah were not exactly welcomed with open arms by the ruling powers.

FRATER ORTHODOXUS: Do you think that you have been exercising the role of a prophet in recent decades?

LUTHER: I am no prophet. Just a participant in the priesthood of Christ, as are all other Christians. I tried to preach the Gospel of Christ, and those who were preaching their own gospel took offense at this.

FRATER ORTHODOXUS: You speak of the "Gospel of Christ" as if it were something easily distinguishable from imitations or approximations. In fact, is it not quite difficult to be sure which is the Gospel of Christ? How can we identify it?

LUTHER: "Where the body is, there will the eagles gather." Where you find a consensus among the body of believers about the Gospel, you need look no further. It is their possession, it is in their keeping.

FRATER ORTHODOXUS: And how can one determine who the believing Christians are? You will tell me that they are "those who adhere to the Gospel." And then we will have a classic <u>circulus vitiosus</u>.

LUTHER: It is not as hard as you think to determine where the true Christians are. All you need do is bypass the ecclesiastical power-mongers, the ravenous and self-serving priests and monks, the sentimental and superstitious followers who try to work magic with relics and statues and mumbo-jumbo-- and as you walk on a little bit further you will catch sight of scattered groups of people who listen to the Word of God and try to make it a part of their life without being tempted into dramatic displays or sectarian rivalries.

FRATER ORTHODOXUS: I think you make it sound too simple. At least you are speaking of the "Gospel" in a very general sense, while I would like to know more specifically what is included in the Gospel. You yourself seem to have had difficulty in making this determination. For example, you have expressed doubt about certain books of the Bible--such as the Epistle of James--which many would include under the heading of the "Gospel."

LUTHER: The Gospel cannot contradict itself. Throughout the Gospel we are told that man is justified by faith in God, not by works. And then the Epistle of James reverses the message, and begins speaking about "works" again. There may be ingenious ways of interpreting this Epistle to bring it into harmony with the Gospel. But, for myself, I think that that Epistle is easily misunderstood and can work against the spirit of Christ which emphasizes grace, by which we are imbued with the justice of God.

FRATER ORTHODOXUS: You place so much emphasis on the idea of "justification by faith alone." Isn't this just one of the "messages" of the Gospel? Are there not other messages equally important--love of neighbor, prayer, the building up of the kingdom of God on earth?

LUTHER: All of these other recommendations of the New Testament can lead to scrupulosity, superficiality or selfishness unless they are vivified by the central theme--justification by faith, which supplies their true context.

FRATER ORTHODOXUS: This is your interpretation of the Gospel's "central theme." Do you want us to adhere to the Gospel, or to your interpretation?

LUTHER: The Gospel must be interpreted. An uninterpreted Gospel is similar to an untranslated

Gospel: if it has not been interpreted with a view to the needs of the people of God in the world in which they happen to be living, it might just as well be couched in a foreign and inaccessible language. The true spirit of the Gospel is revealed precisely in its true interpretation.

FRATER ORTHODOXUS: The Roman Church has always agreed that interpretation is of the utmost importance. But it emphasizes an "objective" interpretation: in order to find the true meaning of the Gospel, one must test possible meanings against the criteria long-established in the ecclesiastical community and continuously maintained through the ages.

LUTHER: The Roman Church, as usual, has completely reversed things. It should be the other way around: the traditions and customs of the "Church" should be tested against the criteria of the Gospel, interpreted in accord with the grace and faith of the believing Christian. What is indifferent or inimical to this spirit of faith should be rejected--no matter how long and loudly it has been ensconced in traditions.

FRATER ORTHODOXUS: You seem to be setting up a very subjective criterion for determining Christian truth.

LUTHER: Where is the kingdom of Christ, if not in the inwardness of our faith? Do you expect to find it in the palaces of Cardinals, in the cathedrals built with revenue from the sale of indulgences, in the writings and rituals of obsequious monks?

FRATER ORTHODOXUS: No. But if every "believing Christian" is just as good an interpreter of the Scriptures, if there is no official or authoritative voice to guarantee some objective standards, one is paving the way for endless debate and sectarian chaos. Take the Anabaptists as a case in point. If I follow their "private interpretation" of the Scriptures, I become a revolutionary, destroying traditional institutions for the sake of establishing a communistic "kingdom of God."

LUTHER: The Anabaptists are lunatics. One should not remove the Bible from people with common sense, simply because of the possibility that a few demented idiots will misuse and misconstrue it.

FRATER ORTHODOXUS: In your opinion, is it permissible to forcibly restrain such "lunatics," to keep them from implementing their own subjective interpretation of the Bible?

LUTHER: That may not even be necessary. Amidst all the ranting and raving of the lunatics, the good sense of God's people will prevail. They will turn the proper "face" to them--their hind end. If the mischief-makers become too troublesome, it may be necessary for Christian rulers to step in to reestablish order by force.

FRATER ORTHODOXUS: In relying on the power of "Christian rulers," aren't you substituting a new and possibly arbitrary and dangerous power for that papal power which you find so objectionable in the Roman Church?

LUTHER: I am not introducing any "new" power. The Gospel tells us quite clearly and frequently enough to be subject to the so-called "secular" authorities. Unlike the Romanist clowns, these "secular" authorities have legitimate power. It is simply a _fact_ that the power of this world, which Christians inhabit, resides in such men. They contrast rather sharply, I think, with the supposed "servants of the servants of God" in Rome who cling nervously to their unwarranted honors and ill-gotten benefices, so that they may continue _in aeternum_ to carry out their intrigues and ever more incompetent administration of the Church.

FRATER ORTHODOXUS: I'm sure you will admit the possibility that a strong Christian prince or king may end up backing the wrong religion? Would you say that a Christian should be obedient to a secular authority when he is sure that that secular authority is "on the wrong side"?

LUTHER: There is only one Christian religion. . . . Disputes may arise, secular leaders may have to oppose other leaders. Christians have no master-strategy for assuring that they will win out. But they have the assurance of Christ that their faith will triumph. And it is _through_ their faith that they will triumph--not through any special human talent or ingenuity, or because they happen to be allied with the strongest prince. Remember that it is the perverted alliance with merely human power that has been largely responsible for the spectacle of the modern Roman Babylon.

FRATER ORTHODOXUS: You seem willing to relegate that Roman Church completely to the devil. Don't you think there are any conditions under which some form of union between the Roman Church and your "evangelical" Christians could be maintained?

LUTHER: I repeat, Christians _are_ in unity. We are showing this every day. One does not have to ally oneself with autocratic popes or effeminate sycophants in the Roman curia in order to perpetuate Christian unity. This would be to compromise the Word of God, to water it down. "God's word is not to be restrained."

FRATER ORTHODOXUS: With or without the Roman curia, you "evangelicals" surely can't expect to maintain a strong and efficacious Christian unity without leaders, official leaders.

LUTHER: Yes, but leaders who do not depend on tyranny or ill-gotten goods for power. Christ relied on none of this and did quite well, through the power of the Word.

FRATER ORTHODOXUS: You seem to take a very hard and uncompromising position regarding the Roman Church. A long time ago, when you first published your ninety-five theses, you considered yourself a loyal member of that Church. You were hoping that proponents of opposing views would come to debate with you, and you no doubt would have been willing to compromise, if Tetzel or perhaps some more gifted and intelligent opponent had come to debate with you. But the debate never took place. Do you think you might have gravitated toward a one-sided position because of lack of constructive opposition?

LUTHER: You are quite wrong. It is true that no one showed up for the particular academic debate that I proposed in the Fall of 1517. But the debate has, subsequently, taken place. It is still taking place. Many divergent voices are still discussing the points which began to be raised by my theses. Where intelligent men have worthy ideas to offer, we are willing to compromise. But when snivelling idiots come giving orders to us as if we were schoolchildren, and spelling out for us what we should believe, we rightly ignore them and proceed with equanimity on the path we have chosen.

FRATER ORTHODOXUS: Then you see no chance for compromise with the Roman Church?

LUTHER: At the Diet of Augsburg the Romanists were willing to offer me all sorts of compromises--a married clergy, release from the jurisdiction of bishops, communion with wine as well as with bread, and so on and so on. My friend, Melanchthon, was interested in negotiating with them. But I never held out much hope for such negotiations. For the Romanists overlooked and continued to overlook the main points: they must give up their arbitrary sham of papal power, put off their airs and their finery, and abandon their indulgences and man-made "sacraments," and their hierarchical priesthood. If they did this, no negotiations would be necessary. Unity would be a fact. But short of this, no negotiation can be meaningful.

FRATER ORTHODOXUS: Aren't you asking for quite a bit? Are you yourself willing to give up nothing for the sake of unity, while expecting such thoroughgoing sacrifices from them?

LUTHER: You are talking the language of secular diplomacy. In the Christian religion, it's not a matter of quid pro quo agreements, redistribution of power, redefinition of jurisdictions, etc. It's a matter of keeping the Word of God in honor. And in this regard we could even say that we have already given quite a bit to the Roman Church.

FRATER ORTHODOXUS: What do you mean?

LUTHER: We've given them the Scriptures. Before our challenge to the Romanists in Wittenberg, there was apathy about Scripture in most elements of the Roman Church. They were more interested in canon laws, papal pronouncements, Aristotle and scholastic philosophy. However, in the last few decades there has been a general awakening of interest in Scripture in all segments of society. Even the Roman priests, for whatever motives, have begun to try to preach the Gospel more often than they preach indulgences and other nonsense. So I feel we have done much for them, and for the people under their control. They should strike a papal medal in our honor, rather than trying to devise new stratagems for getting us "back into the fold."

FRATER ORTHODOXUS: You seem to have a very spiritualistic idea of Christian unity. It is obvious that Christian unity must be based on faith in the Word. But "the Word was made flesh." There must be visible expressions of this spiritual unity. But at present we are faced with two churches, each flying the banner of Christian unity--the Roman Church and the Evangelicals. If this is confusing to the believer, how confusing it must be to the unbeliever. How is one to know where to find the Church of Christ?

LUTHER: The way to find the Church of Christ is indicated quite clearly in the New Testament. First of

all, you won't find it among the self-righteous
Pharisees but among those who acknowledge that they are
sinners before God. Secondly, you must look for those
who are baptized and come together to hear the Word of
God in simplicity and humility, and to commemorate the
Lord's Supper without trying to transform it into a
pagan sacrifice. Even a disenchanted Romanist, who is
used to all kinds of externals, should be able to
locate the Church of God if he searches for those few
simple signs.

FRATER ORTHODOXUS: Doesn't it seem suspicious
to you that, at this moment of history, we should have
to begin to overthrow all the traditions and structures
that have been built up over the centuries, and begin
anew? Do you really feel there is so little worth
salvaging in the Church that used to be--the
hierarchical Church?

LUTHER: We can adopt some of the buildings, the
rituals, the music, the customs of the past. We can
make use of the insights of Augustine and the other
Fathers, where they have rightly expounded the Word of
God. Our freedom as Christians allows us to do this.
But to perpetuate the power of craven Italians and
their confederates was never part of Christ's plan.
You find nothing about it in the Gospel. Like the
tower of Babel, it must be destroyed, and its
destruction will be a lasting testimony against brazen
human pride. At some time in the future when all these
contrived appurtenances of power have crumbled, men
will see that these pseudo-problems about "Christian
unity" will solve themselves, without any special
negotiations being necessary. Christians will
recognize one another! even those Christians who have
just been rescued from captivity.

FRATER ORTHODOXUS: I can tell from our
conversation that you do not consider yourself a
revolutionary. Would you call yourself a reformer?

LUTHER: Perhaps, in one sense. I brought certain
perfidies and prevarications of the leaders of the
so-called Church of Christ out into the open; I put
them on public display for all the people to see. Now
they find it much more difficult to engage in selling
indulgences and bishoprics, and they have to think of
other things to say besides "the Pope says this," and
"the Pope says that." But in a more important sense,
God is the reformer. He awaits the proper time, then
gives men grace and calls them to faith. Once called

to faith, they ally themselves with others in mutual
reverence for God's Word; and they consign those
faithless imposters, who wish to busy themselves only
with sanctimonious and unprofitable "works," to their
own leader--the devil. This is the essence of reform.
It consists of God's work on the hearts of men.

CHAPTER II

FORTY-ONE THESES ON THE CHURCH
AND ON RELIGION IN GENERAL

Note: It is no longer the literary fashion to develop
one's ideas in the form of various "theses."   Perhaps
one reason for this is that now, with the coming of the
age of science, the "hypothesis" has the connotation of
a tentative statement of the way things are, subject to
revision if the facts turn out differently than the
hypothesis envisages. A thesis, on the other hand,
sometimes has the connotation of a dogmatic statement,
demonstrable on "a priori" grounds without any direct
appeal to experience being necessary. This connotation
derives   from   the uses of scholastic philosophy;
textbooks in   scholastic   philosophy traditionally
proceeded to develop themes in the form of theses which
were demonstrated, along with their corollaries.

For Martin Luther, "thesis" did not have this hard
and dogmatic connotation.   He made it quite clear in
many places that most of his ninety- five theses were
simply proposed subjects for disputation, and subject
to revision or reformulation. In a sense, they were
similar to what we call "hypotheses"--except that they
were in a non-scientific area of discourse. From the
reactions which the theses elicited, however, we may
surmise that Church authorities at that time did not
view them as tentative, hesitant or revisable
statements, but rather as dogmatic assertions.

It is interesting to note that Luther's confrere,
Melanchthon, refers to Luther's theses as "paradoxical
sentences." As regards the majority of the ninety-five
theses of 1517, it is not readily apparent why
Melanchthon would refer to them as "paradoxes" (i.e.
apparent self-contradictions which are really not
contradictory).   A few of the theses are somewhat
paradoxical: e.g. the second and third theses, which
state that the Gospel's invitation to penance refers
neither to external penance, nor to mere inner
repentance; the seventh thesis, which states that God
does not remit guilt unless guilt is already remitted
by the priest; the fifteenth thesis, which states that
the fear of punishment felt by the souls in purgatory

is itself their greatest punishment. But for the most part the theses are paradoxes only in the widest sense, i.e. insofar as they are striking statements, which in many cases contradict opinions that are commonly held.

The following forty-one theses utilize paradox systematically, and in more explicit form. It is the belief of the author that paradox is a particularly apt mode of expression for the truths of religion, insofar as it brings into focus some of the mutually contradictory currents in human life. It also seems to be a fact that straightforward theological affirmations often seem to produce paradoxes when subjected to philosophical analysis, as one author has recently pointed out[2]. And, as is well known, paradox is frequently found in the Bible (e.g. Christ tells us that one who saves his life will lose it, that the last shall be first, that it is better to give than to receive) as well as in the scriptures of Eastern religions. So there seem to be sufficient grounds to warrant an experimental use of paradox for developing certain religious topics or problem areas. It should be emphasized, however, that the paradoxes that follow--as was also the case with Luther's theses--are to be taken largely as tentative statements, subject to debate and retraction or revision.

The paradoxical theses will be developed in the following order: 1) theses about the Catholic Church; 2). . . about Christianity in general; 3). . . about religion in general; a) miscellaneous topics; b) God; c) faith, knowledge and Scriptures.

A. Catholicism

1A. Confession of sins should be replaced by reform. .

The "sacrament of penance" used to be a relatively
simple and straightforward thing in the 1950's: There
were fairly well-defined categories and subcategories
of sins--some serious, some less serious.   One went
into the confessional box on Saturdays frequently or
infrequently, depending on his fervor; went through a
list of his personal sins for the priest; received a
"penance" usually consisting of a few prescribed
prayers to say; sometimes received some admonitions or
instructions; and left the confessional, very often
with the conviction that the "slate had been cleared"
and he was starting anew.
Now all this is changed: Theologians are no
longer sure what constitutes a "sin" and the neat
categories of yesteryear have fallen by the wayside.
There has also come the realization that for one to
confess something that is not a sin or is just a
manifestation of weakness or sickness may be bad for
the penitent, resulting in scrupulosity, frustration,
depression, etc.   Then finally, doubts about the nature
of the sacrament--whether it should be public or
private, formal or informal--have crept in, and more
general doubts have arisen about the authority of the
Church, and in particular the authority of priests to
forgive sins with a few ritualistic words.   For
whatever reason, the use of the confessional by
Catholics has dropped off sharply during the last two
decades.
There seems to be no concrete evidence that the
morality or spirituality of Catholics has worsened as a
result.   In fact, one can see possibly beneficial
developments resulting from this trend: After all, if
I really offend my neighbor, it is no doubt much more
salutary and constructive for me to apologize or
better, to make amends to my neighbor, than to attain a
feeling of exoneration by merely telling a priest.   In
fact, it is to be feared that, with most "sins," the
mechanical recital of sins to the priest could be
simply an example of the "way of the flesh"--offering
one an excuse for failing to take constructive steps to
become reconciled with the person one has offended.

If the "sacrament of penance" meant that a person with a really troubled conscience found an adequately trained confessor who could help him, and went to him periodically for advice and consolation, the confessional might rival the psychoanalyst's couch in effectiveness in certain kinds of cases. But to step into a dark box and mechanically recite a litany of sins in anonymity to whoever happened to be listening, in order to receive a blessing, certainly never did anyone any good, and smacks of magic rather than religion.

1B. . . but reform is often impossible without confession.

> The maintenance of secrets acts like a psychic poison which alienates their possessor from the community. In small doses, this poison may actually be a priceless remedy, even an essential preliminary to the differentiation of the individual. . .As is well known, the many ancient mystery cults with their secret rituals served this instinct for differentiation. Even the Christian sacraments were looked upon as mysteries in the early Church (e.g. Baptism). . . However beneficial a secret shared with several persons may be, a merely private secret has destructive effect. It resembles a burden of guilt which cuts off the unfortunate possessor from communion with his fellow-beings. --Carl Jung, <u>Modern Man in Search of a Soul</u>, Ch. II.

The above quotation refers primarily to unconscious secrets, the secrets repressed long ago into the hidden recesses of one's psyche, and later emerging in untoward and uncontrollable ways to haunt their possessor. Sigmund Freud in his psychological theories had pointed out how a burden of repressed guilt breaks out in devastating ways in many mental disorders; and Jung, a disciple of Freud, takes a similar position in the presentation of his own psychoanalytic theories.

However, the principle applies also to consciously guarded secrets: If I have thoughts or have done

something that sharply contradicts the tenets of my own
conscience; if I have done something, or think I have
done something, that is strongly disapproved by
society-at-large; the result may be persistent remorse
or extreme shame; and my remorse or shame may induce me
to so conceal my "sin" from the rest of society that I
must in effect make constant efforts to show only one
side of my personality, or to deal only with those
members of society who are least likely to suspect my
sin. Such contrived efforts may not only cause
psychological problems, but may also serve to cut me
off from my fellow man, from the community. If love
and communion is one of the central messages of
Christianity, one would have to agree that a person in
this uncommunicative stance would suffer spiritual
detriment--a condition that might at least begin to
reverse itself if that person were to make confession
of his sin to the priest in confession, who, with a
guarantee of full confidentiality, would be able to
offer advice, put exaggerated or completely unwarranted
guilt into perspective, and perhaps point the direction
toward reconciliation, mental and otherwise, with
society.

Going beyond Jung's principle enunciated above, we
might also make the following observation: Some men
avoid the ravages of conscience or the disapprobation
of society at large, by allying themselves only with a
selected coterie--those who are engaged in similar
disapproved activities or who are less discriminate in
their moral sensitivities. Such men are also cut off
from community in a wider sense, and could benefit from
an institution like confession in which the confessor,
for them, would represent that "other" element of
society; and by a constructive encounter with one such
representative the path to further constructive and
wider encounters may begin to be revealed.

2. The Church can transcend all times only by taking
    on current political structures

"Thou art Peter and upon this rock I will build my
Church, and the gates of hell shall not prevail against
it." (Matt. XVI, 18)

The Catholic Church looks to these and other words of Christ for proof and assurance that it is a perpetual institution, destined to remain impregnable until the end of time. As if to perpetuate this image, certain atavisms are adopted: church officials wearing garb from ancient times; still using a dead language, in some cases; repeating rituals whose sources are obscure and whose present meanings are only conjectural. Included in this list of atavisms would be the hierarchical semi-monarchical structure of the Roman Catholic Church. Although there is a semblance of republicanism in the election of the Pope by the college of Cardinals, it is quite clear that,once elected, the Pope exercises an authority that is quite autocratic and unchecked by any parliamentary system, popular referendum, etc. This was also illustrated under Paul VI in the promulgation of the uncontestable decisions of the Encyclical Humanae Vitae forbidding artificial contraception--despite a majority opinion to the contrary, among papal advisors.

Although clinging to styles of garb and traditions of the past may be relatively harmless, the maintenance of monarchical or autocratic jurisdictional structures may be absolutely counter-productive in a democratic or semi-democratic society. The message of a person, or of a church, is proclaimed not just by word, but by gestures, habits and other inarticulate devices. If I wish to persuade people in another country to adopt a certain way of life, it matters little that I speak to them in their own language, if at the same time I give evidence of certain habits or customs which are completely foreign to their value system. I am and will remain a foreigner to them. They may make use of me for their own purposes, but they will never be genuinely persuaded by my message (unless, in isolated cases, they are absolutely alienated from their own way of life, and willing to identify with anything sufficiently "foreign"). The point is that, when, after centuries of social and political evolution, a great part of the world has progressed to democratic or quasi-democratic political structures, those who preach a religious message "from behind" the pulpit of other political structures must necessarily seem unenlightened and unconvincing. It is relatively easy to bring about a separation between church and state in the constitution of a country. It is impossible to bring about a peaceable cleavage in the mind, such that one accepts democratic structures in his secular life, and believes in static hierarchies in his religious life. The result may not be mental disease, but it must certainly be an unhealthy separation of the two aspects of life.

It is ironic that in the early Christian Church the belief was prevalent that the "voice of the people was the voice of God," and that bishops were commonly elected by the people. These and other Christian traditions have been interpreted by some philosophers as seminal harbingers of democracy. Now, however, when democracy is becoming a fact in more and more places, we hear the claim that the church is not democratic because it is "changeless." Strange words, coming from strange-sounding voices!

3. **To have an effect on morals, the Church must withdraw from the sphere of morals**

This thesis applies to Protestantism as well as Catholicism. But the problem has become more explicit and well-defined in the Catholic Church.

One of the most recent examples of an attempt by the Catholic Church to influence morals by an overt pronouncement was the Encyclical Humanae vitae regarding birth control. This Encyclical reiterated the traditional stand of the Church that any use of artificial contraceptives was immoral. This stand was backed up by various arguments, philosophical and theological.

It is interesting to note that this Encyclical was issued at a time when various groups were petitioning the Pope to clarify the position of the Church on other moral issues--for example, the question of the right of a large country to intervene with massive force in a civil war in another country (such as Vietnam) to influence the outcome. But the Church does not make official pronouncements about matters pertaining to political and social ethics. In some cases, the reason for this may be the extreme complexity of the issues involved.

As a matter of fact, the only definite, unambiguous ethical positions taken by the Church have been in the sphere of sexual morality--birth control,

abortion, divorce. Rather than trying to rush to
interpret this from a Freudian perspective, we should
reflect that it is a common denominator in many of the
world's religions--Hinduism, Judaism, and Buddhism as
well as Christianity--to make restrictions regarding
sexual matters. The motive for this seems to be the
supposition that excessive or unregulated involvement
in sexual pleasure will hinder one's attainment of
"spiritual perfection"-- a goal which is defined in
different ways in different religions. Thus certain
prohibitions are enunciated --prohibitions which are
relatively strict in proportion to the degree of
perfection that the disciple wishes to attain. The
prohibitions essentially take the form of a
hypothetical imperative: "If you wish to attain a
higher degree of ascetical or mystical perfection, you
should avoid doing such and such." In this form it is
a counsel, appealing to the spontaneous good will of
believers who hear it.

If a religion tries to spell out such counsels in
too great detail, it runs the risk of destroying the
spontaneity and voluntary collusion of wills that seems
to be one of the essential aspects of religion; and we
end up with the classical return to the emphasis on
"works," rather than faith, which so disturbed Martin
Luther in the 16th century. In trying to regulate a
matter like birth control, a kind of <u>reductio ad
absurdum</u> can easily take place, if one tries
to enunciate in legalistic fashion just how the ascetic
recommendations should take place for all classes of
people--potent and impotent, fertile and infertile, men
who come home from work every day and men whose work
involves constant travel, women who menstruate
regularly and those whose rhythms are unpredictable.
In such vicissitudes one must observe that the good
sense of a religion may be judged partially on the
basis of how much it is willing to trust to the good
sense of its adherents.

Because of the traditional association of religion
and morality, some religionists feel that if they cease
to make such explicit ethical rules, the cause of
morality will suffer. Past history would lead us to
believe otherwise. There was a time when the intimate
conjunction of the Christian religion and political
powers was thought to be necessary. The separation of
Church and state took place, and religion was not
appreciably weakened. There was a time when the Church

claimed authority over the domain of science. Science
was emancipated and flourished for the first time. A
similar emancipation has taken place in the case of
speculative philosophy (including speculative ethics)
which, until the time of Descartes, had been bound up
with theology. If the final "emancipation" takes
place--the emancipation of practical ethics from the
domain of religion--should we expect this to bring
about the deterioration of practical ethics or
religion? This could happen, but indications from the
past would lead us to believe that practical ethics
might flourish as a result, and religion, with its
essential concerns and primary domain better-defined,
might grow in stature and respect and influence (even,
indirectly, influence on morals).

4.   Protestantism's split with Catholicism
      necessitated Catholicism's emphasis on tradition
      over Scripture and authority over individual
      freedom

The discussion about the relative priority and
importance of Scripture and church tradition had been
taking place long before the Protestant Reformation.
During Martin Luther's lifetime, the swing had been in
favor of tradition, but opposing views, favoring the
primacy of Scripture, were also represented within the
Catholic Church. A similar observation might be made
with regard to the question of the relative priority of
authority and of individual freedom. Representatives
of both "causes" could be found within the Catholic
Church. But it should be kept in mind that the
movement toward individual freedom was itself just a
nascent effort, conditioned by political and social
changes then taking place, and also, some say, by the
advent of printing, which made individual assimilation
of ideas both feasible and popular.

Since all the values considered here--adherence to
Scripture, adherence to tradition, individual freedom,
ecclesiastical authority--were held in honor by society
at large, the effect of Protestantism's emphasis on
Scripture and ecclesiastical freedom was to polarize
Christianity. If one of the values, e.g. tradition,
had been held in disfavor by large segments of society,
those who championed opposite values would have been

simply victorious, as far as their strength in the
social sphere was concerned. But this was not the
case. In fact, the importance of the opposite values
was recognized even by those who opposed them. The
Protestant reformers tried to make it quite clear that
they were not completely rejecting tradition and the
value of authority, while the Catholic Church, on the
other hand, tried to show that man's freedom was
enhanced by submission to authority and that
ecclesiastical tradition was necessary for the guidance
of individual Scripture interpretation. Therefore,
when Luther "took his stand" in favor of Scripture and
freedom, polarization took place. Other developments
might have taken place: In a great show of power, the
Roman Church might have effectively silenced Luther and
those with similar ideas; compromise might have taken
place, involving a liberal redefinition of Papal power,
etc.; or Luther might have been unable to find powerful
and resourceful sympathizers to support his cause. But
none of these things did take place. Rather, those who
felt as strongly as Luther about the importance of
Scripture or individual freedom now had a place to go.
They need not repress their preferences any longer;
there was a growing contingent of honorable men with
whom they could ally themselves. On the other
hand--and this is important-- those in the Roman Church
who preferred values such as tradition and authority
now were under the necessity of defending these values.
Previously they may have felt a simple preference.
Now, in the face of a substantial challenge from their
opposition, they must take a strong stand, close their
flanks, solidify their forces. This solidification
took place notably in the Council of Trent, in which
the priority of Tradition over Scripture was definitely
proclaimed; and in the First Vatican Council, in which
the infallibility of Papal authority was finally made
explicit. In each case, the proclamation was
anticlimactic, to say the least. Any members of the
Council of Trent who felt really strongly about
priority of Scripture would have already gone over to
the side of the reformers; anyone at the first Vatican
Council who was really adamant about individual freedom
would never have found himself in the midst of the
bishops and cardinals making the decisions there. Such
are the effects of polarization.

5. The church that is "one" is the church that unifies

There is a dogmatic tradition in the Catholic Church that it possesses the four "marks" of the true Church of Christ--it is "one, holy, universal, and apostolic." The fact that these four marks should be the signs of the existence of the "true" Christian Church is variously demonstrated from Scripture and tradition. In the case of "unity," the theologians or apologists can easily point to Christ's prayer at the Last Supper, "I have prayed for them that they may be one, as we are one. . ." (John XVII, 21) as verification of this "mark." (Christ's prayer is certainly efficacious; therefore his Church will be one, they reason.)

But if one wishes to identify the Church of Christ with the Catholic Church, and consequently to show that the Catholic Church has this sign of "unity," some explanation is necessary. In the interests of reality-consciousness, one must deal with the historical facts of the Protestant Reformation and the schism of the Eastern "Orthodox" Churches. The theologians and apologists have done this by emphasizing uniformity of belief and organizational unity under the jurisdiction of the Roman Pontiff. (The practice of pointing to other Christian churches as heretical or apostate is no longer prevalent.)

At the present time, when there is less obvious unity of belief or ecclesiastical discipline than in previous times, it becomes difficult to see how the Catholic Church possesses the marks of "unity," as something plain for all to see. But then, one may wonder whether unity of belief and organization was what Christ had in mind in the first place. He doesn't say this; and if one were to take the prayer about unity in context, it would seem to imply above all a unanimity of spirit, a union of love and fellowship. A quality like this would be much easier to detect for some non-Christian inquirer who took it into his head to locate the "true church of Christ" by using the criterion of "unity."

But if a contemporary searcher were to utilize any of the aforesaid interpretations of unity--i.e. unity of belief or organization, unity of spirit or fellowship--it is conceivable that after an exhaustive search he would have to give up his effort and conclude

that the Church of Christ is no longer extant, if unity
be one of its ineradicable marks. Then, if the
theologians got wind of this, they might be motivated
to redefine "unity" in more liberal terms. An endless
process. . . The days are gone when one could simply
state that those elements in the Christian Church which
were in unity were the "visible Church," while some of
the elements not in unity might still belong to the
"invisible Church" or the "soul of the Church."

In view of the obvious and serious disunities
among Christians, it would seem most rational to take
the "unity" of the Church as an inchoate idea, a
developmental concept , an ideal to be aimed at.
Christians do not have unambiguous "unity," in any of
the usual senses of that word; but they are capable of
attaining it. And--if one were dead-bent upon finding
the church which is the chief exemplar of Christian
unity--he would do best to look for the Church that is
doing most to overcome differences and to unify
Christians. The Church that did this would be, would
prove itself to be, the "true Church of Christ" (in
process).

6A. The way to create more saints is to abrogate the
institution of sainthood

One finds an impressive number of saints in the
rosters of the Roman Catholic Church. These saints are
both male and female and include a considerable variety
of personality types; they are somewhat exclusive,
however, insofar as they consist mostly of clerics or
professed religious or celibates, with only a sparse
sampling of married or single layfolk. At the present
time deceased persons are officially designated
"Saints" only after a lengthy canonical process, which
includes investigation of biographical details, as well
as authentication of miraculous cures of illnesses
taking place after prayer to the proposed saint. The
explicit purpose behind the official recognition of
saints has been to propose certain individuals in
heaven as intercessors and as models for
imitation--although it is quite certain that other
implicit motives (e.g. regional pride) have been
operative in the creation of certain saints. To a

certain extent, both the explicit purpose and the implicit motives have been achieved through the institution of sainthood. But certain considerations would lead us to believe that the institution has become, or is becoming, counter-productive.

An analogy with the political realm may help: Since ancient times there have been societies in which only one man (the Ruler) or at most a few, were really free; the others lived (or still live) in abject subjection to the will of those few who are free. To one who lives under a democratic system of government, the question may suggest itself: How could so many people be content to live out their lives without freedom, without expecting any representation of their views or their will in the conduct of government, without any guarantee against arbitrary interference with their rights to life and property? According to some philosophers and psychologists, the answer to this may lie in "projection." Individuals who are not ready for freedom may still satisfy their natural desire for freedom in a vicarious way--by projecting it upon one man (or a few) whose freedom is identified with theirs. We who live in societies which are at least structurally more democratic, might come to understand the mechanism involved here by turning our own attention to a phenomenon in the socio-economic sphere: namely, the idolization of celebrities in entertainment and sports--something that is extremely common in the United States. We might ask, how is it that a struggling wage -earner in the lower-middle class does not bristle with resentment when he learns that his favorite sports celebrity is doing a few phony fifteen-second TV commercials for ten times the yearly income of the aforesaid wage earner? how is it that the plain young secretary around the corner, who has neither romance nor money, can gain immense satisfaction from reading about the fourth marriage of her favorite screen star, this time to another handsome and fabulously rich young man?--In all such cases, the only explanation for such contentment seems to be that the individual is living, to a certain degree, through another person, the celebrity, whose fortune is their fortune and whose satisfaction is their satisfaction. In the meantime they fail to do anything very decisive to better their own economic or social status because, after all, they are deriving immense vicarious satisfaction from the economic windfalls or social attainments of their "idol."

Returning to the case of sainthood, there can be little doubt that devotion to the saints has been, for many people, a vicarious emotional experience, analogous to the above-mentioned types of experience in the social, economic, or political realms. The devotee of the saint, often enough, may be an individual who has had a few passing desires for spiritual perfection, enlightenment, or union with God, but is content to deal with these desires vicariously, by simply projecting them onto the official "saint," and feeling immense relief that someone has fulfilled these spiritual aspirations. Hand in hand with this attitude goes the static placidity which disinclines one to work for any lasting spiritual fulfillment in his own life, because, after all, he has his saint up there "working" for him and willing to "put in a good word" for him now and then.

In the historical evolution of mankind towards the consciousness of individual freedom, a point of readiness had to be reached before most men were willing to take on political freedom as their mutual right and responsibilty. Until that point had been reached, autocratic or aristocratic governments held sway. In the religious evolution of mankind, have we yet reached the point where a sufficient number of people are ready to take spiritual fulfillment as their own personal goal? If so, the dazzling and often legend-inflated exemplars, the "saints," may be an obstacle to the attainment of this goal; while the low-key and unromantic example of other "ordinary" people working for this same goal, may serve as the highest personal incentive.

6B. A church that can't produce its own saints should import them

The "saint" in common religious usage can be two very different personality-types: on the one hand, the prodigy of altruism who distinguishes himself in the arena of the "active life": on the other, the hero of the inner life, who attains to heights of spiritual experience that the majority of us can only try to comprehend from a considerable psychic distance.

In the Western Church, we have had some saints in the latter sense-- John of the Cross, Theresa of Avila, Meister Eckhart, etc. -- colorful ascetics, often visionaries, who would leave no stone unturned and flinch from no suffering to arrive at their ideal of personal unity with the divine. Some of them left books behind them--books whose contents are clearly geared only to the admiration of the many, but to be imitated nowadays only by the elite or, in some cases, the psychically unbalanced. The supply of saints of this latter type has just about dried up in the Church. If one decided, say, to place himself under some widely recognized master of the spiritual life, one who has "been there" himself and is able to show others the way, one would have a difficult time deciding who to go to in the Western Church. This difficulty would be compounded by the fact that the predominant ascetical tradition in Western Christianity looks upon the highest states of meditation or contemplation as "graces" or "gifts of the spirit" given occasionally here and there, but not systematically attainable by serious people through tried and true methods.

No. The real and undisputed saints of the contemporary Western Church are of the former type -- Mother Theresa, Dag Hammerskjold, Pope John, Martin Luther King--geniuses of the active life whose private spiritual odysseys may be warm, intense, and noteworthy, but are not known to be extraordinary or heroic.

Contrast this situation with that in Hinduism (Buddhism and Taoism also come to mind; but Buddhism is atheistic, and Taoism has now been subordinated to the political realities of Maoism; so Hinduism is more easily comparable to Christianity at present). The Indians have comparatively little acquaintance with our type of active saint, but practioners of the spiritual life are everywhere to be seen, yogis who set up thriving ashrams where great and small alike are presumably initiated into the scientific techniques of spiritual perfection and who are so numerous that India can export her yogis abundantly the way the U.S. exports wheat and the Arabian countries export oil, without suffering any noticeable scarcity at home. The Western observer must seriously wonder whether this is simply a manifestation of extraordinary cheek (spiritual fakir-y) or a sign that the Indians have really developed a sure science of the spiritual life

while we have been busying ourselves building up and proliferating physical science and technology.
Are we to resort to foreign exports in spiritual matters?

7A. "Communion" can be a hindrance to union with God

If a Roman Catholic believes that bread and wine are transformed into the body and blood of Christ during the sacrament of the Eucharist, it is only natural that he should look upon communion--in which he partakes of the "species" (appearances) of bread and wine--as an appropriate means for attaining to union with God (which is the fundamental motive for all religious activity). However, it is quite possible that the act of partaking of communion could be a formidable obstacle to an individual's attainment of the union that he dimly desires.

There is an almost inescapable aspect of magic in some of the sacraments of the Catholic Church, including the Eucharist. By "magic," I mean the claim that by certain mechanical and ritual activities one can obtain effects which transcend ordinary human powers. Catholic theology does not believe in magic, but it does believe that certain sacraments produce their effects, as they say, ex opere operato, i.e. from the very doing of an external deed. For example, an officially ordained priest, even if he has diabolical intentions or a complete lack of faith, can still produce the body and blood of Christ in performing the consecration of bread and wine, provided that he intends what the Church intends in the act. Then again, the layman who receives communion from a priest is truly united with Christ, as long as he meets the bare minimum qualifications for receiving the sacrament (i.e. lack of serious sin). Because of this emphasis on the objective production of certain spiritual effects, it is probable that with many Catholics "going to communion" has become for all practical purposes a magic ritual, scarcely distinguishable in kind from the pagan's use of a talisman to ward off evil spirits.

Since essential union with God can only come about through the intentions of consciousness, it seems to be a foregone conclusion that the most direct means to attaining this union are prayer and meditation. The ascetic tradition in Christianity, as well as in certain Eastern religions, has always emphasized the fact that conscious and systematic effort is the only congruent means to divine union. If this is the case, the impression of many Catholics that they can attain union by the ceremonial act of communion, is illusory and no doubt is an obstacle to their realization of any deeper spiritual aspirations.

It is interesting to note that Martin Luther, although he believed in the "real presence" of Christ in the Eucharist, parted company with Catholic theology in his mode of explanation of this presence. For Luther, the faith of the communicant was one of the essential factors calling forth this "real presence." Perhaps this emphasis on the subjective contribution that the believer must make towards the objective presence of Christ is the necessary and sufficient antidote to the frequent and magic-tinged belief of Catholics that communion is an easy and quasi-automatic way to the attainment of divine union. The Church, of course, does not encourage magic, but the Church's emphasis on the objective transformation of the Eucharist into Christ (through "transubstantiation") may provide unnecessary inducements to the "magical" interpretation.

7B. Union with God may be impossible without communion
     (in the Catholic sense)

If there be such a thing as union with God, there are no doubt many people who would approach this union from the side of pure spirit. That is, because of metaphysical or religious inclinations, they believe that there are certain operations of the human soul which are completely independent of the body and consequently do not need any "stoking" from the external world. If one holds such a metaphysical belief, he would be able to look forward to a sort of divine union congruent to his beliefs. (If he subsequently attains such union, this would also amount to confirmation, for him, of his metaphysical belief.) However, it is unlikely that most men would be able to give more than lip service to such belief: For from

experience most men surmise that all their knowledge,
personal fulfillment, etc. is derived from the external
world in some manner, or requires certain external
conditions or stimuli. If this fact is uppermost in
one's mind, and if he has never had an experience of
acting "independently of the body," he would find it
difficult to believe in any ascetic, purely spiritual
process of divine union. And, if he does not really
believe in its possibility, he could not seriously make
any efforts to attain it.

For such a person (shall we call him an
"empiricist" in a wide and, of course, non-derogatory
sense?) it may be absolutely necessary to meet God
appearing substantively and independently of his belief
(excepting his belief in the reality of the external
world) in order for union to be possible. The Catholic
sacrament of the Eucharist, in which God is believed to
exist just as substantively as any external object,
would supply the necessary prerequisite. If, in
response to his faith, an individual experienced union,
or communion , not only with the "community of faith,"
but with some transcendent source in his participation
in this sacrament, this would amount to evidence of an
"empirical" nature that might be conclusive for that
individual.

8.   The music and rituals of the Church must become
      both foreign and familiar

It is difficult to clearly characterize aesthetic
reactions, but one could say that, in general, the
music and liturgy of the Catholic Church in the 50's
was "foreign, but not unfamiliar." The words were
mostly in Latin, and the vestments and rituals, (e.g.
medieval styles of music and chant) and musical
instruments (the organ) were somewhat strange and
"foreign" to most congregations. (One might also add
to this list the Gothic or Baroque style of
architecture in many churches.) At the same time, this
"foreignness" did not elicit complete incomprehension
or alienation; rather, an atmosphere of mystery,
reverence, and sublimity was preserved (depending, of
course, on such contingencies as the behavior of
babes-in-arms). And altogether, one could characterize
the general atmosphere as attractive and not

unfamiliar, for many people. The Latin language, after all, is not Chinese; Gregorian music is quite beautiful to many Western ears; and the symbolic rituals connected with the offering of the bread and wine have a certain universality about them, which is not necessarily marred by the passing of a collection plate.

In the years following the Second Council of the Vatican in the 60's, the swing was in the other direction, towards greater familiarity-- through use of the vernacular instead of Latin, the license to experiment with more modern musical forms and musical instruments, gradual updating of the liturgy, etc. The result in many cases has been what was not quite expected: alienation. The liturgy now might be characterized as "familiar, but extremely foreign." Church attendance (especially among the youth) has dropped off, despite some noteworthy efforts on the part of both clergy and laity to revitalize the liturgy. Some of the reasons for these developments are evident: A translation, especially a bad translation, cannot reproduce the original sentiments of Latin hymns; a handshake with those around you seems artificial when someone directs you explicitly to shake your neighbor's hand; songs like "Blowin' in the Wind" and "We Shall Overcome" are inspirational, but not in a religious way; chants sound dull and mechanical when their rules of accentuation are simply transferred from Latin into the vernacular language--But there are perhaps other, deeper reasons: the psycho-social development of mankind, secularization and the "death of God" theology, etc. We will not attempt to go into these here.

The ideal liturgy would be "both foreign and familiar,"--that is, combining mystery, reverence and sublimity with a beauty and native ingenuity of expression that congregations can identify with. An approximation to this ideal might be possible if artists and writers were in the service of the Church now as in former times. But the "separation of Church and state" seems to have penetrated to that area, too. In the long run, however, the solution to present liturgical problems may lie in the direction of simplicity--a return to the essentials, the Lord's Supper, the Word of Scripture. In a businesslike and non-ritualistic Western social milieu, the addition of music and various liturgical activities, if not spontaneous and <u>aesthetic</u>, should be considered superfluous and counter-productive.

9.   The most orthodox form of Thomism is non-Thomism

"Thomism," or the philosophical and theological doctrines of St. Thomas Aquinas (died 1274), has been for centuries the standard of orthodoxy in the Catholic Church. Recent Papal pronouncements have reiterated the Church's insistence that the teachings of St. Thomas are still not outdated, and can be taken as a guide for theologians and philosophers in our own times.

There is an unauthenticated legend that St. Thomas at the peak of his career broke off writing abruptly because of a vision. "After what I've seen," he is reported to have said, "it's all straw." The followers of St. Thomas have taken this legend as an example of Aquinas' legendary humility. "Of course, we can't take this comment literally," they would say. But why would it be so outlandish to suppose that St. Thomas, in a moment of illumination, saw that his writings, in spite of the great insight they contained, were essentially of an ephemeral nature, and would begin to lose their value and validity with the passage of time? Or perhaps he realized that his writings could only encapsule one aspect of the truth, which, if taken too seriously by his followers, would leave them with the empty shell of truth, or at least with little content. (As one philosopher put it, "Save us from our disciples!")

The great and unparalleled genius of St. Thomas consisted in his ability to bring about a synthesis of theological knowledge with all the most advanced philosophical and scientific knowledge of his century. His means to achieving this goal was an encyclopedic knowledge of, and mastery over, the Scriptures, the writings of the Fathers and Doctors of the Church, and the writings of various philosophers, especially Aristotle and some commentators on Aristotle. Since the works of Aristotle were a voluminous compendium of new and often revolutionary philosophical and scientific positions, the incorporation of Aristotelian insights into theological disquisitions was a novel and audacious undertaking for those times3

(Several contemporaries of St. Thomas attempted to make similar syntheses, but were not as successful.)

In our own times there are new and revolutionary scientific discoveries and philosophical insights from which profitable theological "syntheses" might be made--e.g. findings in psychology, new concepts of the universe and its formation, the evolution of life, philosophical analyses of myth, of religious consciousness, of God as process rather than as stable unity. Although theological syntheses with such massive knowledge is now a formidable task and impossible for a single individual to complete, partial attempts have been made in that direction--e.g. Teilhard de Chardin's attempt to synthesize Christianity with evolution. More attempts need to be made. The point is, those who make attempts of this sort could be called, in the most veridical sense, the "followers of St. Thomas"--even if they happen to be unfamiliar with or opposed to the doctrines associated with Aquinas. For in the strictest sense they are doing what he did, and following Thomas' own explicit injunction, "The most important thing [especially in philosophy and science, in which "authority" is not a major factor as compared with theology, which relies upon the authority of Scripture or Church leaders] is to examine what has been said, not who has said it." Those, on the other hand, who adhere too strenuously to the synthesis which Aquinas made long ago with largely outmoded scientific concepts and now irrelevant philosophical viewpoints very easily find themselves with a jaundiced eye which (to use one of the favorite examples of St. Thomas) since it already is imbued with one color, cannot see or differentiate colors clearly.

10. The claim of infallibility increases fallibility; the admission of fallibility creates relative infallibility

The First Vatican Council of the Catholic Church, which first propounded the doctrine of papal infallibility, took place, significantly, towards the end of the 19th century, a century marked by the ever-increasing ascendancy of the physical sciences, which had become established as paragons of certitude and the final arbiter of truth. Since men had previously looked to religion for truth and certitude, it is no wonder that a kind of competition with science would emerge in religion--a tactical maneuver to regain that territory of human assent and volition that had been taken over by its formidable competitor. In some forms of Protestantism, reaction was in the direction of fundamentalism, an even stricter adherence to the literal interpretation of the Bible; in other forms, there was a movement towards a more "scientific" religion, a trend with a variety of manifestations--the anthropological- historical reinterpretation of the Scriptures, the revision of religious or ethical practices in the light of the latest psychological or sociological evidence, etc. In the Catholic Church, at that particular time, the movement was in the direction of dogmatism, and the ultimate buttress for the authoritative declaration of dogmas was the doctrine of papal infallibility. (Certain purely logical paradoxes emerge out of the formulation of this doctrine: if the doctrine was authoritatively defined by a Church Council, is it not the Church Council rather than the Pope which must be taken as infallible? If the Council were infallible, this would only be because the Church is infallible and because it transmitted its infallibility to this Council in an infallible way -- a combination of conditions that would be difficult to ascertain or guarantee. If the Council were fallible, its doctrine of infallibility would be revisable and fallible. If, on the other hand, the Papacy itself were taken as defining its own infallibility, would this act of definition be fallible or infallible? It could be taken as infallible only to those who already believed in Papal Infallibility.)

If religion were to learn anything from science, it would be that dogmatism is the greatest obstacle to progress in human knowledge. In the history of science, the adamant and dogmatic adherents to traditionally accepted scientific theories have often been vociferously and mockingly opposed to new discoveries in science, until they were accepted by universal acclaim. On the other hand, it is precisely the habit of thought in science of distrusting hypotheses and reexamining them in the light of new data, and often with unorthodox methods and "heretical" approaches, that has led to new and great scientific discoveries.

An analogous situation obtains in the Church: In the middle ages, for example, theologians such as Thomas Aquinas, backed by long traditions and papal directives, taught that heretics should be dealt with by capital punishment, and that usury was gravely immoral. Later, with advent of new and less autocratic forms of government, and the separation of Church and state, and the transition from feudal to capitalistic economies--the position of the Church was reversed on both of these matters. De facto, if not ex cathedra, it was the ability to recognize the relativity and fallibility of previous positions that gave the Church sufficient latitude and flexibility to avoid flouting common sense when the "handwriting was on the wall." At the present time it is precisely this humility, this willingness to acknowledge error, that is the surest guarantee of true and trustworthy ecclesiastical decisions on the contemporary religious and moral issues: For example, it has been the position of the Church in times past that, under certain conditions, war between nations could be justified. In a nuclear age, when some wars would almost certainly touch off a global holocaust, the theory of the "just war" needs revision, perhaps retraction. Again, the Church in times past has opposed contraception, and in doing so seemed to be defending the divine injunction found in Genesis, "increase and multiply and fill the earth." But now, to all appearances it seems that this divine injunction has been fulfilled--and a corresponding modification of the stand against contraception might be called for. (A small army of celibate priests and nuns might help to stem the tides of population expansion, but one can scarcely expect even the most religious person to embrace celibacy just to help remedy overpopulation.) In such instances, it is the firm insistence on the continuity of tradition and the infallibility of previous stands taken by Papal predecessors which can effectively block the emergence of moral or religious truth. It is perhaps significant that the Catholic Church has never placed too much emphasis on papal infallibility in actual practice. For one thing, the requirements for an "official and ex cathedra infallible pronouncement" have been interpreted so strictly by many theologians, that it is doubtful whether there have been any truly infallible pronouncements made. Then again, there has been a trend against making infallible decisions in the moral sphere; for example, in the encyclical of Pope Paul VI against contraception, indications are given that the pronouncement was not infallible. Therefore, for all practical purposes, the realm of infallible pronouncements seems to be relegated to such purely religious beliefs as the Immaculate Conception, the Assumption of the Virgin Mary, etc. But if religious beliefs are affected (albeit slowly) by the processes that affect other beliefs--evolution, demythologization, reformulation--the need for a conscious and acknowledged fallibility would seem just as important in their regard, as in the realms of scientific or moral "truths."

B. Christianity

11. It is better not to proclaim the Gospel than to proclaim it outside of one's personal revelation

"Work while it is yet day; when the night comes, no man can work." (John IX, 4)

*   *   *   *

In Ingmar Bergman's film, <u>Winter Light</u>, we are told the story of a Protestant clergyman who finds himself in a situation where he is under pressure to speak about religious matters in which he no longer believes. This is indeed a pitiable predicament, but it should never happen. And it does not have to happen. It is both possible and necessary for a preacher to restrict what he says to the personal revelations (using "revelation" in the broad sense) which he himself has had. This is possible, because every preacher will have had insights, including problems and doubts, concerning the Gospel. If one is lacking some positive insights, he may at least concentrate on the negative insights, e.g. regarding sin and the human condition, or on Scriptural passages (e.g. the doubts of Jesus during his final sufferings and Crucifixion) which are in harmony with his personal state. It is necessary to speak from one's own revelation; because otherwise the element of personal witness is lacking, and the power of the Gospel becomes nothing more that purely academic illumination, if not hypocrisy.

But what if the minister finds himself in such a negative state that he feels not just doubt about the Gospel, but rejection and complete disbelief? Should he give vent to these feelings and quit? Or wait for the feelings to pass over? Or content himself with concentrating on the opinions and insights of others; on political, social, or ethical matters which have little relevance to religion; on ecclesiastical beliefs or rules that have little relevance either to the Gospel or to the world? A third possibility is also open to him: to continue meditating on theological matters, and to make use of whatever insights he can skim or glean, even if they do not seem extraordinary. The important thing here is that they are his, and he can vouch for them. And it is through the processes of meditation that "revelation" in the widest and most usual sense takes place. If an individual cannot personally assimilate and vouch for certain elements in the Scriptures --e.g. the concept of personal immortality, the divinity of Jesus Christ, etc.--he should concentrate on other elements.

But what if one simply cannot meditate, or meditation yields nothing? This might happen (a) because one simply does not have the ability to meditate and develop his own insights; or (b) because one experiences a complete "loss of faith"--can no longer accept the existence of God or the divinity of Christ in any sense. In case (a), it is better not to speak than to mouth mechanical irrelevancies or the opinions of others. In case (b), if this be a sustained and irreversible position, one must, when his personal aggravation comes to greatly outweigh his communal instincts , resign his ministry as well as cease to preach. It is much better to be a sincere and reflective agnostic than a mechanical or hypocritical "believer."

12. The split of Christianity and Judaism had the effect of making the Jews "worldly" and the Christians escapist

If one reads through the Acts of the Apostles and the various Epistles of the New Testament, he will gather the impression that most of the apostles of Jesus definitely looked upon themselves as a branch or continuation of Judaism, and perpetuated Jewish ceremonial obligations and religious observances as a sign that they considered themselves full-fledged Jews. However, under the influence of St. Paul and his followers, who were interested in accomodating Christianity to the Gentile world, a wedge was gradually introduced to dissever ritual and organizational ties with the parent-religion, to liberate the consciences of Christians from the yoke of "the Law." With a few exceptions, it is the Pauline conception of what Christianity is that seems to have prevailed in the Christian Church, down through the centuries.

One of the decisive factors in driving the wedge between the Christian and Jewish religions was the belief of the early Christian communities in the imminent coming of Christ and the Kingdom of God, and the end of the world (these three concepts have distinct meanings, but became interrelated in the minds of many Christians). This belief seemed to influence many Christians to abandon sexual ties and their worldly goods, in order to prepare themselves assiduously and ascetically for the Day of Judgment, which was "just around the corner," so to speak. This Christian belief contrasted sharply with the Jewish expectation of a Messiah or Christ who would come to restore the Jews to dominance and power, including political power, in the present world.

The Christian projections proved to be inaccurate. Generation after generation passed, and still--no End of the World! One might expect that this development, and the consequent shift in expectations, would cause some Christians to become more materialistic. And it did. But one would also expect that it might condition the mainstream of Christianity to put less emphasis on escape from the world and concentration on the possibilities of an "afterlife." And this it did not. Rather, whether because of stubbornness, force of habit, or true spiritual perception, Christianity became the religion which emphasized the afterlife, although a few branches (such as the Calvinists and Puritans) were willing to allow a certain measure of material prosperity (as long as sensuality was not encouraged), as a "sign" of one's salvation in the next life. In the Jewish religion, on the other hand, from which many of the idealistic and "spiritual" adherents had been drawn into Christian other-worldliness, there was a gradual shift towards concentration on survival in this world--a concentration nurtured to a great extent by the tendency of various dominant host nations of making the existence of Jews difficult, and their material prosperity precarious. Nowadays, even among practising Jews (who are greatly outnumbered by more secularist coreligionists), one will find many who are sceptical about "other-worldly" orientations, such as a belief in personal immortality or the resurrection of the body after death.

It was finally a baptised Jew, Karl Marx, who pointed out quite forcefully that it was the concentration of Christians on reward in the "other world" that had subtly, and almost in an unconscious manner, had the effect of making them disinterested in social and economic progress and reform. Now, after about a century of pressure from Marxism in its various forms, there is a movement afoot in the Christian Church to identify (or "re-identify") the Christian message with social progress and reform. If this movement gathers and maintains momentum, would the consequent convergence of interest pave the way for the so-called "conversion of the Jews" that many Christian interpreters of Scriptural prophecies projected or prophesized? But perhaps relations have too far disintegrated for this to take place.

13. The ultimate goals of communism can be attained only through Christianity, and vice versa

Teilhard de Chardin, in an essay entitled, "The Heart of the Matter,"[4] depicts Christianity and Marxist humanism as two polar extremes in the world today. On the one side, the devout Christian is dedicated to attaining his salvation and spiritual perfection, as well as the ultimate fulfillment of all men, in the "Kingdom of God"--which is usually relegated to a great extent to an afterlife. Directly contrary to him is the dedicated Marxist, who works assiduously for the complete unity of all mankind--a union attained through the obliteration of class differences, the abolition of private property, and the redistribution of wealth.

The Christian, on his side, is willing to admit that the love of God should result in, and foster, the love of neighbor. But the love of neighbor is interpreted in the main as a spontaneous outpouring, taking the form of private charitable contributions and voluntary public service. The idea of reorganizing completely to redistribute wealth and eliminate artificial class restrictions (and thus make private charity somewhat superfluous) is thought to be inimical to the spirit of Christianity--although some minimal approximations to this goal may be found in the "welfare states" of Scandinavia and elsewhere.

The Marxist communist, on the other hand, is willing to admit that social progress should be accompanied by individual fulfillment. But the freedom of the individual must be temporarily restricted, during the phase of the "dictatorship of the proletariat," in which the gradual re-training and

reorientation of individual men takes place. For the
time being, force and outside pressure must be employed
to scientifically lead men towards final socialism, in
which individual men will no longer be alienated from
their own work on account of class divisions and profit
structures. When this time arrives, the restrictions
may be eased, the dictatorships ended, for the ordinary
man will have become reeducated, completely socialized,
no longer petty, provincial or selfish.

Thus the Christians are long on good will towards
mankind in general; but short in their practical
organization and mobilization towards the attainment of
the universal minimums of material welfare that are
necessary to make "spiritual fulfillment" something
more than a luxury. The Marxists are long on
mobilization towards social welfare and complete
equality; but short on spontaneity, as is verified by
the continued necessity for harsh surveillance and
"walls," literal or metaphorical, in communist regimes.
(Ironically, with the walls and the orthodox beliefs
and the enforced communal living and the ritual
silence, Marxist regimes have ended up with something
like monasteries, but on a scale never dreamed of by
St. Benedict or St. Bernard.)

There is some dispute among Christians as to what
sort of thing the "parousia," or final appearance of
the Kingdom of God, will be. Scriptural evidence
allows the interpretation that the Parousia will be
something beginning, and perhaps even brought to
perfection, on earth. If this interpretation be
adopted, there can be little doubt that Christians have
something to learn from the communists about the
practical implementation of the Scriptural commands to
feed the hungry, clothe the naked, etc.

As far as communism is concerned, one can
visualize an impasse being reached, where some Marxist
theoretician might say to himself, "if only we could
attain greater inter-personal spontaneity, something
like love for neighbor, along with our present
socially-oriented political and economic structures.
Then we would no longer have to worry about capitalism
or individual avarice rearing again its ugly head. We
could relax the restrictions and show the capitalist
nations what a truly 'free' society looks like." The
point is that an abstract ideal of universal equality
is not sufficient of itself to elicit the voluntary
sacrifice of personal interests and personal

aggrandizement. An almost superhuman energy would be required to sustain such a spirit subjectively. And it is perhaps with this in mind that the French revisionist Marxist, Roger Garaudy, admits,

> It is not out of the question . . .
> that Christians, who have always emphasized subjectivity and the interior life of the person--sometimes to excess, to the detriment of social commitment and of the historical and practical dimensions of life--will formulate demands which are happily complementary to those of Marxists, who for their part emphasize historical efficacy, at the risk of working for it unilaterally--not because they deny the role of subjectivity, which both Marx and Lenin stressed, but because they both have a tendency to underestimate it.[5]

It is this "principle of subjectivity" which will be the decisive factor as to whether the human atoms are to be moulded by force into a giant international organization, or brought through the power of internal attraction into the ambit of an ever more complex and universal social organism.

14A. Private charity is at a maximum only when it is completely organized

The notion that "marriage is the enemy of love" (which was a a slogan in the nineteenth century romantic-existentialist tradition, and can be traced back even further to the days of chivalry) is still prevalent today, as evinced especially by the life-style of the "hippies" of the '60's and their present-day ideological descendants, commensals and sympathizers. And there is, it seems, a sense in which marriage, by introducing custom and routine and familial necessity into "the love which began it all," gradually causes the flames to apparently wave and sputter, the waves to ebb and lose their crest. How many married couples do we consider to still be "in love" after 10 years or so of marriage and child-bearing? We don't expect to discern really romantic sentiments in most of them. Thus we may still

be infected with the old romantic-existentialist bias,
although we give lip-service to its opposite.

A similar situation prevails in regard to the
attitude of many Christians towards "charity." When
they hear the admonitions of the New Testament, "feed
the hungry, care for the sick, clothe the naked," etc.,
they think primarily of spontaneous outpourings,
frequent or less frequent depending on the character
and temperament of the individual Christian, in
response to perceptions of need in the less fortunate
or among equals. To a Christian who thinks this way,
the idea of the absolutely complete organization of
charity, such as might be found in a welfare state,
would seem contrary to the whole spirit of
charity--even if this "complete organization" were
accompanied by a minimum of bureaucratic waste. To
their mind, the organizing and systematizing processes
themselves would be inimical to the essential
spontaneity and good-will which should characterize
charity.

But nothing could be further from the truth.
Marriage (to use our earlier analogy) can and should
maintain, foster, and extensively elaborate the love
with which it began, even though the passional
sentiments of the "first love" will gradually grow less
dramatic in most cases. And in like manner the citizen
who calmly and deliberately and voluntarily pays a
heavy load of income taxes with the knowledge that the
taxes are being used to make "private charity" rare or
superfluous in certain selected categories (e.g. food
and health care), is no less spontaneous or "Christian"
than the impulsive benefactor who, inspired by feelings
of benevolence or oppressed with the pangs of
conscience or the need to atone for injustices
committed, offers his charitable contribution in a
more direct and "personal" way to the needy or
unfortunate victim he happens to come across. The only
way that the sentiment of charity could be maintained
at a constantly high and extensive level would be
through a vast organizational network.

14B. Organized charity can be effective only to the
extent that it is personalized and non-systematic

The whole modern scientific organization of charity is a consequence of the failure of simply giving alms. . .and yet you are sure, as I am sure, that were the world confined to these hard-headed, hard-hearted, and hard-fisted methods exclusively, were there no one prompt to help a brother first, and find out afterwards whether he were worthy, no one willing to drown his private wrongs in pity for the wronger's person, no one ready to be duped many a time rather than live always on suspicion; no one glad to treat individuals passionately and impulsively rather than by general rules of prudence; the world would be an infinitely worse place than it is now to live in.
    --William James, The Varieties of Religious Experience

One can imagine a world-wide bureaucratic charity organization that is so efficient that it has complete and instantaneously available information on all the people it serves, and distributes to them exactly what they need, no more, no less; utilizing and applying strict criteria of eligibility for determining who receives what. If such an organization maintained its outstanding efficiency and functioned for a few generations, the later generations might develop without ever knowing what charity really is. For in order to really experience charity, you have to receive it when you are unworthy, or receive more than you deserve, or be given something abundantly without any antecedent examination of how much you deserve. An example from the psychological sphere may help to clarify this point:

In The Art of Loving (New York, 1956), Erich Fromm makes a distinction between "motherly love" and "fatherly love." Motherly love is unconditional, bestowing services and favors aside from considerations of what the child actually deserves or earns. Fatherly love, on the other hand, bestows its gifts on the basis of accomplishment and merit, and withdraws them in the absence of requisite conditions. (This dichotomy of unconditioned and conditioned love is not necessarily partitioned between mother and father, respectively; rather, both types of love can co-exist in various proportions in both mother and father; and it is presumed that this is what usually happens.) Both

types of love are necessary. But it is especially
through our being the beneficiaries of the
"unconditional" type of love that we develop a notion
of our intrinsic worth, aside from our accomplishment;
and of the intrinsic worth of others. The child that
has not had ample experience from some source of a love
that is occasionally blind, and misses the mark, and
gives more than expected, will grow up never really
knowing what love is and can be.

In the religious sphere, the situation is
analogous. We find it emphasized frequently throughout
the New Testament that it is precisely because God did
and does more than is expected for sinners who never
even ask for his gifts that we come to really
understand the goodness and mercy of God (see e.g. Luke
XV, 11-32).

Returning, then, to the hypothetical example of a
world-wide supremely efficient charity organization:
If its goal were not just to solve messy social
problems but to demonstrate genuine charity, it would
have to program into its system a regular departure
from system and spontaneous excesses here and there
over and above what its clients expected, needed, and
deserved. It is because of the extreme difficulty, and
perhaps impossibility, of this type of "programming,"
that "private charity" will probably continue to be
necessary, no matter how large and fail-safe charitable
organizations or welfare states may become.

15. We can perceive the "true Christ" only if we come
    to de-emphasize and de-centralize the question of
    the Jesus of history

At the present time, after much ground-breaking
has been done in Scripture studies by Albert
Schweitzer, Rudolph Bultmann and others, the search for
the "historical Jesus" has reached a denouement. Every
word and event in the Gospels has been sifted, tested
for cogency and accuracy, compared textually and
contextually with what are taken to be source
materials, and with what science can tell us
historically and archeologically about Gospel events
and circumstances. The result of all this research is
that now every single word reported in the Gospels as
spoken by Jesus is subject to dispute; and many

historical facts--the place and time of Jesus' birth, his geneology, the number of his siblings, the real character of his deeds, cures and miracles (after the outer core of legend or myth has been peeled away) and (most important) his resurrection from the dead--are all also in doubt. Such a state of doubt may seem a major and perhaps insuperable obstacle to a Christian's attainment of a viable faith in the man-God. For how are we to direct and formulate our faith, if we are unable to fill in accurately many of the most important concrete details about the object of our belief? This would seem to be the logical line of thought; but not necessarily so.

The nineteenth century existentialist, Soren Kierkegaard, following up on some ideas of G.W.F. Hegel, tells us that a man whose faith is supported by historical proofs about the existence and activities of Christ--is a man without faith. Such a reliance upon historical evidence is an insuperable obstacle to that personal encounter with Christ, which is indispensable for a solid and lasting faith-commitment. A man who has never been affected and changed by his own subjective experience of the Christ "who was, is and will be" -- the ever-present, essential Christ who emerges from the interior of man's soul -- cannot have authentic faith, and is not a Christian (although he may be a churchgoing member of "Christendom").

Some authors have taken Kierkegaard a step further and asked, how does one attain this personal, existential encounter with Christ? They focus on the fact that in early Christianity, Christ seemed to identify himself with his followers (e.g. in the conversion of St. Paul, Jesus informs Paul, who had been persecuting Christians, that he had indeed been persecuting Jesus himself); and vice versa, Christians identified themselves with Christ, whose spirit lived within them, and who was the head of a "Mystical Body" of which they were members. Thus these authors conclude that a "personal encounter" with Christ is ordinarily attained in one's present Christian community -- not in nostalgic remembrance of some primordial, uncontaminated Christian community far off in time. These are hard words. At times when what we take to be "the Christian community" (something which may be hard to identify, since multiple communities claim that title) no longer affords us strength, inspiration, or comfort, it would seem desirable to have solid historical facts; some definitely inspired and infallible scriptural quotations; some well-authenticated dogmas and traditions going right back to the beginning -- as a source of and sustenance for, our faith. The Scripture scholars have been in the process of removing these props from under our feet now for some time. If, however, we are to believe the latter authors, this conspiracy of the Scripture scholars may not be such a bad thing after all.

16. "Universal love" can become a reality only when the enmity in the world is complete

At the present time, an indubitable and inexorable polarization seems to be taking place in the world. Led by the two super-powers, the U.S. and the U.S.S.R., the Western democracies and the Eastern socialist republics continue to define and differentiate themselves, establish "territoriality," and bring as many countries as possible into the ambit of their respective influences. The Chinese communists, who used to be allied more or less with the "Eastern bloc," now are developing claims to leadership of the "third world." One also hears mention of a "fourth world." But the point is: the world is being simplified into three or four fundamental ideological and political oppositions; and the opposition and rivalry is rising to a crescendo and intensity that is fraught with danger for the world.

Those who are advocates of universal peace and brotherhood and some kind of international order, are dismayed at this situation. To their mind, the attainment of a world government or some kind of international federation is interminably delayed by the perpetuation of such rivalries. But in truth, the very opposite may be the case: as the rivalries and polarizations become complete, a stable equilibrium may develop (foreshadowed now by the concept of the "balance of power" in international politics); and then finally a steady state of constructive opposition may develop, analogous to the "political party" system prevalent in Western democracies. Communism will not "defeat" democracy or vice versa. But their oppositions will become organized and institutionalized; and at some crucial point "the circuit will be closed," so to speak; and as the positive and negative poles make electricity possible, so the international ideological and political polarization will (when proper conditions obtain) give rise to a viable and progressive international order.

It is only under such hypothetical conditions that the Christian ideal of universal love could become operative once and for all.

Sigmund Freud, in Civilization and its Discontents (New York, 1962), sees the Christian injunction to love all men, including enemies, as a natural result of the sublimation process that takes place in civilization as more and more disparate units are drawn by circumstances to live side by side. But--in Freud's opinion--the concept has become, in the hands of Christians, an unrealistic and psychologically regressive abstraction: for it is quite impossible to love all men. (The ordo caritatis in the much-maligned manuals of Catholic moral theology of yesteryear could be taken as a judicious attempt to deal with such practical impossibilities; but the concept of charity is more usually left undefined and amalgamous.) Effective and meaningful human love often requires discernment of proper objects, differentiation of those who are more worthy of one's love from those who are less worthy, discrimination of those who are close to one ideologically, aesthetically, etc., from "enemies." The person who, instead of particularizing and provincializing his love, tries to extend it indiscriminately towards "all men," will end up with a watered-down love, an ineffective sentimental orientation that has little in the way of practical consequences and expression.

We might agree with these observations of Freud, but add "at the present time" as a qualification. The Christian ideal could be implemented if the above-mentioned properly polarized world order, in which even inveterate hostilities were organically concatenated into its "constitution," came about. For, in this case, although the love of most men would be limited to the provincial and natural boundaries dictated by the "laws of attraction," these provincial boundaries would be themselves woven into the fabric of a very complex global political network. In such a situation, individual loves would be (as ever) provincial; but the provincial contexts, by dint of new international relationships, would be so interconnected

with, and explicitly dependent upon, other provincial
contexts and oppositions, that the word, "provincial,"
would come to lose its meaning. "Universal love" would
become a fact because all mankind's particular loves
would be caught up in stable and unavoidable
international equilibrium. Isaiah prophesied that "the
wolf shall dwell with the lamb" (Is. XI, 5). Does this
mean the wolf will become pacified and non-aggressive?
More probably, it means that properly stabilized
versions of natural human aggression will come to
coexist with human love, which (we must not forget) is
also natural.

17. The final object of the Church is to do away with
    itself as an institution

"The time is coming," says Jesus in John's Gospel
to the Samaritan woman[6], "when the true religionists
will worship neither here nor in Jerusalem, but will
worship God in spirit and in truth." Many authorities
interpret this passage as referring to the Christian
religion, which was (they say) foreseen by Jesus to
supersede the Jewish religion and other sects prevalent
then, such as the Samaritan sect. Only a few
interpreters read this as a veiled reference to some
future time when all formal religions will be rendered
superfluous, and everyone will be able to find access
to God without the interposition of any professional
human mediators or guides. Is Christianity the
religion in which man is finally able to worship God
"in spirit and truth"? Or should we look forward to
some final stage superseding Christianity?
    One obstacle in the way of an unbiased and
objective discussion is the very human tendency of any
vested or semi-vested interest to perpetuate itself.
If, for example, one were to suddenly confront the
automobile manufacturers with the sudden availability
of materials or processes that would make their
products last three times as long at no extra cost, we
may well expect the manufacturers to give some
deferential lip-service to the idea and then return to
whatever they are doing with a slight shudder and a
renewed feeling of satisfaction in the conviction that
their way is the best way. If one were to confront the
physicians or dentists of America with the immediate

availability of methods which would reduce by 90% the prevalence of the pathologies they are interested in (i.e. the various diseases, or in the case of dentists, tooth decay), we may expect something less than an enthusiastic reaction to this news from most doctors and dentists (they would, of course, explain their negative reaction by pointing out the scientific reasons why this or that is "impossible" -- but one wonders whether most men would be unbiased enough to admit the evidence for something which would be likely to take away their livelihood and their claim to social prestige).

What if priests and ministers were similarly confronted with the stark and imminent possibility of doing away with -- yes-- sin? or even with the <u>fait accompli</u> (sin being completely abolished through a massive miracle or an outpouring of the "Holy Ghost")? It is, of course, hard to conjecture such an event coming to pass. But if it did, one might expect even the good and sincere among them to adopt every defensive mechanism in their repertoire to discountenance or disprove the evidence. They would not, of course, come right out and say that it is impossible to ever bring about any dramatic reversal of the prevalence of sin in the world -- since, after all, their job is to obliterate sin as much as possible. But other, more subtle types of negation might be expected from them. This last, and rather extreme, example was meant to illustrate our main point. Just as a parent's main role is to render his child independent even of the parent, so also the main role of the Church has been to lead individuals to direct and constant union with God -- a union unencumbered with the need for any finite pedagogue. But just as many parents have difficulty in actually leading their children to independence and accepting that independence as a fact when it comes, so also the Church is quite interested in perpetuating the notion of its own indispensability (in conjunction, of course, with the Holy Spirit). But the final test of the perceptiveness of the Church would be to recognize, if and when it comes, the stage at which the seed can perpetuate itself only by dying to itself (John XII, 24).

18A. Sin is the unconsciousness of sin

In Matthew's Gospel (XII, 31), Jesus speaks of a sin which cannot be forgiven either in this life or in another life -- the "sin against the Holy Spirit." Various interpretations have been given concerning what this sin might be -- apostasy? despair? suicide? obstinate infidelity? But, if we reflect for a moment, it becomes quite obvious what this "sin" must be: namely, the unconsciousness of any sin. The person who is conscious of sin, admits to it in any way whatsoever, is always somewhere within the parameters of "forgivability." On the other hand, one who is not conscious of sin, and refuses to become conscious of sin, is (by definition) beyond forgiveness. An example of this sort of situation emerged some years ago in American politics, when President Ford issued a pardon to his predecessor, Richard Nixon, for the crimes of "Watergate." The question was raised, after the pardon, as to whether the acceptance of the pardon implied an admission of guilt; and the consensus was generally that, yes, it did. However, while an individual accepting a pardon for various infractions of a legal code may do so for merely pragmatic motives, a person seriously accepting forgiveness for "sin" would have to be imbued with the consciousness and acknowledgement of sin. If he were unaware of any sin, it would be meaningless and, indeed, impossible for him to solicit and/or accept forgiveness. If forgiveness were offered to one who saw no need for it, the most appropriate reaction on his part would be to laugh, or perhaps even feel pity for the misdirected and misinformed agent who saw something that needed "forgiveness" in the first place.

Thus we might say that the unconsciousness of sin is both the epitome of sin and the element in any transgression which renders it relatively heinous and unforgivable. In this sense, the unconsciousness of sin becomes the essence of sin, i.e. that which makes it what it is.

18B. The consciousness of "sin" has no efficacy without the consciousness of particular sins

There is a tendency in various forms of Protestantism (e.g. original Lutheranism, Calvinism) to place great emphasis on a general feeling or consciousness of sin, as the sine qua non for salvation. All one need do (the various persuasions tell us) is attain a wholesome awareness of personal sinfulness, of our human inability to accomplish anything good without God's grace -- and the floodgates of God's assistance will be made available.

But -- one might continue this line of thought--what if one is not conscious of any particular sin? If there is nothing definite that he can "put his finger on," can he still attain the general consciousness of sin which is supposed to be a prerequisite for salvation? The "general consciousness of sin" seems to be comparable to "anxiety" in the psychological sphere. Some psychologists differentiate anxiety from fear on the grounds that fear is related to definite, particular objects, while anxiety is vague and dangerous precisely because its source is unknown. If the "consciousness of sin" is to be any more salutary than psychological anxiety, it would seem necessary for some specification of, and orientation towards, particular sins. As St. Paul put it, "if the trumpet gives an uncertain sound, who shall prepare himself for battle?" (1 Cor. XIV, 8). There is no doubt that the tendency in Catholicism to categorize and define endless genera and species of sins was untoward and counter-productive to an extreme degree. But the opposite tendency--to inculcate awareness of "sin" but not of "sins"--is equally ineffectual and even self-contradictory.

19. Sin in some sense was necessary to establish man as an independent being

At the beginning of the Bible, the origin of sin in the world is explained in very simple terms: Adam and Eve in the state of innocence were commanded not to eat from the Tree of the Knowledge of Good and Evil. They broke that command. And now, as a result, they experience evil (including the evil of sin) as well as good.

This story has been subjected to many interpretations. One of the most common interpretations has it that the "knowledge of evil" implied is a practical knowledge; thus one would actually have to do evil to gain this knowledge. What, then, if Adam and Eve had obeyed the command? Would they have just a theoretical knowledge of good and evil? How could there be a dichotomy between the theoretical and practical knowledge of evil, when there was yet no practical knowledge of evil possible? No. If we accept this interpretation, consistency would lead us to expect that, if Adam and Eve had obeyed this command, they would have had no knowledge whatsoever of good and evil. In other words, they would have no necessity or opportunity at all for making what we call "moral decisions." Unless God were, by a special act, and as a reward for their obedience, to infuse some moral knowledge into their minds (some Fathers of the Church leaned towards this hypothesis), they would have remained strictly amoral agents. We could put it more strongly: They would have lived and acted as mere extensions of the will of God. Not having the power to make personal decisions on the basis of their own value judgments, about what they should do, or not do, they would certainly not have possessed "freedom" in any of the usual senses of that term. In fact, we may well doubt whether they could have had any consciousness of the fact that they were indeed distinct from God (without some minimal decision-making power, freedom or "independence" would seem to be an unintelligible and meaningless word.)

Thus, if we accept this line of interpretation, the primordial or "original" sin was necessary precisely to establish man as an independent being. In fact, it would be true to say that the attainment of independence was man's first sin. If man had "chosen" to "reject" the fruit of the Tree of Knowledge of Good and Evil, it is impossible to comprehend how this could have been a free and independent choice (how could a choice be made freely without any knowledge of the "pros and cons," so to speak?) Perhaps it was a mistake for Adam and Eve to choose as they did. Perhaps it would have been better and wiser and even more progressive to continue to function sinlessly in organic and (as it might seem to us) semi-mechanical unison with the great Spirit that walked through the Garden of Paradise. We tend to look upon freedom-as-independence as the primary value, but others, in other cultures, do not thus emphasize it.

Perhaps our very emphasis on the independence of each individual is keeping us from a degree of fulfillment that we can barely imagine. But it is just as hard to imagine how a being who never actually asserted his independence from God in any significant way, could be considered free and independent.

Someone will object: Why would they necessarily have to choose or do something forbidden in order to be free? As long as they knew of the possibility of disobeying the command, this would be the necessary and sufficient condition for their experience of freedom. But this objection supposes that one could know the possibility of evil, without ever experiencing evil in any shape or form. It is a conjecture that is self-contradictory, or at least vacuous; because one can't meaningfully talk about the "possibility of evil," unless one has some idea of what evil is, through experience. We are led to the conclusion that the primordial experience of freedom, in the sense of "independence," is not only the source for the idea of the possibility of evil, but is also, at least unconsciously, considered to be the source of evil. This conclusion is mitigated and qualified, however, by the fact that in the Christian dispensation, freedom, in the sense of independence from "the powers of darkness," becomes a new source for the reversal of evil by free (independent) assertion of one's dependence on God.

C. Religion in General

20. One can convert others only by being converted

"To convert X to Christianity," as an expression used by religionists, has always had a one-sided, and a somewhat hierarchical, connotation. One who has a peculiarly privileged access to the truth bestirs himself to share this truth with others less fortunate, who are still situated in darkness. The "converter" here is the active and initiating source who decides, out of altruistic motives, to lift others up to the higher level of existence and illumination at which he has already arrived.

Carl Jung makes the very important observation that in psychoanalysis the therapist can effectively change the patient only to the extent that the therapist himself is influenced and changed by the patient. In the more specifically religious context, we have the example of Paul the Apostle who "becomes all things to all men" (1 Cor. IX, 22). Christian missionaries have followed this counsel to some extent in times past, by learning the language, and taking on some of the customs and mannerisms of the people they were trying to influence. And the more successful missionaries seemed to have followed the advice even more thoroughly. But there were still pockets of "resistance"; the adherents of some oriental religions seemed almost impervious to conversion efforts, and the Mohammedans gained the reputation of being almost impossible to convert. But one thing still remains to be done: Let the missionary become -- as far as is possible without compromise -- a Mohammedan, a Jew, a Buddhist or Confucian. Who better could represent to them the merits of Christianity than a co-religionist? Who could understand the spiritual needs of the potential convert better than one who shares the same religious rituals and insights? Or are we to say flatly that Christianity is completely incompatible with these other persuasions? To be sure, the Mohammedan predilection for polygamy seems to conflict with the Christian injunction of monogamy, the lack of a formal concept of God in Buddhism seems to pose an obstacle to Christian theism, and so forth. But there are areas of broad spiritual agreement; and who is the best judge of incompatibilty, if not the one who has made persevering efforts to adapt himself to the needs of the other faith?

Many have observed that communism now takes on the aspect of a religion. If we look upon it in this light, then the same principle holds: the best hope for "converting" a communist would be to become one.

Obviously, the main thrust of this line of thought is that missionaries should cease to look upon themselves as transmitters of illumination from "on high," and begin to perceive themselves as sharing truths and commitments with others who also have their own valuable spiritual traditions and insights to share.

One should never be "converted" as a means to converting someone else, however. A "missionary" who did this would be the religious counterpart of the international spy--one who is "passing" as a citizen of a foreign country while trying to foster the interests of his native country. Obviously, this is nothing but a sophisticated species of deception, and could accomplish nothing substantial for the furtherance of truth in the world. As the viable alternative to this kind of "religious espionage," stands the missionary who sincerely strives to synthesize two religious persuasions, and seriously believes he can do so--as Peter and James tried to synthesize Christianity and Judaism in the early Church.

21. Natural religions are the result of inner revelation; revealed religion can be effective only through correspondence to natural needs and insights

The distinction between "natural" and "revealed" religions has been traditional in Christian theology. The natural religion is defined as a religion which emerged out of man's basic emotional and intellectual needs. The ancient Greek and Roman religions, as well as "philosophical" religions such as Confucianism and Buddhism, are offered as examples of natural religions. A revealed religion, on the other hand, purports to show how God himself, by using human instruments, deigned to establish a certain religion on the face of the earth through a remarkable sequence of visions, miracles, prophecies and other "interventions" which seem to bypass natural laws and transcend natural needs. The major religions which claim to be "revealed" are Judaism, Christianity, and Mohammedanism. Judaism gives us perhaps the most graphic example of what it means for a religion to be "revealed": for in Judaism every major detail in the development of its creed and organization, including even the architecture of the temple, the dates of holidays and the proper sequence of acts in ritualistic observances, was "revealed." In the United States, Mormonism makes similar claims. Hinduism claims that its two major Scriptures, the Vedas and the Upanishads, are "revealed"; but its development, creeds, hierarchy and organization were certainly not "revealed" in the manner and to the extent that these things were "revealed" in Judaism.

What is it that signalizes the "revealed" religion, if not the transcendence of the divinity? God takes on the aspect of a hard and fast objective entity who buttonholes certain creatures through visions, locutions, dreams, and miracles, in order to confront them with a message and/or a mission that they had presumably not thought about before, or at least takes them by "surprise." This God may become present to the believer in such ways and also in rituals or sacraments, but he "comes from afar," so to speak. In contrast to this, the "natural" religion is characteristically immanent. Certain natural needs become personified in a religion like that of the ancient Greeks; certain perennial philosophical insights become codified and systematized in a religion like Buddhism. If there is a God in a natural religion, it is certainly not the single and unique, personal, eternal, almighty Father who stands outside history but takes a keen interest in, and exerts a decisive control over, historical and personal events.

However, the distinction that has been made between the natural and revealed religions is patently artificial. Subjected to further analysis it breaks down; and the two distinctions merge into each other. A "revealed" dispensation that did not conform to man's basic and intimate needs, "revealed" truths which did not conform to man's conscious insights or unconscious attitudes or archetypes would never have a chance of success, with or without prayer. On the other hand, the whole force of "natural" religions derives from the fact that they reveal to man some astonishing truths about himself and the world about him: the fact that these truths have been unearthed by human ingenuity, and may be somewhat slanted to a particular culture and somewhat tainted by the scientific and moral

presuppositions does not in any way derogate from their
revelatory force. (The truths that an individual, or
a group, discovers through its own efforts about itself
may turn out to be the most astounding revelations and
produce lasting and irreversible "conversions" in the
way of life of the individual or group.)

The collapse of the distinction between revealed
and natural religions has its implications: Let your
religious enthusiast boast to his heart's content that
the truths he is expounding are revealed by God; if
they do not conform to basic human needs and
inspirations, he might as well save his breath; for
those to whom he is preaching will not accept any truth
in a lasting and thorough way that is not a revelation
to and for them. In like manner, if this or that
"natural" religion reveals as much or more to us about
ourselves and the world than the "revealed" religion to
which we have been adhering , we would be foolish to
reject it because it seems to lack the highborn
pedigree of "revealed" origins, that we have come to
attach so much importance to.

22.   The supernatural is the truly natural

The French Jesuit paleontologist, Pierre Teilhard
de Chardin (died 1955), was ostracized during the last
couple decades of his life for "confusing the natural
with the supernatural". For example, Teilhard
hypothesized that the production of the human soul was
simply a result of a certain stage of evolution when
hominids began to reflect on themselves, and thus
became "men"; and he also speculates about a future
state of mankind, in which all individual
consciousnesses as a result of a natural evolutionary
process will be gathered together to produce a
super-consciousness or "Mystical Body," which will
endow all its participants with powers far above and
beyond presently "normal" capacities.

The controversy caused by such Teilhardian ideas
reminds one of the endless speculation about the
condition of Adam and Eve in the "Garden of
Eden"--speculation which began in the patristic era and
still continues. Down through the centuries, the
majority opinion in the Church seemed to hold that Adam
and Eve were endowed with some extraordinary privileges

and powers-- freedom from sickness and death, infused scientific and theological knowledge, perfect control over their own impulses and over their environmental conditions. But were these powers and privileges "natural" or "supernatural"? Some authorities saw them as supernatural endowments which were forfeited when man "fell from grace" by original sin. Others characterized them as endowments natural to man, but unfortunately lost by their sin--so that now man would require supernatural help ("grace") to regain them. Contemporary Scripture scholars often interpret the story in Genesis as a myth of some primeval state of innocence, fondly enhanced and embellished into "supernatural" proportions in the memory of those who have developed to a higher stage of civilization and were struggling with the everyday realities of that higher state.

Obviously, the dispute as to what is natural and what is supernatural is largely semantic. Hindu Yogis claim that by following their methods of meditation and ascetic practices, individuals can acquire the powers of performing miracles, prophecy, levitation, bilocation, living without eating or sleeping, etc. If these claims were true, would these powers be "natural" or "supernatural"? We find the same sort of powers described as "supernatural" in the Christian Lives of the Saints; but Yogis generally prefer to see them as natural powers which are latent and need to be activated by Yoga or other techniques.

With a minimum amount of intellectual adjustment and compromise, one can perceive that the "natural but latent power" which the Yogi purports to "activate" is one and the same thing with those inner powers, states or gifts which are often described as "infused" or "supernatural" in Christian saints. But the Yogic approach is more optimistic: one who thinks that such powers are latent in everyone is more optimistic about human nature than one who looks upon them as "exceptions to the rule."

23. Angels can approach us now only after some wing-trimming

Whatever happened to the angels? There is scarcely any reference to them any more by preachers, philosophers, theologians and religious people in general. It is as if they had become outmoded in the modern world. And, indeed, the traditional concept of the "angel" is particularly unsuited to our age of technology.

Consider the "profile" of the angel: He hovers above us, is capable of swift movement anywhere (symbolized by his wings), has a comprehensive knowledge of what is going on in the world (thus being able to protect his charges from evil), and has a predilection for the ancient and medieval cultures (as we may surmise from his depiction in long, flowing garb). In our day there is nothing wonderful anymore about swift movement, even through the skies; we have instant knowledge of events taking place throughout the world (through television, telephone, etc.); and we are so proud of our contemporary stage of progress that we would probably not expect to receive any usable and progressive advice from a creature who is identified even clothing-wise with the ancients. It is hard enough to maintain a viable concept of an all-powerful and all-knowing God in our powerful and eminently enlightened civilization; it is even more difficult to be serious about angels. . .

The fact is, in order for people to conceptualize any entity as "divine," this entity must have some aura of mystery about it. If it so happens that, with the advance of science, things which were formerly considered "mysterious" are no longer seen in that light, eventually a point will be reached when former divinities, associated with former mysteries, must be relegated to the shadows of myth.

Is there in our day a "revised version" of the angels? The closest candidate for this honor seems to be the flying saucers. Consider the current folklore about flying saucers: They come to us from an extraterrestrial civilization which is supposed to be far advanced beyond us, not only technologically but morally (why don't we simply presuppose that they are creatures like us, with a strong tendency to evil and self-aggrandizement?). They are coming to protect us from destruction by some catastrophe, nuclear or otherwise (a function strangely similar to that of the angels of yesteryear). They move instantaneously and are even able (according to some) to "stop on a dime" and to make abrupt turns at a 90-degree angle (accomplishments which are wonderful even to denizens of space-age earth). They are continually observing man all over the world, but after decades and decades of observation they still seem to have no inclination to land and deal with earthlings in some publicly recognizable and verifiable way (the most feasible way of explaining this reluctance to "mix," is that they consider themselves a completely different and superior species, such that communication with man would be deemed as inappropriate as man's communication with plants is deemed inappropriate by us. They are supposed to have the power to read thoughts, and to completely control the behavior of human beings without resorting to guns or other coercive devices. They appear only to isolated individuals or small groups of individuals (just as the visions of angels in the Ages of Faith were always private or semi-private visions). And finally, they are depicted as utilizing super-advanced instruments of conveyance (now it is the flying saucer, which goes beyond all our technology, using a motive source and energy unlike anything we know; in former days, it was the wing--which had never been put to use as an instrument for human conveyance).

Can one considering such resemblances fail to suspect the "blood relationship" between the flying saucers of today and the angelic hosts of yesteryear? They have had to relinquish their ancient garb and change their habits, but they are still with us, out there in the skies.

24. Spiritual alienation can be dissipated only if social alienation is overcome; and vice versa

There are currents or schools of thought in most major religions, which regard personal, spiritual or ascetic activities such as meditation, prayer, fasting and/or reading of Scriptures, as panaceas for "spiritual" alienation-- which might be defined as the doubt, disquietude and purposelessness that seems to characterize human life. Overemphasis or over-reliance on these remedies is a mistake, however, because spiritual alienation tends to be inseparably intertwined with deep-seated and almost ineradicable social alienations. Two reasons of a philosophical nature can be given for this:

1) In our introspective knowledge of ourselves we tend, consciously or unconsciously, to compare

ourselves with others; the value judgments which we
make about ourselves are conditioned by the (often
unthinking or biased) value judgments we have already
made about those with whom we compare and contrast
ourselves.

2) If we may believe the psychoanalysts, we tend
to project the things we love or hate about ourselves
onto other people. Thus, if there is some aspect of
myself that I loathe, instead of examining and
re-evaluating this loathing, I sometimes transfer it
onto another person who reminds me of this aspect of
myself; and this other person bears the full brunt of
my fury or disdain. Likewise, if there is some aspect
of myself about which I feel particularly smug or
proud, I will sometimes tend to gather around me others
who also reflect that aspect also and thus admire that
aspect--so that any serious critical re-evaluation of
myself might call for a critical redirection of my
social propensities (a consideration which may
naturally prejudice me against critically re-evaluating
myself in the first place.)

Thus, paradoxically, the quickest and most
"direct" way to overcome spiritual alienation may be to
alter the direction and distibution of our social
involvements. Christ seemed to have something like
this in mind when he said, "If you go to the altar to
offer your gift to God, and then remember that you have
some unresolved difficulty with your neighbor, go first
to be reconciled with your neighbor and then you may
make your sacrifice profitably to God" (Matt. V, 23).
In other words, if you read your Bible, go to Mass or
recite your Buddhist mantras in the morning, and (by
action or apathy) contribute to racial, civil, or
community strife in the afternoon, you may be
increasing rather than diminishing your personal
alienation.

On the other hand, the hostilities and rivalries
that take place between individuals and groups have
their own momentum and are often self-perpetuating.
What is it that prevents individuals from extricating
themselves from this web of "social alienation," if not
their own alienation from themselves? Aristotle in his
Nicomachean Ethics remarks that one must be on friendly
terms with himself before he can effectively befriend
others. Kierkegaard, in Either/Or, applies a similar
observation to the modern world: there are too may
people rushing headlong into mindless and destructive

external relationships because of their simple fear of
being by themselves, without anything or anyone to
distract them. For such an individual, perhaps the one
thing necessary and sufficient for helping them break
out of their own cycle of social necessities, is some
form of spiritual introspection, recommended by this or
that religion.

The major conclusion to be drawn here is that
individual spiritual alienation and interpersonal or
social alienations are absolutely interdependent. A
religion will generally avoid recommending that a
devotee rush into his house to pray while people are
dying or houses are burning outside his front window.
We may expect that most religious persuasions will also
avoid the other extreme, of recommending complete
immersion in efforts for civil and social amelioration,
regardless of the spiritual and personal depth of those
who are to so immerse themselves. But between these
two extremes -- which theologians sometimes call the
incarnational and eschatological dimensions of
Christianity -- there are more subtle variations of
emphasis on the one extreme or the other, which are
equally self-defeating, and more dangerous because less
obvious.

25A. Laws in religion are in a certain sense
     superfluous (or counter-productive) because
     spontaneity is of the essence of religion

If religion has any purpose and goal, it is to
free men from laws--from the laws of the passions and
inclinations which control human behavior, and often
prevent them from following reason; from the laws of
conventional thought, which tie men down to a certain
narrow view of reality, rendering them unable to raise
their sights beyond their own limited perspectives; and
from the laws of force, power and war, which tend to
extinguish even the basic natural attractions and
affinities of men, and prevent the unification of men
and mankind. In order to facilitate the accomplishment
of these goals, religions will offer various
options--counsels of fasting, almsgiving and other
ascetic practices, to help assure the ascendancy of
reason over inclination (self-mastery); beliefs
concerning the nature of the world and the destiny of

man; beliefs calculated to illuminate man about his purpose and place in the world (items concerning which the average man is in darkness); and more or less sophisticated ways of regrouping and unifying men--if not in the service of Universal Love, then at least as a means to transcending individual, familial, and provincial enmities and rivalries. There is a well-known tendency in religions, however, to extrapolate these recommendations and supererogatory measures into new laws--laws concerning ascetic practices, dogmas to be believed, rituals to be performed. This has happened in all religions--Judaism with its numerous dietary laws, purifications and endogamous injunctions; Roman Catholicism, with its elaborate code of Canon Law, and its definitive moral pronouncements; Protestantism, for which proper interpretation of, and adherence to, Scripture, often takes on the aspect of a new law; Hinduism, with its ritual and dietary observances and the present remnants of the former caste system; Mohammedanism, which still inculcates a somewhat passive acceptance of fate, and the subservience of women in society; and so on. A law or injunction, of course, would be meaningless and ineffective without some sanction. In order to give "clout" to its laws, religion must thus either ally itself with the secular power (which can chop off heads, if necessary), or develop more subtle sanctions--social ostracism, threats of punishments in this life or the next, etc. The dangerous thing about such laws, of course, is that they can be observed in a purely mechanical fashion, without any particular show of freedom or spontaneity. This is an ironical development, to say the least, since the purpose of religion in the first place was to free and illuminate its adherents. When all religions are encumbered with laws or provincial perspectives, and this becomes manifest, shall we expect another super-religion or meta-religion to appear on the scene and once again fulfill the task of freeing and illuminating men? Or, as the skeptics prefer to suggest, should we expect religion to finally "self-destruct" under the sheer weight of all this peripheral apparatus?

25B. Laws are necessary in religion to inculcate spontaneity of spirit

The goal of religion, to state the matter summarily, seems to be a state characterized by preeminent knowledge of the self, and its relationship to the world and/or God--not the abstract, theoretical knowledge that philosophy and psychology offer us--but an experimental and practical knowledge which will spontaneously result in congruent and sustained personal and social expressions of one's true self. Some religious sectaries downplay the arduousness of this goal: the gnostics, the illuminati and pseudo-mystics who claim secret, privileged, wholesale and immediate access to the divine arcana; and the semi-Dionysiac pseudo-charismatics, ancient or modern, who pride themselves on their talents for producing spontaneous, emotional outpourings of truly inspired, divine sentiments almost at will, in the proper setting. However, most mortals, even if they accept the above-stated goal of religion, will see it as a distant goal (because of their awareness of their own limitations); and will approach it in the way that they approach any other rationally projected and seriously contemplated goal in life--by devising laws, methods, systems, roads, ways, or strategems for attaining it. There is, of course, the ever-present danger and almost the inevitablility that such laws, methods, etc. will become vulgarized, misunderstood, needlessly embellished, or, worst of all, ends-in-themselves instead of means. But what are we to say of the St. Pauls, the Wesleys and the Siddarthas who seemed to have attained illumination, serenity and freedom of spirit in a few moments, bypassing all the systems and laws? Miraculous conversions and spontaneous illuminations cannot be categorized or accounted for, of course, precisely because they are supposed to go beyond the usual, beyond the laws. But if we examine such cases we usually find that the devotee thus favored has been using various methods, whether useful or ill-advised, to attain his projected religious goal, and had either almost despaired of reaching this goal or at least had no particular intimation that it was imminent. Those who devise methods and set sail for their goals will occasionally catch a particularly propitious wind with comparatively little effort; those who don't set sail would, of course, not be able to harness the wind, even if it came their way.

26. Marxism is an alienated form of religion

Karl Marx, following the German philosopher, Feuerbach, used to say that religion and the belief in God was an "alienated form of true human existence." He based this thesis on the conjecture that "God" was simply an objectification or projection of man's most creative and productive capacities: Man's capacity for goodness was projected into a God who was the Supreme Good; man's capacity for gaining power over the world and nature was projected into a God who was all-powerful; and so forth. After the projection took place, man was simply dealing with himself, his own capacities, but in this projected or alienated form. This process brought about a form of escapism. Men, fascinated by this divinized image of their own abilities, were content merely to admire and worship it, calling it "God"; there was no urgent need to develop their potentialities, because these potentialities had already reached absolute perfection in the God-image.

Marx felt that this was an "upside-down" view of reality, and he proposed to re-focus man's attention on his own powers of productivity, thus restoring a "right-side-up" view of reality. It is possible, however, that Marxism itself is an upside-down view of reality. And then, from the right-side-up perspective, it would be valid to say that Marxism is an alienated form of religion.

Most major religions have as their goal the attainment of universal brotherhood, the unification of mankind. (In Christianity, the most explicit formulation of this goal is the notion of the "Mystical Body," an organic unity of Christians as a body under Christ as their head--a concept which was intended by St. Paul to be more than a metaphor.) But the means taken to this goal by religion have been twofold: 1) devotion to God as Father, or as the absolute reconciler of differences; 2) the attainment of illumination, self-knowledge and self-reconciliation on the part of the religious devotee (in Christianity, the supposition has been that if I see God as "Our Father", brotherhood will ensue with others who actually or potentially recognize the fatherhood of God; and if I struggle to overcome my sins and attain spiritual integrity for myself, I will more readily see the way toward reconciliation with my "other selves," i.e. my neighbors.)

One could say, then, that the Marxists, impatient
that the goal of mutual reconciliation and universal
unity might be attained, chose to bypass the methods of
worship and individual ascetical practice, which
prevailed in religion, and substituted their own
methods--a scientifically engineered world-wide
revolution, which would obliterate class differences
and facilitate the reappropriation of their own
productivity by the working people of the world. This
goal would be attained by force, if necessary; although
in certain instances force might not be necessary.
Thus Marxism took over a goal of Christianity and
other religions; but, because of a complete reversal in
priorities, this goal was hardly recognizable in
Marxian form; i.e. it existed in "alienated" form in
the Marxian ideology.

In line with this thesis, we can then see an
explanation for the animosity of Christians to Marxism:
nothing is more obnoxious to a person (or a group) than
to see another person (or group) flouting and
capitalizing on prerogatives that had always been
reserved to oneself. We can also see clues of a hidden
attraction: the jealousy of inveterate enemies is often
caused by a latent desire for the qualities or
characteristics manifested by the "enemy."

27. Belief in the afterlife is most effective if it is
vague

Let us suppose for the moment that the traditional
religious belief in an "afterlife" is exactly
true--that there definitely is some abode of light,
bliss and perfect harmony somewhere in some universe,
to which men with the requisite qualifications can go
after their death. Let us also suppose that there is a
benevolent and all-powerful God who both desires all
men to enter into this supernal state and is willing to
do anything necessary to help them get there. On these
suppositions, it would seem a natural "first step" on
the part of this God to give men a clear and distinct
idea of this possible destiny--would it not?
Otherwise, how could they seriously strive for it and
fulfill the prerequisites for attaining it--which may
involve considerable sacrifice? As Paul says, "If the
trumpet gives off an uncertain sound, who will prepare
himself for battle?" (1 Cor. XIV, 8).

This line of thought seems logical. But reflect for a moment on what might be necessary for this God to give men a clear and distinct idea of their afterlife. . . For one thing, they would possibly have to die. At least, there is a tradition in Christianity, Hinduism and other religions that man's usual, unmodified body and senses would be an impediment to perceiving the higher spiritual reality of "heaven." On the other hand, St. Paul was supposed to have been transported into the "Seventh Heaven" while still living; and the question naturally arises, could not God perform a similar feat for all men, thus affording all of them the "clear and distinct" idea of where they are going, or where they could be going if they proceed properly along the way?

No doubt an omnipotent God could perform such a feat (although in admiring his omnipotence we might begin to have serious reservations about his prudence, in failing to regulate the laws of human nature from the beginning in such a fashion that he would not need to intervene miraculously in every person's life to provide adequate goal-orientation.) But if He did intervene in such a fashion, the intervention would no doubt be counter-productive with most of us. One person, after coming face-to-face with such incomparable bliss, would be unable to get interested in ordinary life and duties any more, and would pine away in neurotic hankering for the "next world." Another person, a hedonist by temperament, would no longer be able to enjoy the pure sensual pleasure which he prefers, and would be perpetually cursing the memory of the divine experience that distracts him from the serious business of immersing himself in momentary enjoyments. Such examples might be multiplied.

What, then? Are we to opt for a concept of the afterlife which is highly dubious, incapable of eliciting intellectual assent except from the most credulous denizens of this world? This would be equally unfortunate; for it would have the effect of immersing man completely in his temporal situation. Utopian and futuristic concepts--which are often just "demythologized" versions of religious notions of an afterlife--would no doubt be few and far-between. Man in general would be more prosaic, more provincial.

No. The best possible situation for most of us is undoubtedly one in which the afterlife is a sufficiently viable belief to tantalize us, and make us

wonder now and then what sort of a future is really
attainable by man and whether some Transcendental Force
"up there" is going to crown our efforts with success;
but likewise sufficiently vague to force us to rely on
our own efforts, develop our own methods, and devise
our own solutions, for dealing with the enigmas and
conflicts of concrete existence.

28. Religious "self-surrender" and secular
    "self-determination" are identical in essence

"Self-determination," as we usually employ the
term, has a connotation of initiative, resourcefulness,
spontaneity and/or individualism; it is contrasted with
subservience in any form, and is supposed to be the
secular virtue of modern, democratized man.
"Self-surrender," on the other hand, is frequently used
in a religious or quasi-mystical context; and has the
opposite connotations of passivity, subservience,
helplessness and anonymity. Thus the extremely
religious exemplar of self-surrender is often
contrasted with the non-religious or anti-religious
exponent of self-determination.
     At their worst, self-surrender and
self-determination do tend in completely divergent
directions, and are validly contrasted. At its worst,
self-surrender can mean the unthinking and
unquestioning adherence to certain religious rituals or
concepts, or the purely emotional abandonment to some
higher force of inspiration which one feels--extreme
passivity being implied in all of this. At its worst,
self-determination loses its halo of enlightenment and
liberty and becomes stubbornness, willfulness,
capriciousness, egocentrism.
     In their essence, however, and at the apex of
their meaning, the two concepts converge: in
self-surrender, the God to which one subjects himself,
duly de-objectified and internalized, is none other
than one's own higher Self (a concept of the Self which
merges at its acme with the notion of
God-within-consciousness, e.g. the Christian notion of
the Holy Spirit). Thus the ultimate justification of
the religious man's stance of self-surrender is that he
is surrendering himself (his lower self, by definition)
to that which is best and highest in himself. In

self-determination, on the other hand, it is also
important that a similar distinction be made between
differently valued aspects of oneself. It would
certainly not be beneficial or progressive for one to
"determine himself" on the basis of every whim,
impulse, passion or craven desire. If it is to have
meaning at all, "self-determination" implies the--yes,
the surrender of that which is considered to be the
inferior self or the inferior aspects or elements of
the self, to that which is considered to be higher.

Whether in practical life the self-determiners and
the self-surrenderers will ever find themselves joining
in common cause is "another question." But, on a
purely conceptual and admittedly abstract plane, they
seem to be kinfolk.

29. The most complete miracle would require the
    complete perfection of science

In order to perform a thoroughly effective and
convincing miracle at any time, God would have to do
something that was completely beyond the reach of the
science and technology of those for whom he performed
the miracle--e.g. curing illnesses for which there was
no known cure, knowing things which would be considered
beyond the knowledge or even the educated guesses of
mortal men, performing feats that could not be
duplicated by teams of magicians and/or
scientist-technicians. In our day, for example, it
would no longer be extremely impressive for God to
speak in a thundering voice from behind the
clouds--since we all know that a movie mogul like Cecil
B. DeMille, with the help of a few weather balloons,
some off-duty Air Force specialists and his own sound
technicians could do something like this quite
convicingly (it goes without saying that in the
aftermath of the movie, The Ten Commandments, the
parting of the waters of the Red Sea or any other sea
is passè). Likewise, even if some apparition or
emissary of God were to hover or fly above us, without
any visible means of support, this would excite little
admiration in an age of aviation and space technology:

in our day we have Buck-Rogers-type rocket apparatus (visible but capable of further refinement) worn on the back and capable of carrying individuals up and away.

On the other hand, if God were to restore brain segments to former lobotomy patients, replenish all the world's oil supplies, inspire all millionaire capitalists to distribute their wealth to charity, and/or motivate all corrupt politicians to spontaneously confess their secret crimes and resign, people would no doubt sit forward and take notice, and belief in God would no doubt become publicly admissible and fashionable again, since such accomplishments as these are well beyond the grasp of our scientific technology or our sciences of behavior and human engineering.

For the grandest, most overwhelming miracle, however, we have to wait until the end--that is, until that day when all the sciences (physical, behavioral and social sciences) have gone as far as they can go. Then God (if only He is willing to avail Himself of this opportunity) has the possibility of performing the "absolute miracle"--i.e. a miracle not relative to the imperfect state of science in a particular era, but beyond the reach of science in any era. Three possibilities present themselves: 1) In the event that science will have overcome all the physical obstacles (disease, pollution, lack of natural resources, gravity and inertia, etc.) but never been able to control and harmonize society through behavioral engineering, the dictatorship of the proletariat, or any other means--the chance for the absolute social miracle would naturally be the final harmonization and pacification of mankind, at a time when authorities from all nations were throwing up their hands in disgust, saying that such a goal was impossible. Or 2) let us assume that the social, behavioral and political sciences had been equally successful as the physical sciences, and had produced ultimately a harmonious, crime-free, poverty-free world social order: God would still not lose His chance to perform the absolute subjective miracle. The miracle, in this case, would be to cause or foster belief in God at a time when mankind had absolute proof of its consummate competency and self-sufficiency. Or 3) if and when the science of psychology finally attains disciplinary maturity and perfects its techniques for bringing humans to personal maturity, we will be ready for the absolute miracle in psychological order -- the abolition of sin without the abolition of freedom. Or 4) when science has finally reached its limits in life-prolonging and resuscitation techniques, we would be best disposed to appreciate that absolute physical miracle, which would obviate the necessity for any further miracles--namely, the abolition of death itself.

30. Religious toleration is at present the greatest nemesis of religious unity

The religious toleration prevailing now in many parts of the civilized world is without doubt a great improvement over the persecutions, executions, malignments and malefactions prevailing among Catholics and Protestants, Christians and Jews, Christians and Moslems, etc. in days gone by. The diminishment of such open hostilities is taken as a presage of the dawning of an age of relative sophistication and enlightenment. Indeed, this may be the case. Enlightenment may be one of the contemporary world's chief virtues. But religious toleration, with all its enlightenment, is no great help to the cause of religious unity; and, in fact, it is at present the most formidable and subtle barrier to the latter.

In order to understand this, one should first realize that "religious toleration" has two divergent connotations now, both of them somewhat pejorative: On the one hand, it can imply an attitude of superiority, one smugly convinced religionist condescending to recognize the rights of other persuasions to earn for themselves a lower place in heaven, or a higher place in the nether regions. On the other hand, among the less dogmatically and orthodoxically inclined, it can mean the watering-down of one's beliefs and the dampening of one's zeal, to the point that, like a super-unitarian, his religion is neither offensive nor very vibrantly attractive to most others. The first brand of toleration is merely a more modern and polite form of repression, which nevertheless has its nasty practical consequences now and then, when it comes to choosing individuals for jobs or promotions, deciding on one's social equals, or espousing plans or policies

which embody ideological presuppositions or social
value-judgments. The second kind is much more amicable
and egalitarian, but so secularized that religious
motivation is an afterthought, if indeed it is present
in any degree. Either of these forms of religious
toleration is inimical to the realization of true
religious unity.

To achieve religious unity, ecumenism worthy of
the name, the first prerequisite is to go beyond
toleration. Transcendence of the attitude of mere
toleration takes place in three equally important
steps:

1) A deepening of personal religious commitments.
If one has religious beliefs which seem on an
intuitive basis, to be attractive and worth preserving,
then these beliefs should also be worth exploring and
examining, through reading, meditation, discussion,
etc. When one arrives at the deeper roots of his own
commitments, he may find to his surprise that he shares
these roots in common with what were thought to be
other ideological saplings. 2) Criticism and debate.
It is interesting to reflect that in the Middle Ages,
which are not particularly recognized for enlightenment
or sophistication, public disputes on matters of
religious dissent were frequent and proportionately as
well attended as football games in our own day. In our
"advanced" era, debates which delve into essential
religious differences are rather rare and elicit only
spasmodic interest (depending on conflict with
prime-time TV and other considerations). It of course
does little good to let our aggressions "hang out" in
shouting matches, but for a society trained in
toleration it should not be too difficult to engage in
debates on serious religious issues, with discipline
and dignity. The alternative to this is the repression
of one's inchoate religious inspirations and
enthusiasm, in the name of toleration, normality and
etiquette--a repression which may have equally serious,
if not morphologically similar, consequences as the
sexual repressions which have received most of our
attention. 3) Negotiation: The art of negotiation,
which has been widely practiced by politicians,
defeated generals and businessmen since time
immemorial, seems for some reason to be relatively
unknown and unpracticed by religious leaders.
Otherwise, no doubt, tiffs between Catholics and
Episcopals regarding the formal validity of their

ordinations to the priesthood, between Roman and
Orthodox Catholics concerning the center of
ecclesiastical authority, between Catholics and
Lutherans regarding the correct theological formulation
of the "Real Presence of Christ" at the Lord's Supper,
between some Protestant evangelicals and liberals on
the interpretation of the Scriptures--might have been
resolved in a creditable way long ago. Religious
authorities, when questioned about this lack of
negotiation, will often point out the importance of the
beliefs they are defending--one cannot compromise them
lightly, they say. But one who is less optimistic
about human nature might suspect that their motives are
just the opposite: a conviction that their beliefs are
unimportant, and don't affect world affairs much,
anyway. If a precise formula of belief, or ritual, or
organizational patterns is not going to change man or
the world, why bother negotiating about it? But we
might ask them, "what about ecumenism? does this, or
would it, have a beneficial effect on the world as a
whole? if so, why not begin serious negotiations?"

D. God

31A. The logical conclusion of theism is atheism

The history of religion is an incessant succession of human efforts to represent the transcendent or divine in various ways: as the sun or light; as plants, trees, or animals; in abstract symbols--pyramids or obelisks; in concrete symbols, talismans, statues, and finally as incarnate divinities (Jesus, Krishna) or men who have become immortalized (Buddha, Confucius, Mohammed). But throughout this long history rather frequent warnings have come, from within even the most "transcendent" religions, that God wears various guises and must not be confused with any of them. Thus in Judaism there was reticence about even naming God, for fear of hypostasizing him and making him, for all practical purposes, a highly conceptualized idol. Christian Fathers such as Dionysius the Pseudo-Areopagite and theologians such as Thomas Aquinas remind us that it is impossible to form any positive concept of God; and in fact, that what we call the God-concept is derived by a process of intellectual negation--thinking of the totality of beings and perfections, and then asserting that "God" is not any of these things or qualities, and indeed surpasses them all. No doubt the most extreme form of this counterbalancing trend is found in Buddhism, which comes close to neuroticism in denying the reality of any perfections, then denying the validity of these denials which are made, and even denying that the ultimate state of quiescent denial (Nirvana) is a reality (e.g. a positive concept of "God") or a negation (an ultimate product of human asceticism or stoical mysticism). In Buddhism we find perhaps the most admirable and honest attempt to come to grips with the notion of transcendence; and the result has often been characterized as an "atheistic" religion.

31B. But the culmination of reflective atheism is a return of theism

The message of enlightened atheism, in spite of numerous peripheral differences in emphasis, has been essentially the same: If there is anything divine, it is in man; let's forget about these unsubstantial projections of God, and devote our attention to the true source of man's own consciousness, his own ingenuity, creativity and resourcefulness. In propounding this message, our atheists are performing a role something like that of the Freudian psychiatrist who tries to bring his patient to a realization that, in his pursuit of love-objects, he is really just projecting his internal "mother-image" onto this or that suitable or not-so-suitable "carrier" of the image. But--following out this analogy a little further--our hypothetical Freudian patient might object to his analyst: "Now that I know it's my mother-image that's causing the trouble, I'm still not satisfied; I need some external content for this image, and I'm having trouble finding suitable content." So also, our dedicated and enlightened atheist, realizing that his new-found internalized "divinity" must be externalized, projected, objectified in some way, consciously or unconsciously directs his attention to some new and more properly atheistic absolute, but nevertheless an absolute. Thus Marx the atheist projects outwardly the supremely utopian concept of a perfectly unified society without greed, in which individual egos almost forget themselves in their altruistic absorption in something higher than themselves (this utopian concept, by the way, is not too dissimilar in its larger outlines from the Pauline concept of the "mystical body" of Christ in the world). So also Nietzsche the atheist, quite different in temperament from Marx, projects the ideal of a consummately perfect individual or individuals, a veritable "Superman" who will transcend ordinary men as much as God is assumed by theists to surpass man (in fact, Nietzsche's Superman will function as a God, a new focal point for the aspirations of men, a supreme arbiter of values and ideals prevalent in human society). Christians who are particularly devoted to the Holy Spirit (God as man, God immanent in human consciousness) perhaps undergo an analogous experience with this "immanent" concept: the idea of the divine must be projected in some fashion (images of the dove and the tongue-of-fire are not completely satisfactory), and thus they find themselves relying on some of the more transcendent and traditional images of God--even sometimes the Father and the Son. "Death of God" theologians nowadays, if they want to avoid a merely negative and funereal mood,

must perhaps follow either the Marxian or the
Nietzschean model--culminating either in utopian
concepts of a completely harmonious divine social order
or an overly optimistic conception of the creative or
psychic potential divinity of the individual man. If
this is unsatisfactory, they can always try God again.

32. God can only be our absolute "other" insofar as
     he is our absolute self-identity

     From existential-phenomenological theologians we
sometimes hear it said that God is the "Absolute
Other". By this, it is generally meant not only that
God is something absolutely different than man, but
also that there is something attractive, mysterious and
fascinating about this difference that makes it seem
worth investigating. (One could say that absolute
nothingness, if it could be conceived, is as different
from man as the most exacting existentialist would
require; but one could hardly get excited about
nothing. Or again, if a man contrasts himself with all
the rocks in the world, there is quite a chasm of
difference, but nothing to "write home about.")
Granted that God is not an indifferent or uninteresting
type of otherness, it must also be granted that He is a
person--since only a person could be both sufficiently
complex to merit sustained and everlasting fascination,
and sufficiently different to challenge the ego and its
parameters. But not any kind of person will do. After
all, it is only a handful of persons or personality
types that fascinate or intrigue us; and for some
reason or the other, it seems that these persons happen
to exemplify traits or virtues that we either are
conscious of in ourselves, or would like to think we
have; or else identify with in a purely unconscious
way, in potentialities that are present but never
actualized or expressed. In short, the persons that we
find interestingly "other" tend to be those with whom
we identify in one way or another. But if there is an
aura of mystery associated with our attraction or
interest, this is generally attributable to the fact
that the identification is unconscious. Thus Carl
Jung, in theorizing about the ideals of attractive
sexual objects which individuals formulate for
themselves, hypothesizes that these ideals result from

repressed and unconscious sexual potentialities; for example, a man who has certain female characteristics and tendencies, but will repress them in deference to his male role and society's expectations, will project his own repressed tendencies as a female "ideal," and will tend to find females who conform to this ideal "fascinating" (the converse case holds for females with repressed masculine traits). Following on this line of thought, we may say (Jung and others have already said it) that the idea of God as a n ideal divine person results from our individual projection of our own most fundamental and superior, but as yet unfulfilled, potentialities. Each of us has a feeling for what is our highest potentiality and our key to ultimate perfection, and we absolutize and conceptualize this feeling into "God." This idea is characterized by mystery and an image of unknowability, however, because we can never really know potentialities until they have become actualized (if we were cocksure about our God, and found nothing mysterious about Him, we would no doubt be projecting conscious, rather than unconscious, attributes--i.e. virtues that we are quite proud of in ourselves, and would like to see absolutized and properly divinized). Once we formulate this idea as a general impression or intuition, we will also tend to associate it with certain eminently suitable ideas, symbols, representations of the divine--which provide proper content or vehicles ("carriers") for the idea.

What, then? are we to say in Marxian-Feuerbachian fashion that God as supreme Person is just a projection of the ultimate possibilities of human nature? Why "just" . . . human nature? If God has any traceable genealogy, what better Bethlehem could He have than some of the cleaner and better-equipped caverns to be found in the interior of human consciousness?

33. God can only become present through his absence

Writers of religious and mystical books sometimes speak of the "practice of the presence of God," and recommend this practice to their readers. They also make mention of a concrete, emotional feeling of God's presence, which may come to a person now and then as a "gift." But "way down deep" these writers generally realize that such practical or sensuous experiences

could never be very effective encounters with God.
God, after all, is a spirit; and an encounter with God
on the plane of feeling and sensuous experience would
be comparable to a conversation with a great mind, in
which there is nothing more than an exchange of
pleasantries and talk about trivial matters. In both
cases there would be, in the strict sense, no
encounter.

In an earlier section (#31) it was mentioned that
we reach the idea of God through absolute negation--we
think of all perfections in this world, then negate
them by thinking of something "beyond" them, and that
"beyond" is God. To this intellectual process, it
would seem there corresponds an emotional process. To
reach towards God emotionally (and here again we have
corroboration from many mystical writers) one must
engage in successive emotional detachment, withdrawal,
disengagement and disillusionment, until one's psyche
is sufficiently refined to be capable of a meeting with
God "spirit-to-spirit." But in fact the term,
"meeting" is in this context a misnomer. For as
sources as disparate as Buddhist scriptures and the
ascetical writings of St. John of the Cross tell us,
the very process of successive emotional negations and
rejections is itself the gradual manifestation of the
Absolute (which in Christianity, is called God). Or,
another way of putting it--it is the Spirit of God
which impels the soul to transcend the finite and the
sensuous; and, in the process of doing this the soul is
spiritualized or divinized, so that talk about
"encounter with the divine" becomes superfluous and
inappropriate (one is the divine, i.e. encounters the
divine in oneself).

And so--is our would-be mystic to resign himself
to a life of negation and absences, and call that God?
Not quite. There is a mystical-theological loophole in
this process: if one successfully transcends all his
emotional and sensual attachments, or is gradually
weaned away from them, his final state is essentially
one without pain, negation, or absence. In Buddhism,
the attainment of "Nirvana" (emptiness of the self) is
the attainment of final bliss and peace. In Christian
mysticism, the "dark night of the soul," in which one
suffers the complete absence of God, results in the
"unitive state," in which there is such constant
identification with God that the dualism implied in the
term, "presence," becomes completely inappropriate and
inapplicable.

34. God is a projection of the future of man: but he
    must be present now, in order to be projected

     It is not too uncommon to hear from psychologists
and Marxians that God is a "projection." The Marxian,
as we indicated above (Thesis #31), held that God was
simply a projection of man's as yet unfulfilled
productive potentialities. Freudians, in a somewhat
parallel way, say that the idea of God is simply the
farthest extension and reification of man's own
super-ego (our unconscious notion of the moral "oughts"
bearing on our behavior); while Jungians prefer to talk
about an unconscious archetype of the union of
opposites, which is projected onto certain "divine"
entities or persons. In all such cases, the term,
"projection," is used to describe the
semi-objectification of something which is purely
subjective: God is really just a conscious or
unconscious idea, but becomes embodied in, or confused
with (or "projected into"), what is really _real_. . .
     Such theorists no doubt perform us a service in
offering some plausible explanations as to how the idea
of God is formed. If the idea of God is to be
something more than a vague intimation of "otherness"
or the "Unknown God" that St. Paul found so piteous, it
has to be complemented with positive attributes, drawn
perhaps quite liberally from our own intuitions about
our fundamental positive capacities (whether actualized
or as yet unfulfilled.) (The "devil," of course, would
be the suitable "carrier" for our projected negative
capabilities.) If such a mechanism does take place,
then the idea of God also becomes a very subtly masked
notion of man's own _future_ ("man" here can have either
an individual or generic connotation): our idea of God
can be an idea of our own _personal future_ in terms of
potentialities unfulfilled or only partially
fulfilled--and/or an idea of the future of the race or
culture whose attributes we identify with and personify
in our god or gods. Thus the various ideas of God
which have developed from the dawning of man's
pre-history can be interpreted as exemplifying an
evolution in human consciousness itself, and
particularly consciousness of the future: at first
there are only vague ideas of good and evil

attributes, states and powers, "anthropomorphized" into
a divinity; gradually, the idea of the divine becomes
more complex in personality traits and/or embodies more
definite, sophisticated and abstract virtues (thus
reflecting the more sophisticated self-consciousness of
later generations and their clearer ideas of "where
they are going" and what is possible to them).

But, granted that man's idea of God may be a
useful index for gauging his goals and what he
considers progress--is it "just an idea"? Man's future
possibilities embodied in the idea of God are based on
an intuition, faulty or veridical, of his own present
capacities, trivial or important, good or bad,
all-too-human or transcending the human. It is
possible, just possible that man at the present has the
power of eventually breaking out of the human state,
transcending it, becoming divinized individually and/or
as a race. If so, our ideas of the divine may prove to
be something more than merely carriers for our dreams
and foibles--they may prove to be objectifications of
nuclear forces really within consciousness now, to
which man is very slowly and laboriously giving birth.
If and when these forces are released, we shall realize
that the God who becomes manifest is the God who was
within us all along. The Alpha is the Omega.

35. God is neither transcendent nor immanent but a
    limiting case for both transcendence and immanence

Philosophers and theologians in our day, when
discussing the "God question," often refer to the
traditional distinction between transcendence and
immanence. In general, the "transcendent" is that
which is "other" than the ego, and thus is capable of
being taken as an object by the ego. The "immanent,"
on the other hand, is simply an aspect or possession of
the self, or that which has been reduced to this
status. With reference to God, then, it is said that
man previously considered God as an entity transcendent
to, and independent from, man; while the trend now
(reaching its culmination in "death of God" theology)
is to reject the idea of a God "out there" in favor of
a new emphasis on man and human consciousness, which
(so it seems) is the source of divinity as well as the
"God-idea."

Following this distinction, we would tend to say that that which is transcendent cannot be immanent and vice versa--for example, the "world" as contrasted with the self is other than the self and could never be completely assimilated to it, and personal experience as contrasted with the "objects experienced" is thoroughly immanent and the source of immediate certitude. But, as applied to God, the distinction does not hold up. For God is the exception, the "limiting case."

Take, for example, the idea of God as "beyond the skies" or the Creator of the Universe--certainly a bona fide old-fashioned "transcendent" idea if there ever was one. Yes, the individual who portrays God in this fashion is thinking of something "other" than himself. But there is a "catch": in thinking of God in this way, he is thinking of God precisely as the source of his own human nature and his own consciousness. If an infant being born could recognize the umbilical cord still attaching him to his mother, he would perceive it ambiguously, as that which is in a certain sense external to himself, but also in a very real sense the source of his own physical life. Those for whom the idea of a transcendent God is a "living" idea (to use William James' term) similarly do not perceive God just as an interesting external object, but as the source of their own intimate mental life and self-consciousness.

On the other hand, those who try to reduce God to the parameters of human experience, if they do not completely succeed in humanizing and demystifying God, are left with an unassimilable "divine" element within human experience itself. Religious and mystical experiences of all sorts are a case in point: those who report such experiences and seem to be level-headed and objective, often emphasize (a) that the experience was sudden and unprepared for, i.e., completely outside one's subjective control; (b) that it was unconnected with ordinary feelings, sexual or otherwise; and (c) that it was the experience of something absolutely other, i.e. not just the perception of an aspect of oneself as in proprioception and self-consciousness. These reports are often received with skepticism, because, if taken seriously, they seem to imply that man is something more than himself, or, more precisely, that there is something more than the ego in man-- which seems to be a self-contradiction. But, paradoxes aside, the experience of God as immanent would have to be different from every other immanent experience.

E. Faith, Knowledge and Revelation

36. Faith emerges only in the absence of knowledge

The defenders of Reason in all eras have shown a tendency to accuse religious people, "believers," of ignorance. To a certain extent they are correct, but their criticism is not quite as devastating as it is intended to be.

Before proceeding any further in a discussion of "faith," it is necessary to distinguish three different usages of this word which are often confused (references will also be made to these different senses in a few of the Theses which follow this one): 1) "Faith" sometimes means mere belief or "opinion." This is the sense in which philosophical analysts and logicians often understand the term, "faith," when they are discussing the validity of religious beliefs. Thus their analysis of faith is similar in procedure to their analyses of beliefs such as "it is going to rain tomorrow." For the serious religious person, on the other hand, "faith" does not usually have this meaning, although he occasionally lapses into it: For example, the fundamentalist will speak about his faith in a non-evolutionary creation of the world by God, the Catholic will assert his faith in infallibility, transubstantiation, or sacerdotal celibacy; but in either case, if you pressed the individual concerning the extent and seriousness of the "faith," and confront him with the fact of certain "in-house" theological disputes, he may be willing to admit that he was just speaking about his personal opinion. 2) "Faith" often implies an intuition about reality which goes beyond accepted and factual knowledge, but is not just a guess or a "stab in the dark." The scientist who formulates a new and formidable hypothesis to explain certain hitherto unaccounted-for phenomena is operating on the basis of a kind of "natural faith." In the religious or supernatural realm, a similar process of hypothesis-formation concerns itself with the ultimate reality, and this somewhat cerebral and intellectual aspect of faith is what Catholics (especially) seem to mean by "faith." In this sense, the idea of God as an explanation of the creation of the universe, of "original·sin" as an explanation of man's weakness and/or perfidy, of the "Virgin Birth" and Incarnation as an explanation for the origin of such an unusual and exemplary individual as Jesus Christ--are "ultimate hypotheses" based on a certain intuition of the human situation and the mysteries associated with this situation. 3) In a third sense, faith is almost synonymous with trust. This seems to be the foremost Biblical sense. When Christ asks his disciples or his audience to "believe" in him, or commends the centurion or the Gentile woman for their "faith," he is not speaking so much about an intellectual assent to certain interpretations of reality as about a trust which, presumably, is based on one's intuitional or emotional <u>love</u> for him as a person. Since this non-intellectual, non-dogmatic sense of faith is the one most frequently represented in the Gospels, it is natural that Protestants, emphasizing the importance of the Bible, have also emphasized this connotation of "faith."

It should be noted that these three senses of faith (we shall call them $faith_1$, $faith_2$, $faith_3$) are not necessarily mutually exclusive. $Faith_3$, for example, if it is a belief in the "mercy" of God, converges with $faith_2$; $faith_3$, if it is a trust precisely in God's "words" or doctrine or prophecy, becomes $faith_2$; and both $faith_2$ and $faith_3$, if they are primarily conditioned by social and cultural traditions rather than any strong personal convictions, may border on becoming $faith_1$.

*   *   *   *

It should be noted that it is only in sense #1 that faith is, strictly speaking, a species of ignorance. Thus $faith_1$ (opinion) is defined precisely as an imperfect state of knowledge; and naturally those religious people who would devote themselves to this type of faith are contrasted unfavorably with the devotees of reason and science. In the "Catholic" sense (meaning #2), however, "faith" connotes a serious hypothesis about the world and the mysteries of human life. Though it emerges in a context of defective scientific knowledge, it is based on some positive intuitions and insights about certain ultimate puzzles. Thus the proponents of science cannot accuse <u>this</u> kind of believer of ignorance in a pejorative sense, i.e. superstition, since science itself is in a similar state of ignorance about the same questions. The scientifically oriented person may choose to adopt other theses as explanatory devices, but they are just hypotheses and there are no "universally accepted" hypotheses concerning such ultimate questions; thus at base science shares a state of ignorance with regard to these mysteries, in common with religion. [8]

Finally, in the "Protestant" sense, again, "faith" does not necessarily imply ignorance in the pejorative sense, but emphasizes other values than knowledge, and other functions than knowing. There may be ignorance, as is the case with the neophyte who submits himself with trust to the respected master, but--even in this example--ignorance is not the necessary motivation, since the neophyte may submit himself because of his affection and love for the master, and not precisely because of his desire for knowledge or his consciousness of relative ignorance. Therefore, we could say that although knowledge or progress in knowledge may be a concomitant or by-product of faith, knowledge is never an important consideration or motivating factor--and thus, in this case also, faith emerges in the absence of, i.e. outside the sphere of, knowledge.

37. Faith can only exist in a "credibility gap"

We are speaking here of faith, (see p. 83 above), i.e. faith-as-trust. Faith of this[3] kind implies and even requires a certain degree of doubt or "nervousness" about the object of faith. If the object of my faith, were completely and incontrovertibly a "sure thing," there would be no merit in my believing in that person; in fact my actions in deference to that person might better be described as prudence or pragmatism, rather than faith,. On the other hand, if I went about believing in everybody, or believing in some one person in every respect at every time, this faith, would certainly be no compliment to the person towards whom it is directed; rather, it would be looked upon with annoyance or contempt, as a sort of mindless dependence. Thus a realistic and bona fide concept of trust implies, objectively, a less than "perfect" and "perfectly obvious" worthiness in the trustworthy person; and subjectively, a residual diffidence and reserve on the part of the individual placing his trust in someone.

Thus the faith$_3$ which Christ valued so highly and tried to elicit from his disciples was essentially characterized by a kind of dialectic. It was continually receiving setbacks when Christ enunciated unintelligible teachings and parables, and was being continually subjected to indignities that seemed incongruous with his Messianic kingship; but the same faith$_3$ was spurred on, conversely, by periods of lucidity and victory. If it had been more or less than this, it would not have been human, conscious, developing and dynamic, meritorious trust. A more abstract and subtle dialectic is often found in the relationship of Christian mystics to God: the pathway to religious perfection and "union" is strewn with rejection and "dark nights"--God seems to be very hard, cold and unapproachable towards what (one would think) are his "best friends," but then, every once in a while, when the situation has become almost intolerable, seems to reveal Himself a little bit or offer a little bit of consolation. In the Catholic Church, faith in the ecclesiastical leadership falls in this same category. "He who hears you, hears me," Christ tells his disciples; and Catholic theologians look upon the present-day Church hierarchy as successors of the disciples and Apostles. Thus (they conclude) faith is due not only directly to God and Christ, but also in a general way to Christ's "mediators," including the Pope, bishop, etc. If what they tell us is true, we may observe 1) that this would be another instance of faith$_3$; and 2) that, analogous to the other application of faith$_3$, a "credibility-gap" would be essential in this area of faith also: If, for example, the Pope began to make pronouncements on birth control, war, civil rights, etc. that most men agreed with and thought to be eminently sensible, they would nod agreement to the principles that they themselves already accepted, but there would be no faith$_3$ _ipso facto_ required, nor would there necessarily be any trust in the personal integrity and veracity of (in this example) the Pope. In order for us to be cast precisely in the attitude of "faith$_3$," a certain amount of what the trusted person does or says has to be "above us," in some way unintelligible, unassimilable.

38. The dissolution of faith leads to the dissolution
    of knowledge

Here we are again discussing $faith_2$ (see p. 68
above). $Faith_2$ is concerned with forming ultimate
hypotheses, quasi-conceptual constructs concerning the
world and man's situation in the world. The "man of
$faith_2$" confronts mysteries concerning the origin of
the universe, the purpose of life, etc., and tries to
make them intelligible through myths, legends, or
religious theses. As he proceeds to do this, "science"
in its various forms comes on the scene to cast doubt
upon the formulations he has made. The man of $faith_2$
subsequently tries to reformulate his ideas in a more
sophisticated way. Science then attacks these
reformulations--and so on. Sooner or later, the man of
$faith_2$ may become discouraged and cease to formulate
any "ultimate" hypotheses, because "science is going to
refute them, anyhow." But such disillusionment with
faith is a mistake. Yes, one may expect one's $faith_2$
to be continually challenged and modified because of
the findings of science, but never abrogated--because
science per se avoids the consideration of ultimates.
For example, the English cosmologist Fred Hoyle has
proposed a doctrine of "continual creation" of matter,
in order to account for certain realities in an
expanding universe; but has continually dismissed such
questions as "creation out of what?" or "how did it all
start?" as uninteresting and irrelevant. If a
scientist allowed himself to delve seriously into such
ultimate mysteries, he would be delving and
hypothesizing not as a scientist but as a man of $faith_2$
(since there can be no precise, scientific knowledge of
such things).
     Thus science never contradicts a truly ultimate
hypothesis, i.e. $faith_2$.
     But it is one thing to say that science and $faith_2$
do not come into conflict. It is another to say that
$faith_2$, in spite of the necessity for its continual
revision or demythologization, is a prerequisite for
science-- and this is the main point we intend to make
here. In order to understand this, reflect on a
fundamental dictum of Gestalt psychology: the
comprehension of the context or whole determines the
order and import of the comprehension of the parts.
This dictum applies primarily to the perceptual order,
but it also has an analogate in the conceptual or

scientific sphere: one's basic view of man and the universe dictates the kind of scientific questions which will be considered relevant, the criteria on the basis of which solutions are accepted or rejected, and the general succession of problems which are posed. And, even more important, this basic view provides the sine qua non context for knowledge: to perceive objects pertinent to a room without perceiving the fact that they are set in the context of the room, would be an incomplete and misleading perception. To comprehend a host of scientific facts without having any positive notion of, or interest in, their ultimate context would be to willfully ignore the meaning, value and intelligibility-potential of the facts which are "known." The scientist who says "there is no beginning," "no purpose," "no ultimate meaning" is taking an extreme position in regard to the "tree," which will cut him off from the "forest." He may challenge prevalent theories about the beginning, purpose, etc.--but to deny them out of hand without offering any positive and constructive counter-thesis is to ignore the all-important whole, the context for knowledge; more precisely, it is to deny that there is any whole. And to such a person we must simply point out (reverting to our previous metaphor) that one who "knows" a tree while ignoring the forest does not really know that tree (provided that the tree is really in a forest).

39.   One who insists on seeing before believing will end up neither seeing nor believing

Here, also, we are speaking of faith$_2$ (see p. 83 above), which has to do with the horizons, the peripheries of knowledge. It is concerned primarily with intuitions or visions about those murky areas for which there is no scientifically precise or determinate knowledge, the areas in which we face up to some of the ultimate mysteries about life and existence. Mystery, we repeat, is not the same as nothingness, and is not entirely an "unknown." The explorer who is making his way through uncharted territory for the first time in history does not expect to disappear at any moment into a vacuum of nothingness or into "negative matter." This sort of thing happens sometimes in science fiction, but in real life the explorer--whether in a literal or figurative sense--has certain indefinite expectations about what he is going to find. If he is a good explorer, his beliefs or hunches are something more than merely clever calculations of chance expectations or statistical probabilities; they are intuitions which prove to be true with uncanny regularity--and this is what makes him a "good" explorer. Applying this "exploring" metaphor to the intellectual realm, we can say that the man of enlightened faith$_2$ (as opposed to mere superstition or credulity) is one who has certain personal insights or intuitions about the unknown horizons of our knowledge (which, from another point of view, are the horizons of the knowable world); but has sufficient honesty and realism to avoid confusing these indefinite intuitions with definite knowledge. And we should add that, if some of the indefinite areas become clearer as he moves forward, he must have sufficient pliability to avoid forcing these clearer areas into the mold of pseudo-scientific dogmas, failing all the while to avert to the new unexplored areas which still remain before him. (Here we come to the limits of viability of the "exploring" metaphor: the explorer can transcend and thus dissipate his [purely geographical] horizons as he arrives at the goal he sets for himself; but one who "explores" cosmic mysteries can entertain no such hopes with regard to his own species of horizon). Thus the individual who draws nigh cognitively to these horizons in order to "see," i.e. in order to capture and comprehend what is unknowable in definite logico-empirical formulations, is doomed to failure from the outset. For one thing, he is in the wrong "place": he has mistaken the sphere of mystery for a sphere of puzzles whose solution could easily be worked out by a gifted person (such as himself) using appropriate methods. For another thing, even if he were in the right place, he would tend to interpret whatever happens in terms of the familiar images and constructs he already possesses, just as the dreamer tends (as they tell us) to interpret various noises, sensations, smells, etc. during the night in terms of happenings which he has already experienced in his conscious life. Finally, the saddest reflection of all: the person who misuses the perceptual-conceptual approach with regard to matters of faith$_2$ could be using this approach with regard to more^2 suitable content, and make great progress. <u>Quelle dommage</u>. Such a waste.

40. The primary "object" of faith is faith itself--that is, the belief in faith

Faith$_2$ (see Thesis #36 above) is to some extent analogous to cognitive functions. Just as sensation is oriented towards sense objects, and the understanding is oriented towards conceptual or conceptualizable objects, so also faith$_2$ is directed towards certain ultimate religious explanations of life and existence. But these analogies must be qualified by some very considerable distinctions: in sensation there is maximum dependence on external objects, and there can be no veridical sensation without congruent objects. In understanding, there is somewhat less dependence on objects--I could be confronted with intelligible objects all day long and still comprehend them hardly at all, unless I make definite subjective efforts to reduce them to intelligibility. In faith$_2$, finally, there is minimal dependence on suitable objects, and maximal importance accrues to one's subjective dispositions, attitudes, and efforts. Yes, "objects" are required for faith$_2$. But these objects are characteristically so overladen with obscurity or ambiguity that they hardly can be said to "force one to believe" through the sheer weight of evidence. Perhaps this is the reason why Paul, in one of his Letters, asserts that faith$_2$ "<u>is</u> the evidence for things unseen"--in other words, <u>the</u> evidence for our faith does not come from its admittedly dimly seen objects, but rather from faith itself.

In line with this understanding of faith$_2$, the existentialist, Søren Kierkegaard, observes that it is a mistake for religious persons to base their faith too much on miracles, e.g. the miracles recorded in the New Testament: for the main miracle <u>is</u> faith$_2$ itself. He goes on to say that the man of faith$_2$ feels himself drawn along, he knows not how, to believe and suffer--so that he becomes unintelligible to himself, as well as to his fellow men. Christian mystics such as Theresa of Avila and John of the Cross, with their own peculiarly ascetic emphasis, point out that in an advanced prayer of faith, called the "prayer of quiet," the individual feels his intellect and/or imagination to be held attentive by some object--and should not interfere with this state by trying to direct his thought to _specific_ religious images or concepts. Such portrayals of faith$_2$ seem to indicate that the experience of faith^2 essentially involves a powerful subjective impulse to believe, along with very little evidence concerning the credibility of any corresponding objects--a state of affairs that would no doubt prove frustrating to many men, particularly intellectuals.

If we wanted to try to render such a state intelligible, perhaps the only way to do so might be by offering an analogy with _instinct_. In examples of complex animal instincts--e.g. bees working on their hive, beavers building their dam, spiders spinning webs, etc.--something seems to "take over" the intelligence of the animal and program it to carry out these completely unlearned but certainly not irrational activities with infallible precision. Anthropologists and psychologists tell us that there are no such complex instincts discernible in human behavior. But men of faith$_2$ such as Kierkegaard or John of the Cross, might, if they spoke the language of anthropology, disagree with such an assessment. They would say that, in paradigmatic faith$_2$-experiences, the intellect is supervened and overruled to a greater or lesser extent, and the individual is "programmed," not to perform various concrete successive activities, but to grasp, in a discursive and/or intensive way, his own existential situation in the universe--a very complex operation in the abstract, cognitive sphere. (Kierkegaard would say that such an experience does not damage but rather enhances human freedom.)

Whether or not faith is comparable to a "complex instinct," the most important thing is that it depends for its validity primarily on subjective inner criteria, and perhaps may never be satisfactorily explained or defended on objective premises. Thus the man who might wish to foster or perpetuate faith$_2$ in himself might do well to pay less attention to the various "objects" of his faith$_2$ than the subjective dispositions which make faith$_2$ possible. The most important of these dispositions is a certain belief or faith in _faith itself_. One who does not believe in the possibility or validity of faith$_2$ would _ipso facto_ no doubt place obstacles in the way^2 of recognizing or appreciating an experience of faith$_2$, if it came his way. There is no guarantee that believing in faith$_2$ will cause one to have an authentic faith$_2$-experience; but it seems almost incontrovertible that ^{2}disbelieving in the possibility of such an experience would make the advent of this experience impossible or improbable.

41A. We can only understand the Scriptures by disregarding the literal meanings

God did not speak to us in the Scriptures. No claim is even made to that effect. God spoke to Moses, and David, and the prophets, we are told, and the New Testament tells us that God spoke through Jesus to Peter and Paul and Mary Magdalene and the Samaritan women and quite a few others-- but not to us, specifically. It is true--in one place, Jesus says, "what I say to you, I say to all. . ." (Mk., XIII, 37) But what is meant by "all"? Does it include us? Actually, the extent of "all" would be known best by the "you" to whom the statement was addressed, those who immediately heard the words, experienced the self-revelation that resulted from these words, saw miracles, both objective and subjective, confirming the truth and validity of these revelations. To others, in distant lands and cultures, the words themselves may provide little or no revelation, and then a fortiori there will be no miracles of any sort to corroborate any revelations. If there is to be any meaningful and efficacious revelation to us, in our day, it must be made by God, or by some intermediary, directly to us. A second-hand revelation is no revelation at all.

41B. . . .but the revelations of the Scriptures can become clear only through emphasis on the written word

On the other hand, let us suppose that God wished to speak to every open-minded person, individually and as directly as possible. How would he go about this? The mystical visions and heavenly locutions that were supposedly granted to the prophets and saints would not provide the best medium--they are too esoteric for the ordinary person, and require perhaps an unusual sensitivity and/or imagination (and, even after you've had such a subjective experience, can you really be sure it was <u>God</u>?). No, something more exoteric would be called for. The most feasible and direct way for God to achieve such a goal (with the emphasis on "direct") would be to come Himself, at some particular point in time, and speak in some particular language which would be burdened down with finitude and fallible connotations and cultural nuances and colloquialisms. Into this language (unless He wanted to face up to the confusions and no doubt insuperable complexities of multiple incarnations), He would have to pack a concretion of multiple revelations, sufficient for all to whom He wished to communicate, but of course needing to be dislodged or unpacked. This process of dislodgement or unpacking would be presumably furthered (if it is to be furthered at all) by later interpretations or revelations, the revelatory value of which would have to be judged in terms of the effects--subjective or objective, intellectual or volitional or affection-wise, theoretical or practical--that accompanied them. But the bedrock upon which all such revelations would have to be built would be the actual words, enunciated in person, "way back when. . ." And for the person who really experienced significant effects, the question, whether that person speaking "way back when. . ." was really God, would be an uninteresting historical speculation.

CHAPTER III

PRIVATE INTERPRETATION OF THE SCRIPTURES

During the last hundred years, beginning with some faint rumblings in Germany, a revolution has taken place in Scripture studies. This revolution is considered a cataclysm by traditionalists and fundamentalists, liberation and enlightenment by the liberals--and there is every shade of reaction in-between. At any rate, at the hands of such men as Strauss, Niebuhr, Bultmann, Schweitzer, Barth and Küng the pendulum has swung full circle from the treatment of the New Testament as Revelation and the inspired and infallible Word of God to the contemporary cautious and scholarly consideration of the myths, sayings, anecdotes and stories of the New Testament according to the canons of historical criticism and "higher" criticism and approved hermeneutical methods. And so, while in the "old days" almost every Christian theologian, Protestant and Catholic, used to believe at least that Jesus rose from the dead after being put to death by crucifixion, at the present time not only this "pivotal fact" is called into question but also the factuality of Jesus' birth in Bethlehem, the virginity of his mother, whether or not his mother really sang the "Magnificat" hymn during her visit to her cousin Elizabeth, whether or not Mary and Joseph really traveled seventy miles at the bidding of Caesar to register for a census, whether or not Jesus was really responsible for the miraculous cures reported in the Gospels, and really made some of the apocalyptic predictions which are recorded there and so forth. There is in particular such tremendous disagreement about the doctrines of Jesus that Adolf Holl in <u>Jesus in Bad Company</u>[10] observes that "modern exegetes question the authenticity of every single word attributed to Jesus, and unanimity on any particular point is rare." One whose faith is tried and bewildered by all this disagreement has at least one consolation: It would be <u>impossible</u> for anyone who takes all the scriptural <u>controversies</u> seriously to be "killed" by a too faithful adherence to the "letter" of the New Testament (although the well-known admonition of Jesus that "the letter kills, but the spirit gives life" is itself subject to interpretation, and could be quoted both for and against modern Scripture interpretation).

If a justification were necessary for the reapplication and reinterpretation of Scripture, perhaps the best case could be established from the New Testament itself; Matthew is so intent on reapplying Old Testament prophecies to the birth and family circumstances and travels and death of Jesus, that he is often accused of forcing the facts into the preconceived mold of his own personal understanding of Old Testament literature (for instance, in Matt. XXI, 17, where Jesus is described as riding into Jerusalem on two different animals, because of Matthew's misreading of a passage from the prophet Zechariah); Jesus himself is often quoted by the evangelists as offering unique applications of Old Testament stories and teachings--e.g. the creation of Eve to be "one flesh with Adam," King David's seizing of the "loaves of proposition" in the Temple, the Queen of Sheba's journey to visit King Solomon, the prophet Daniel's predictions about the destruction of certain kingdoms, and the prophet Jonah's three-days' sojourn in the belly of the whale (sometimes there seem to be literal inaccuracies, as, for instance, the placing of the King David incident "in the reign of Abiathar," and Jesus' prediction that his burial after death would last the same time as the confinement of Jonah--three days and three nights); then again, the Apostle Paul continues the same process of reinterpretation on the Gospels (or the oral traditions concerning Jesus), recommending celibacy to everyone (1 Cor. VII) because of his personal feeling that the "end of the world" that Jesus referred to was something that was going to come any day (so why procreate the human race any further?); the Apostle James (Acts XXI) offered what turned out to be a "minority opinion" that baptism and conversion to Christianity did not free one from obligation to follow Jewish customs and traditions, and the Apostle John when he finally came to write his "fourth gospel," felt impelled--no doubt because of persecutions of, and irremedial hostilities to, the young Christian communities--to reinterpret the "universal love" recommended by Jesus in the first three gospels as referring primarily to fellow Christians and not to enemies and outsiders.

Perhaps Paul's advocacy of celibacy, although it seems to us to be based on a misreading of future events, was an enlightened suggestion at a particular time when family ties were so strong as to be able to dull and counteract even the most progressive and inspired movements. Perhaps John's notion of love, which seems rather "cliquish" to us, was the one thing necessary at a particular point of time for maintaining and consolidating the sense of community among Christians. Who knows for sure? The point is, the Scriptures must be interpreted and reinterpreted, applied and reapplied to different places and times, if they are to have any meaning at all. Bultmann states that the word of God becomes the "word of God" only as it happens here and now. The function of the interpreter is to make it relevant here and now, in order to facilitate its happening here and now. Some interpreters offer a key idea which will unlock the concealed meanings of the sriptures and make them relevant to their particular era. For Bultmann, this key idea is the insight that the New Testament Scriptures in various ways are telling modern man to abandon the temptation to human security, which is vain and existentially enslaving. For Luther (as was pointed out in Chapter I), the key idea was the notion of "justification by faith."

We, like Luther, Bultmann and others, must be bold enough to explore, reinterpret and re-apply Scriptures to our present condition, if we believe in these Scriptures at all (but perhaps, paradoxically this effort is a prerequisite and precondition for any vital belief at all). This does not necessarily call for the development of any single exegetical "key to interpretation." For one who is not a professional theologian or Scripture scholar, it may involve simply focusing on some key New Testament texts that seem to present some special significance for our times. And this is what we will try to do in this chapter, in the unashamedly subjective mode of a Calvinistic "Scripture commentary."

A. Greatness

1.   Matt. XXIII, 8: Do not
                      call anyone on earth your
                      father. Only one is your
                      father, the One in
                      heaven!

In view of Jesus' admonition here to his
disciples, it is interesting to note that it is the
custom in the Catholic, Orthodox and Episcopalian
denominations to call priests "Father." Such a
practice seems to be in direct contradiction to Jesus'
injunction, at least if it is taken literally.

Medieval and patristic Scripture commentators,
when confronted with this passage, used to simply
explain that there was a warning here against "carnal"
glorying in titles, but (they were quick to add) the
Christian practice of calling certain individuals
"Father" is based on a purely spiritual relationship,
and thus is not culpable. But is that a sufficient
explanation?

Imagine, if you will, Karl Marx shortly before his
death, saying something like this to his followers:
"Now, my friends, I would like you to keep one thing in
mind after I'm gone. Avoid capitalistic titles like
'Master' and 'Boss.' I know these are just names, but
titles like these would be contrary to the spirit of
comradeship that we should show for one another."-- And
then imagine that after Marx's death, the custom crept
in of calling all communist party leaders "Boss."
"Extraordinary," you would say--especially if Marx's
specific admonition against this were well-known among
his followers, and especially if there had been no
custom among communists previous to Marx's death of
using that title. It could almost be interpreted as a
sign of contempt for Marx and his teachings.

Christians who call their priests "Father" will
point out that this practice has to be taken in
context: it does not weaken the spirit of equality and
brotherhood that Jesus meant to inculcate and
strengthen by the above-mentioned admonition. . .

But doesn't it? In Catholic monasteries, for
example, distinction is made between the ordained
priests, who have greater privileges and the rights of

97

succession to leading offices, and "lay religious," who are usually less-educated and often specialize in manual labor--by calling the former "Father," and the latter "Brother." The title, "Brother," in this situation certainly does not have the egalitarian ring that it has in certain types of evangelical Protestantism, in which everyone calls everyone else "Brother" and "Sister." There is a definite class distinction implied in such communities by the use of the title, "Father."

The practical-minded traditionalist will object: "But how can I, in the monastery or in the "world," distinguish an ordained priest from others, if they do not wear distinctive clothes and call themselves by a distinctive title? What would I call them, if not "Father"? Would you want me to call them 'Reverend'? or 'Bob' and 'Joe'?"

One answer to this can certainly be given: don't call them "Bob" or "Joe" unless you feel you are in a position of equality with them.

2.
Matt. XX, 26: Anyone among you who aspires to greatness must serve the rest, and whoever wants to rank first among you must serve the rest.

Luke XXII, 26: Let the greater among you be as the junior, the leader as the servant.

Passages such as these supply grounds for the hypothesis of some political scientists that Christianity was a major factor in the evolution of democratic equality--the idea that all of us, including our leaders, are in some deep and spiritual sense "equal," and should structure our societies and our social behavior in such a way as to reflect that basic truth. Taken literally, the principle as stated by Jesus might imply that leaders, at least religious leaders, should be distinguished not by superior garb, titles of preeminence, authoritative demeanor, greater wealth, etc., but only by knowledge of the needs of those they are serving, and the ability to minister

centuries before Christ, suggested that the leaders in
an ideal state should do without the things that are
generally considered luxuries and special signs of
distinction, in order that they can dedicate themselves
more seriously to the business of leading. However, in
Plato's paradigm, although the leader lived a more
abstemious life than others, there was no doubt about
who was in charge: the leader's power even extended to
such matters as regulating who could marry whom--and
thus Plato has been criticized by some philosophers as
advocating a dictatorial regime. In the original
Christian paradigm, there is no question of
dictatorship or even authoritarianism. The closest to
a "test of authority" in the gospels is the incident in
which Jesus at the Last Supper insists, over Peter's
protestations, on washing Peter's feet, warning him
that otherwise it would be all over between them.

If we would search the history of Western society
for examples of leaders who really conceived of
themselves as servants and acted that role, our
candidates would have to be few and far between. In
the religious realm, St. Francis of Asissi, with his
spirit of sacrifice and self-forgetfulness, comes close
to the ideal, although he is hardly very imitable. In
the secular sphere, we who advocate a democratic form
of government think of a leader like Abraham Lincoln as
one who looked upon high office simply in terms of
service and duty and not at all as a means for personal
aggrandizement. Those of a communistic persuasion might
point to a leader like Fidel Castro, who not only looks
like a worker, but conceives of himself in this fashion
and acts the role (but still, there is a difference
between being a worker and being a servant).

No doubt there are good grounds for the reluctance
which leaders, secular or religious, show in
interpreting the ideal of a servant-leader literally.
The doubt uppermost in their minds is probably: what if
I threw aside all appurtenances of privilege and claims
to distinction? who would take me seriously, listen to
me and respect me? These seem to be valid questions.
If a leader--president, premier, or pope--decided to
live in a small house, dress plainly, take public
transportation to work, eschew all special privilege
and the overt use of power, and simply offer his
services where they seemed to be needed, there can be
little doubt that a crisis of authority would develop
in no time at all. For such a leader would be relying

little doubt that a crisis of authority would develop
in no time at all. For such a leader would be relying
on "power" in a more subtle sense--the "force" of
example, the "power" of love--and it would be
reasonable to conjecture that the sensitivity of most
people would not be sufficiently refined to be capable
of responding to such subtle signals. But still, we
may hope that at least some leaders may try something
like this, just so we can have empirical evidence now
and then that such a noble egalitarian ideal really _is_
possible.

3.   Gal. II, 11: When Cephas
                            (Peter) came to Antioch I
                            (Paul) directly withstood
                            him, because he was
                            clearly in the wrong. He
                            had been taking his meals
                            with the Gentiles before
                            others came who were from
                            James. But when they
                            arrived he drew back to
                            avoid trouble with those
                            who were circumcised.

     It is hard to imagine how mature adults could get
into intense disputes about what seems (to us, now) a
trivial matter: whether Jewish Christians should be
permitted to eat at the same table with Gentiles.
However, it is obvious from Paul's description of the
incident that it took considerable courage for an
individual to withstand "those who were regarded as
important" (Peter et. al.) on such a matter.
     The really extraordinary thing about this incident
is that Paul won. Imagine a similar scenario in which
an individual cleric in the Catholic Church withstood
the Pope on the matter of celibacy, or in the Episcopal
Church withstood the Archbishop of Canterbury on the
subject of whether females should be ordained bishops,
or in the Russian Orthodox Church withstood the
Patriarch on the subject of whether ties with the
communist regime should be maintained--and won! It is
almost impossible to conceive of such a thing happening
right now. For one thing, it is scarcely probable
that a Pope or prelate would allow a dissident

individual to come into his presence and debate him
from a position of equality about embarrassing matters.
But even if that did happen, it is rather inconceivable
that, after a certain interval of heated debate, the
Pope or prelate would decide to...give in, change the
policy. Perhaps the reason for this is that Church
organizations are so much more massive now that sudden
changes in policy might have extensive and traumatic
effects. Or, a more disturbing thought: perhaps there
are just no individuals now of the mettle and caliber
of a Paul, who are enlightened and forceful enough to
confront an established authority directly about
established values, and walk away with the victory.
Or, the most disturbing thought of all: perhaps there
was just a greater sense of equality among Christians
then at a time when there was very little interest in,
or thought about, what we call "democracy." We could
probably all give abstract intellectual assent to
Paul's final observation summing up the incident at
Antioch--"God plays no favorites." But anyone with
even a moderate hankering after hierarchy, stability
and order, will in his "heart of hearts" find it
difficult to believe that God will equally favor the
authorities who support long established dogmas,
practices and policies; and the dissidents who
disregard them.

4.   Matt. XXIII, 4: The
                      Scribes and Pharisees
                      bind up heavy loads, hard
                      to carry, to lay on other
                      men's shoulders, while
                      they themselves will not
                      lift a finger to budge
                      them. As to you. . .

     Here is another Christian idea which has been
incorporated into the democratic tradition. For in
democracies there is the unwritten maxim that leaders
should not deliver oracular pronouncements from "on
high," from some aloof position out of contact with the
people. If they do this, and do it blatantly, they
will have a rebellion on their hands (this is perhaps
another of the numerous "lessons" that can be gleaned
from the "Watergate" incident in U.S. politics).

In the political realm, this cardinal idea has been interpreted in various ways. Among some leaders it means dressing or speaking like the common man, for others it means playing proletarian games or working at proletarian hobbies; for still others it means keeping in contact with the masses and with the opinions of the masses. Communist regimes, starting from Marx's thesis that true democracy can be found only in a classless society, have tried to emphasize in various ways that their leaders are just "workers"--but, in general, they haven't been very convincing. The sole exception to this latter generalization was found perhaps in Maoist China, where the Marxist notion that leaders should share in the work of the people they are directing was sometimes applied in a literal way. Our own leaders, secular or ecclesiastic, will seldom go that far; they will claim that the important thing is the "spirit" of union and empathy with the average man. However, they still have one unsolved ideological problem on their hands: how can a leader avoid "in spirit" the appearance of directing others from "on high," unless in some way there is in concreto an obliteration or neutralization of the class differences (and the difference in wealth, privilege, and duties associated with class) which cause real differences in understanding and empathy between members of the different classes?

5.   John, XIV, 12: The man
                       who has faith in me will
                       do the works I do, and
                       far greater [works] than
                       these.

To one who believes in and emphasizes the divinity of Jesus, these words may seem incongruous, especially if one pictures God as all-powerful, all-knowing, etc. How could one really surpass such a God? This person's tendency, accordingly, will be to treat this statement as hyperbolic, and "tone it down" for purposes of interpretation. Thus our orthodox interpreter might say: "Jesus is speaking in terms of an organic concept. He is the "Vine," other Christians are the branches; he is the head of the Mystical

Body, others are the various members. Obviously, the vine is greater and more important than the branches, especially the outermost branches, and equally obviously, the head (brain) is greater than the other organs which it directs or controls. But in a certain sense the branches are "greater" than the vine, insofar as they receive credit for bearing the fruit; and in a certain sense, the subordinate members, e.g. the hands, are "greater" than the head insofar as the reactions and plans that have their origin in the head receive expression and sometimes public exposure in the other organs. . ."

But to those who would like to do away with the qualifier, "in a certain sense," there is still the option of taking the words quite literally: to wit, some of Jesus' followers will perform greater miracles, make more accurate prophecies, expound a purer and more refined doctrine of spiritual perfection, establish a stronger, more soundly based and more effective religious community, and perhaps even endure more severe and profound sufferings than the Master himself.

This latter interpretation, which sounds blasphemous to the "divinist," nevertheless has much to commend it: For one thing, it seems to be the only interpretation consonant with a belief in the real, bona fide humanity of Jesus (although there is still the problem of reconciling the humanity and the divinity, those two apparent contradictories). For another, it jibes better with our concept of a teacher or master. What father is there that would not want his children to surpass him in perfection and achievements, what teacher is there that would not want at least some of his proteges to go beyond him to new and greater discoveries or accomplishments? These are rhetorical questions, of course. We know, in fact, that the greatness of a Master as a Master consists in this ability of teaching others to go beyond him. Short of doing this, he may be considered a great person, but to be a really great teacher, one must give rise to progress beyond and above his own state of perfection.

It is because of these latter considerations that a literal interpretation seems in this case to be the best, the most creditable way of understanding this statement.

6.   1 Cor. XII, ----- God has
                      so constructed the body
                      as to give greater honor
                      to the lowly members.

In this passage, Paul is drawing an analogy
between the "Mystical Body" (consisting of Jesus and
the members with whom he is united through the Spirit)
and the physical body of the
ordinary man. Just as the more sublime members of the
body (head, eyes, ears, etc.) are left unadorned, while
we garb our feet and other inferior parts with
sometimes elaborate ornamentation, so also in the
Mystical Body the lower members are in some sense given
greater honor. This analogy is not completely lucid in
all respects: don't we often adorn the head even more
elaborately than the other members? Just exactly what
are to be considered "lower" members, and why? And so
forth. But the main point of the analogy is clear: by
some sort of divine dispensation of justice, those in
the Church who are less gifted, less spiritually
favored, are allotted a greater portion of secular,
external honor, to make up for this deficiency, so to
speak.

This notion of equilibrium and justice is similar
to principles expounded in the social philosophies of
Plato and Nietzsche. In Plato's ideal Republic, the
"guardians" (the leaders and most noble members of the
state) will give up the right to riches and luxury and
will live a conspicuously plainer life than the
ordinary citizen. Nietzsche's "Superman" is similarly
conceived as an individual who is less interested in
riches and secular pomp, the more exalted he becomes in
his personal spiritual stature.

There seems to be one main difference between the
Pauline and the Platonic and Nietzschean concepts: in
Plato and Nietzsche, the superior individuals, while
bereft of external luxuries and distinctive insignia of
importance, nevertheless are portrayed as receiving
greater than average recognition than others in
society. The recognition that they receive, although
less external and superficial than the honors others
are interested in, is nevertheless "honor" in a very
real sense. In the Christian-Pauline model, on the
other hand, the "saint" not only gives up the external
vestiges of honor but also (often) is deprived of
social recognition: he is typically subject to abuse,

misunderstanding, ridicule, or indifference. And so
the superior "members" of the Mystical Body are often
cast as tragic figures-- spiritual leaders like Jesus
or Paul, who are through the greater part of their
career recognized by only a minority of those whom they
are addressing themselves to.

B. Sex and Marriage

1.
> 1 Tim. II, 12: I do not
> permit a woman to act as
> a teacher, or in any way
> to have authority over a
> man; she must be quiet.
> For Adam was created
> first, Eve afterward;
> moreover, it was not Adam
> who was deceived but the
> woman.

It should be noted that this passage, which is naturally odious to feminists, is based on a certain specific interpretation of certain Scriptures. St. Paul goes on elsewhere to observe that Eve, having been created from Adam's rib, was the image of Adam, not directly of God, while Adam himself (and the male in general) is the image of God. This thesis, as interpreted by Christian theologians, has led more often than not to the conclusion that women must be excluded from ordination and the higher forms of ecclesiastical ministry. In Catholic theology, the same thesis, sometimes coupled with the Aristotelian notion that women, although equally as rational as men, are nevertheless ordinarily prevented by their emotionality from fully using reason, has led Thomas Aquinas and almost all orthodox theologians to insist on the exclusion of women from the priesthood. A recent (1977) pronouncement of the papacy reiterated fundamentally the same position, minus the Aristotelian overtones, in claiming that women "do not bear a natural resemblance to Christ." Some who are interested in changing this state of things suggest that we must start with hermeneutics and the demythologization of Scripture. However, the best way to hasten a fresh understanding of such Scriptures (by removing culturally-rooted prejudices) might be to ordain women and see whether they meet up to the exacting standards set for reflecting and representing Christ and mediating the divinity. There's nothing comparable to a fait accompli for proving the existence of the potentiality or capacity which produced it. The actual is pre-eminently possible.

2.   Matt. XIX, 6. Have you
                            not read that at the
                            beginning the Creator
                            made (human beings) male
                            and female and declared,
                            "For this reason a man
                            shall leave his father
                            and mother and cling to
                            his wife, and the two
                            shall become as one"?
                            Thus they are no
                            longer two but one flesh.
                            Therefore, let no man
                            separate what God has
                            joined.

An individual hearing this anti-divorce statement
might think, "sure, this is the way God joined the
'first man and woman' together but does he still have
anything to do with the 'joining' process now, in our
day?" A skeptic in Jesus' time might object that the
"joining" process takes place chiefly through external
contingencies such as interfamilial arrangements, as
well as through natural attraction. A skeptic in
Western culture in our own day would no doubt emphasize
the importance of "romantic love" in bringing about
marital unions. A believer, in Jesus' day or our own,
might seize upon the same factors (external
contingencies and/or internal physical and
psychological attraction) and point to them as evidence
of the "workings of God." In this vein a contemporary
version of this anti-divorce injunction would be:
"Since God himself joins people together in marriage
through the processes of what we call 'romantic
attraction', any attempts to dissolve such a union
would be contrary to God's implicit intentions."
Having heard this new formulation, however, the
legal specialists, together with their clients--couples
contemplating divorce--would step up with some
observations they consider to be obvious: granted, God
may have joined X and Y together in the first place,
but now Y has changed substantially, and the cause for
Y's attraction has been removed. . .Granted, God joins
many couples together by a combination of physical and
psychological attraction, but in the case of X_1 and
Y_1's marriage, the motivating factors were obviously
predominately physical, because at present they have

hit upon deep-rooted and irresolvable psychological incompatibilities. . . Granted, God joins <u>most</u> couples by "romantic love," but the marriage of X_2 and Y_2 was a "marriage of convenience," and thus, according to these theological premises, was not, strictly speaking, a "marriage" at all, even in the beginning. . . .And so on.

Anyone who tried to specify <u>just how</u> God "joins couples together" will find <u>himself</u> encumbered by a similar jumble of legalistic problems. The saying of Jesus, in this as in so many other instances, is by no means a definitive and unambiguous solution to a complex human problem.

3.   Eph. V, 28: Husbands
                        should love their wives
                        as they do their own
                        bodies

Offhand, this seems a strange comparison. What could Paul <u>mean</u> by it? In order to understand this meaning more <u>fully</u>, we have to consider some of the connotations of the term "body":

On the one hand, the body is conceived as the <u>instrument</u> of the mind (or soul). In this sense, its <u>connotation</u> is ambiguous: 1)We are masters over our instruments, and love them as extensions of ourselves. (Could this be what Paul meant by the wife analogy?) But 2) we are also, in a very real sense, dependent upon our instruments: the man who uses instruments to accomplish an arduous task will admit that his accomplishments would have been difficult or even impossible without the instruments he used. Such a man will no doubt view his instruments with the patronizing pride that a master may have for a very efficient slave, and love them with a full realization of the dependence which he has on them. (Could this be the meaning that Paul had in mind?)

On the other hand, the body is also considered to be an <u>expression</u> of the self. And here another ambiguity, or perhaps a paradox, enters in: 3) As our expression, our body reveals our thoughts and feelings through its words, gestures and actions, and if we have any basic egoistic impulses we love and instinctively take pride in these expressions of ourself, if and when they are a credit to us. (Perhaps this is what Paul had in mind.) But 4) our body is also an opaque and limited expression of the self, and serves to conceal our thoughts and intentions and even (sometimes with difficulty) our feelings and desires; in other words, it is a mask. (Surely this is not what Paul meant by his analogy.)

It should be noted that another possible, somewhat esoteric connotation, could be attributed to the body: the body could be viewed as cooperator, equal to, and equally important as, the mind. If one were to give up the hierarchy of values which places mind and spirit on top, and matter and the body on the bottom, an interpretation of Paul's statement which would be acceptable to even the most adamant of women's liberationists might be possible. However, in view of the whole Judaeo-Christian tradition which served as Paul's context, such an interpretation would be impossible. (Paul certainly did not mean that!)

4.   1 Corinthians VII, 9: It
                     is better to marry than
                     to burn.

The context of this statement is clear: the community at Corinth had asked Paul's advice about certain matters, including sex and marriage. Paul, strongly influenced by his conviction that the world was going to end soon, favored celibacy as a means of preparing for the final day. However, he could not completely ignore the fact that the "burning" concupiscence of some men would make the state of celibacy impractical and intolerable; and so, for these cases he recommends marriage as a palliative or "cure" for their concupiscence. (It seems fairly clear that the "burning" here does not refer to punishment in the afterlife.)

It is interesting to reflect on what consequences would follow if some young man, feeling the tension of sexual desires, took this advice. Hopefully, our young man would not interpret the advice in an extremely literal fashion, i.e. "going out and marrying" the first person who offers herself, simply to quench his ardent desires. No, we can expect our young Christian gentleman to have sufficient circumspection to seek out someone who is at least physically attractive to himself (provided, of course, that he himself is attractive enough to find someone of this sort). We may be less sanguine, however, about our young man having the patience to search for someone who is also attractive intellectually, spiritually, and personality-wise. This search could take years, and patience is not a signal characteristic of sexually frustrated young men. And so we may presume that physical attractiveness will be the necessary and sufficient impetus to marriage, for many or most such young men. In this case, unfortunately, there would arise an indubitable conflict with the principle (referred to earlier) that God "joins couples together" in marriage (at least in contemporary Western society) through a combination of physical with spiritual attraction. But even if our hypothetical young man were patient enough to wait for this appropriate combination, there still would seem to be a conflict: on the one hand, we are led by Christ's words to believe that the attraction is something sacred, coming from God himself; while the Apostle's words here portray God as condescending to tolerate the weakness of human nature in some impetuous adolescents or adolescent types. Paul would not, of course, deny the principle that God "joins people together" in marriage through natural attraction; but he would have to argue (if he were consistent) that prior to each of these "divinely ordained" marriages, God theoretically had a much better plan (celibacy) in mind, if only the creatures in question had been strong enough to follow that plan. Here again, in defense of Paul, it must be reiterated that he was apparently motivated by a strong personal conviction about the imminent end of the world, when he penned the abovementioned words. However, it must be presumed that some Christians have taken and are taking the advice in a literal fashion. And so, in the interests of perpetuating a more positive and constructive concept of Christian marriage, perhaps your New Testament should have a directive in red in the margin alongside this passage in Corinthians stating, "Paul advises this only for those who are expecting the world to end in a few years" or something to this effect.

5.   Matt. V, 32: [In general,
                    divorce is not permitted,
                    but] lewd conduct is a
                    separate case.

This injunction of Jesus is variously interpreted by Christian denominations. The official Roman Catholic position is that in the case of a valid marriage between Catholics the exception made for "lewd conduct" simply amounts to permission for one spouse to initiate separation proceedings, in case the other spouse is addicted to adultery. In some Protestant denominations, divorce is granted only for adultery; in others, for sexual misconduct; in still others, on grounds both sexual and non-sexual.

Some Catholic theologians have objected that to interpret this statement as authorization of divorce would be to offer special privileges where there is sexual misconduct. But the obvious response to this is that the privilege is granted not to the guilty party, but to the other spouse who is offended by the conduct of the guilty party (although, once divorce is granted, the guilty party will presumably share in the privilege, since A cannot morally divorce B unless B is divorced from A).

However this may be, it is important not to miss what seems to be the main point of the passage: adultery and perhaps some other types of sexual misconduct can so seriously disrupt a marriage that the divorce which follows is just a formality. "What God has joined together" has already been "put asunder" by the action of one of the spouses. A divorce, whether or not it is authorized by Church authorities, would in this case in a certain sense be superfluous and anticlimactic, because the alienation of affection (which is the essence of divorce) has already taken place.

6.   Matt.V, 28: Anyone who
                    looks lustfully at a
                    woman has already
                    commited adultery with
                    her in his thoughts.

This statement by Jesus <u>could</u> be taken as a mere tautology: "If anyone looks at a woman with adultery in mind, he has already committed adultery with her in his mind." Construed in this way, it obviously doesn't say much. However, in view of the fact that, in the context, Jesus is contrasting his own ideas with the Mosaic law as then interpreted, and in view of the fact that one of the Mosaic "ten commandments" was "Thou shalt not covet thy neighbor's wife" (in other words, "Don't think about adultery") it is important to bring out the precise sense in which Jesus thought his ideas differed from previously held ideas, or added something to them.

This difference seems to lie precisely in the fact that thoughts are made equivalent to deeds. In the "Old Testament" there were injunctions against "coveting" a neighbor's wife or property, and against hate. But those to whom this law was promulgated were never told that thinking about adultery or stealing was sinful to the same degree as committing adultery or theft, or that hating a person so much that you wished he were dead was tantamount to actually killing him.

To our legalistic minds, this sounds a bit far-fetched. Our "gut reaction" would be: it is better to think about murder, or theft, or adultery, or anything that one considers wrong, than to go ahead in broad daylight and commit a crime. But in this reaction we are thinking primarily about the social consequences of our acts. As far as regards personal integrity and purity of heart--which is Jesus' main concern--there is no difference: the man who <u>seriously</u> delights in contemplating a crime is just as <u>defiled as</u> if he actually perpetrated it.

C. God

1.
> Acts XVII, 23ff. Paul
> stood up in the Areopagus
> and (said) ... As I
> walked around looking at
> your shrines, I. . .
> discovered an altar
> inscribed, To God
> Unknown. Now, what you
> are thus worshipping in
> ignorance I intend to
> make known to you.

In this incident Paul seizes upon the inscription on the statue in Athens, as a springboard for contrasting the "Unknown God" of the Athenians with the revealed and known God of Christianity.

It does not seem that Paul was entirely fair in setting up such an absolute contrast between the two concepts of God. As theologians such as Thomas Aquinas have pointed out, we can have no definite, positive concept of God or the attributes of God. The German philosopher, Johann Gottlieb Fichte, carries this same idea one step further by saying that our concept of God is essentially a concept of the horizons of intelligibility, i.e., those bordering areas of consciousness in which things are no longer seen clearly, and which we lump together as the "mysterious unknown," or God.

But Paul was not thinking of any such speculative concept of God when he was speaking that day in the Areopagus in Athens. He was thinking, of course, of his own sudden illumination some time past on the road to Damascus, and perhaps of other mystical experiences or revelations that he had had of "God." It is a characteristic of such experiences, according to students of mysticism, that they endow the mystic with a certitude about God, based on an indubitable but indescribable inner vision. But for those who have not been granted any such privileged access to the arcanum of divine revelation, the position of the Athenians must be taken as essentially accurate: God, as the subject of one of the most abstract, vague and theoretical concepts we have, is quite unknown and perhaps unknowable on the conceptual level.

2.   Revelations IV, 8:. .
                   .the God who was, and is,
                   and is to come.

It is not completely clear whether John, the
writer of Revelations, is here speaking about three
aspects of one and the same God; or about three
separate aspects, each particularly identifiable with
one of the three "persons" of the Trinity--Father, Son,
and Holy Spirit. In the latter case, "who was" would
describe the Father as creator; "and is" would describe
the Son as redeemer and mediator; and "and is to come"
would designate the Spirit gradually taking root in
individual men and the human race as a whole, as human
spiritual perfection progresses.

The traditional concept of God in the major
religions of the world has characteristically
emphasized the first two aspects of God, but in our
day--no doubt because of the revolution in thinking
instigated by the theories of evolution and
spacetime--the "process philosophers" and "process
theologians" of our day would like to seize upon this
latter aspect--the futurity of God--as the primary or
perhaps sole attribute in terms of which God can be
understood. Their position is quite understandable.
The traditional idea of God as eternally perfect,
unchanging, all-knowing, was perhaps adequate for,
appropriate to, and assimilable by a culture or
civilization which was more concerned with its origins
than its future, and in which a stable and static
conception of the cosmos prevailed, and in which the
chances for choice and change were relatively fewer for
the majority of individuals, than is the case at
present. But in the more developed technological man
of our day, who has become increasingly aware of the
future, as well as his own power in shaping it, the
idea of a God for whom, so to say, the future is "old
hat," is harder to accept and live with. And
conversely, the notion of a "mystical body of Christ"
produced by the individual and communal efforts of
generations of evolving men (compare, for example, the
"Omega God" described in Teilhard de Chardin's
Phenomenon of Man) becomes more and more attractive as
the individual and group self-consciousness of our race
advances. Perhaps the God for the future is the "God
of the future"--no disrespect being intended to. . .
the other gods.

D. Faith

1.

Luke XVI, 31: If they do
not listen to Moses and
the prophets, they will
not be convinced even if
one should rise from the
dead.

In one of the parables of Jesus, a rich man who
dies and is sent to hell for his neglect of the poor
requests permission from "Father Abraham" to return to
earth to warn his comrades to avoid his fate, and
receives the above response.

In our day, some scientists and philosophers
interested in ESP and psychic phenomena have
conjectured that an "empirical" proof for "survival
after death" might be possible if we could apply rigid
scientific controls to the seances conducted by mediums
and still gain reliable information. This
information-gathering process would involve acquiring
very detailed information about the "afterlife" from
spirits, after ascertaining that they were identical
with some individual who had previously lived on earth,
and after eliminating the possibility that the "medium"
conducting the seance might be deriving information
about this individual (now a "ghost") indirectly from
the world around him, by telepathy or clairvoyance.

The problems preventing the attainment of this
objective are formidable and perhaps insurmountable.
But, in the above-cited parable Jesus is telling us
that--even if such "empirical evidence" could be
gathered--it would have no effect one way or the other
on the belief (of those presently living) in an
afterlife, with its rewards or punishments. In a very
real sense, one must already believe in an afterlife,
on the basis of religious traditions, before he would
benefit from, or be enlightened by, any praeternatural
revelations about, or evidence of, an afterlife.

This basic idea also applies, of course, to Jesus'
own resurrection. Those who look upon Jesus' physical
Resurrection as the primary basis for the Christian
faith in salvation and heaven are overemphasizing the
factual and empirical element. One must already
believe in resurrection, before a resurrection can have
any positive significance for him. If any astute
disbeliever in resurrection--whether an ancient

Sadducee or a modern skeptical philosopher--were granted an eyewitness encounter with the newly-risen Christ, they could find some way to explain away their perceptions as a trick or an illusion.

2.   Romans XIV, 23: Whatever
                         does not accord with
                         one's belief is sinful.

The context of this Pauline admonition is a dispute which arose among some of Paul's converts, concerning whether there was still any obligation of conscience for them to adhere to Jewish dietary laws. Paul does not offer any final definitive pronouncement about this problem, but says, in effect, "If you believe it's wrong, it's wrong; if not, it's permitted."

In The Concept of Dread, the Christian existentialist, Søren Kierkegaard, refers to this passage as an important statement about faith, and the fact that faith delivers us from sin. If we see it as a statement about faith, however, the usage of the term, "faith" (i.e. belief), here does not seem to fit in precisely with any of the main connotations of "faith" which one finds in the gospel (see above, Ch. II, #36). It might be best to simply consider Paul's admonition as a statement about what some philosophers have called "natural faith," which means--in the moral sphere--simply that one should do what he thinks is right at all times, living in accord with his conscience. (Thus, in the specific case Paul is addressing himself to, those who consider it sinful to eat certain things should abstain from them; and those who do not consider it sinful may eat in private, but in charity should try not to offend the consciences of their more fastidious and scrupulous neighbors.)

Paul also utilizes this somewhat subjective interpretation of faith and/or morality as his "rule of thumb" in the resolution of the knotty problems which arose concerning the rite of circumcision (see Acts XV, Gal. I-II, Rom. IV, etc.) He comes to a similar conclusion: those who do not feel themselves bound by the Jewish obligation to be circumcised should not be circumcised. (In this matter, fortunately, adherence or non-adherence to the obligation was less publicly observable, so that auxiliary problems concerning social scandal were avoided.)

Unfortunately (or perhaps fortunately) Paul was not troubled by that problem which plagues modern moral philosophers: how can you distinguish between what you think is right and what is <u>really</u> right?

3.   James II, 26: Faith without works is as dead as a body without breath.

This passage has been used, especially in the "old days," as a refutation of Luther's interpretation of Paul's Epistle to the Romans IV, 13-25, which served as a basis for the assertion that a man is saved by "faith alone," not by works.

Scripture scholars tell us that "James" himself (whoever this writer was) may have intended such a refutation of Paul, or at least tried to counterbalance some mistaken impressions that Paul may have given rise to, by asserting that faith without works is dead.

At any rate, this passage offers us a classic example of the possibilities and groounds for purely semantic misunderstandings. The "faith" that Paul is referring to is faith-as-trust (see our reference to Faith$_3$ in Ch. II, V, 36, above). The "faith" that interests James, on the other hand, seems to be the more intellectual, cerebral brand, or Faith$_2$ (see <u>ibid</u>.) The "works" that Paul is referring to are the rituals and ceremonies connected with the Mosaic law--circumcision, abstaining from certain foods, etc. The "works" that James has in mind, as can be seen from the context of his Epistle, are works of charity, mercy, etc.

It is depressing to reflect on the very real possibility that many of the "deep-rooted" doctrinal differences that Christians now point to as causes for in-house disputes among Christians, or even between Christians and non-Christian religions may be similarly based on purely semantical misunderstandings.

4.   Matt. XVII, 20. If you had faith the size of a mustard seed, you would be able to say to this

> mountain, "Move from here
> to there" and it would
> move. Nothing would be
> impossible for you.

For those of us who have experienced difficulty in moving real or metaphorical mountains, and who feel that we have at least a modicum of faith, these words may seem dismaying. But there's a "catch" in the statement, as you might expect: the mustard seed analogy is not meant to express a little or a "modicum" of faith, but quite a lot, as can be seen from an examination of the whole context of the statement. In order to understand Jesus' use of the symbolism of the mustard seed, a very small seed, to stand for a lot of faith, we might profitably look to Hindu religious writings, where a similar analogy is frequently used. In the Svetasvatara Upanishad, Parts 4 and 5, for example, we are told that God is "smaller than the smallest atom, and yet the Creator of all. . ." And the soul, when it identifies with its own egoistic desires, "is a flame the size of a thumb; but when one with pure reason and the inner Spirit, it becomes in concentration as the point of a needle,. . . .as the part of a point of a hair which divided by a hundred were divided by a hundred again; and yet in this living soul there is the seed of Infinity."

This passage helps to clarify the "mustard seed" imagery. It says that the concentration of the soul must be reduced to, and focused upon, a single point of intensity in order for a veridical perception of God to take place. The idea in Matthew's Gospel is not too dissimilar: the faith that can move mountains is not any big Cecil B. De Mille production, but results from an attitude of simplicity and single-minded devotion to God--all of which is typified by the immense potential concentrated in the tiny mustard seed.

There are those of us, however, who are only able to move mountains with bulldozers and other heavy equipage. What are we to conclude from this analogy? We may conclude 1) that our faith is lacking in the requisite intensity; or 2) that Jesus in making the above statement was not precluding the use of bulldozers and similar instruments. However, it is important to realize that the "mountains" Jesus is referring to here are not the usual sort of obstacles, but precisely the obstacles which stand in the way of

the coming of God's kingdom on earth. And whether or
not "bulldozers" could be of any help in overcoming
such obstacles is another major question.

5.   Mark XI, 23: Whoever says
                        to this mountain, "Be
                        thou lifted up and thrown
                        into the sea," and has no
                        inner doubts but believes
                        that what he says will
                        happen, shall have it
                        done for him.

     This passage in Mark is no doubt the original from
which the passage cited immediately above was derived,
with some further embellishment, presumably and
hopefully from another saying of Jesus.
     One point needs to be made with reference to the
emphasis here on a trusting faith which casts out doubt
as a prelude to casting aside mountains: the person who
possesses such an undoubting faith would have to have a
long history of experiences in which his faith was
rewarded--smaller achievements attributable to faith,
before confronting major objectives such as moving
mountains. If a person has not had such a long series
of previous experiences, then his possession of the
"faith that moves mountains" would be a greater miracle
than the actual mountain-moving itself.

E. Prayer

1.

> Matt. VII, 11: If you,
> with all your sins know
> how to give your children
> what is good, how much
> more will your heavenly
> father give good things
> to anyone who asks him.

Often in taking a battery of psychological tests a person will come upon a statement like, "I believe in a God who answers prayers," and will be asked to rate this statement positively or negatively. Presumably, those who rate it positively have given evidence that they are "religious," while those who give a negative response will be categorized as a-religious or ir-religious.

What can one say when he encounters persons who would have to answer that question in the negative, not because they haven't prayed, but because their prayers seem to consistently go unanswered? Should one keep in mind paradigmatic examples such as the mythical Job or the real Jesus with their many trials, and reply that God often takes a long time to answer? This would not be appropriate, because the exemplary individuals that we usually hear about in Scripture and the lives of the saints, etc., are those who have already experienced the bounty of God quite amply, and then are subjected to some long and arduous trial or apparent abandonment. Presumably God the good father doesn't launch into this sort of thing immediately with neophytes. Are we to tell them that God only can be depended upon to answer requests for spiritual benefits? This seems an overly smug answer, and indeed unwarranted, since those who complain about persistently unanswered prayers are generally not materialists, in any case (materialists will soon find other means than prayer to pursue their goals, after the first few prayers go unanswered). Here is obviously a problem that no one can solve in an a priori way. Every man must be his own scientist, conduct his own experiments with prayer, and develop his own hypothesis concerning the nature and degree of God's response to these prayers.

2.   Matt. XVIII, 20: If two
             of you join your forces
             on earth to pray for
             anything whatever, it
             shall be granted you by
             my father in heaven.
             Where two or three are
             gathered in my name,
             there am I in their
             midst.

       This might almost be taken as a reply to the
often-heard question, "why should I go to church, if I
pray on my own?" Jesus' answer seems to be that there
is an especial efficacy in group prayer or liturgical
prayer. The size of the group indicated--two or three
people--seems to be a minimum limit: it is implied
that an even greater moral force would be constituted
by greater numbers.
       Something like a democratic principle is
inculcated here: the individual tests his own desires
and petitions against those of others, and it is the
petitions which they have in common that must be
considered the most viable and worth pursuing.
"Majority rule" in the spiritual realm. But in order
to differentiate the kind of congregation he has in
mind from a mob or group of fanatics, Jesus adds the
qualification that they have to be gathered "in his
name."
       A few years ago a group of experimenters in Boston
with no particular religious motivation reported that
after a year of concentration sessions they had
produced an artificial "poltergeist" which would cause
loud tappings and lift tables by the sheer power of
their thought. Whether or not this is factually true,
it has symbolic value: Perhaps some sustained
experiments should be initiated by religious groups, to
subject the hypothesis of the efficacy of group prayer
to some rigid empirical testing. In the "old days"
almost all religions used to conduct such "experiments"
in times of drought, but praying for rain is not a very
prevalent practice now in our technologically-oriented
society. But we have even more substantial problems
than drought, and some of these problems may be
sufficiently objective and measurable to form the basis
for properly controlled experiments of the power of
group prayer in comparison with individual prayer, and
in comparison to no-prayer-at-all.

F. Suffering

1.
> Matt. XI, 29-30: Take my
> yoke upon your shoulders
> and learn from me, for I
> am gentle and humble of
> heart. Your souls will
> find rest, for my yoke is
> easy and my burden light.

In one of his parables Jesus talks about a servant whose master gave him some money to invest. The servant, instead, took the money and buried it in the ground. When his malfeasance was discovered, he excused himself on the grounds that his master was a hard taskmaster who would no doubt severely punish any injudicious investments that he made. The master, far from taking exception to this description of himself as a "hard taskmaster," corroborated it to the hilt by having the fearful servant cast out and perhaps exterminated. No doubt the offending servant, if he happened to survive, would be difficult to re-educate concerning the lightness of his master's burdens.

Obviously Jesus, in speaking here of his own "yoke," did not consider himself anything like the hard and exacting master in the parable. What if one of his disciples had spoken up then, and said something like, "Your burden is light? I don't understand. My burdens have been overwhelming for a long time, and the fact that I'm trying to follow you has only complicated things further." Perhaps Jesus might answer that the burdens his disciple felt were actually burdens he was imposing on himself, or others were imposing on him--and if the disciple would just stick to the burdens Jesus himself was imposing, he would find them quite light. But more probably Jesus would emphasize the fact that following him brought about some inner state of peace and strength which made all one's burdens easier to bear.

What is the secret of attaining this inner calm or refreshment? In Christianity, as also in Hinduism and Buddhism, it consists in overcoming unruly desires, passions, "sin"--which are characterized as the real and most severe burdens troubling man. Now, if we call burdens in the usual sense Burdens$_1$" and burdens as sinful desires, etc. "Burdens$_2$"--from the point of view of religion the onerousness of Burdens$_1$ would almost disappear if one could concentrate on avoiding Burdens$_2$.

From the viewpoint of the imperfect or sinful disciple, on the other hand, it is precisely the onerousness of Burdens$_1$ which saps his energy and keeps him from loosing Burdens$_2$. The catalyst for breaking up this vicious circle would have to be either a lightening of Burdens$_1$ or a new burst of energy ("second wind") for dismantling Burdens$_2$.

2.   Peter, 10: God. . .will himself restore, confirm, strengthen and establish those who have suffered a little while.

The imagery here, as elsewhere in the Bible, is that of gold ore or some other impure substance which must be purified by fire or some drastic agent or process, as a prelude to bringing out and solidifying what is most precious and important in it. So also, Peter is telling us, the soul and body of the Christian must undergo all kinds of torments, setbacks, frustrations, burdens, and/or attacks as a means to acquiring perfection, peace and establishment in faith.

Perhaps it is with respect to this notion of the necessity of suffering, more so than any other teaching, that Christianity differs from the Eastern religions. Although Buddhism and Hinduism teach voluntary renunciation and asceticism, these are just considered means to attaining the joy and peace of contemplation as quickly as possible. In none of these other religions is any great emphasis placed on suffering in the form of persecutions endured, diseases incurred, failures met consistently, catastrophes weathered, feelings of abandonment by God and men, etc.--i.e. the more "passive" types of suffering over which we have less control than we have over fasting and other forms of voluntary mortification. This whole emphasis culminates in the personage of Jesus Christ, who seems to have suffered in a way and to a greater extent than the founders of any other of the world's great religions. If advances are ever made towards a world ecumenism, perhaps it is with regard to this notion of suffering--rather than dogmatic formulas such as the Virgin Birth, etc.--that the most serious problems for discussion and negotiations will develop.

3.

> Luke XIII, 4: [Jesus, speaking about some tragedies and natural disasters taking place in his time:] Take those eighteen men who were killed by a falling tower in Siloam. Do you think they were more guilty than anyone else who lived in Jerusalem? Certainly not! But I tell you,
> you will all come to the same end unless you reform.

It is long established in the Judaeo-Christian tradition that calamities, sickness and suffering in general are in some degree causally related to sin: if sin diminished, so we are told, the evils in the world would diminish to a like degree.

On the other hand, a belief in divine providence and mercy is also part of the same Judaeo-Christian tradition. Thus the Judaeo-Christian God finds himself, so to speak, in a very tight situation: if he punishes sin immediately and severely, he becomes the Great Exterminator rather than the merciful God; if he does not punish at all, men would lose respect for his justice and forget that in the end they will be held accountable for their sins. Accordingly, God's solution" is something of a middle course: punish just enough to remind men that life is short and they must repent if they are to avoid personal tragedy and spiritual failure. What about the actual victims who are singled out for punishment--the people who are crushed to death by towers, etc.? Putting the matter in the best possible light, we surmise that these are sinners who would not have repented anyway, or else innocent victims who become living holocausts as a call to repentance for relatives, friends, onlookers, and hearers of their fate who are not-so-innocent. In the actual case that Jesus is referring to, the accident was to be taken as a warning to the Jewish nation as a whole that they were courting some kind of extraordinary and summary punishment for their sins (the imminent destruction of Jerusalem seemed to be on Jesus' mind).

In the story of the Fall of man in the beginning of the Bible, we are told that Adam's expulsion from "Paradise" and all evils and sufferings of this world are due to that original sin. In the contemporary world, now that we have the benefit of a very well-established theory of evolution as well as evidence gathered by Scripture scholars concerning the mythical nature of the story about Adam, it is hard to accept the religious hypothesis that, if there were no sin, there would be no suffering (i.e. the world would be a veritable paradise). Neverthless, in the face of bloody disasters, horrible natural calamities and threats of nuclear self-destruction that confront our generation, perhaps that age-old religious hypothesis should be reinvestigated and tested along with the other hypotheses and rules of thumb we use to assess such evils and avoid their repetition. Although it does violence to current concepts of causality in science, it might turn out to be viable and more explanatory of the phenomena than competing hypotheses.

G. The Christian's way of life

1.
> Rom. XII, 20: If your
> enemy is hungry, feed
> him; if he is thirsty,
> give him something to
> drink; by doing this you
> will heap burning coals
> upon his head.

It should be noted that Paul is counseling the Christian in this passage to play a role diametrically opposite to that supposedly played by the devil. The devil is depicted (in the Book of Job and elsewhere) as being allowed by God to test the moral and spiritual fibre of individuals: if a man is going to be rendered worthy of the favor of God, he must at least have the spiritual muscles and know-how to survive the onslaughts of the carefully-proportioned temptations permitted by God. So also, in Paul's characterization here, the Christian is not bound by the law of talion ("an eye for an eye and a tooth for a tooth") that applied to Old Testament Jews, but, liberated from this law, is exhorted to subject the enemies of Christianity to the ultimate test--the test of kindness, forebearance and understanding--to "tempt" the enemy of God and God's friends to a change of attitude. If the enemy is converted, fine: it is a victory for the Christian. If the enemy, far from being converted, becomes hardened and even more stubbornly established in his own viciousness, fine again. It is still a victory for the Christian: his enemy, by resisting the most overt and potent displays of goodness, has increased his own guilt and made himself subject to even greater punishments from God (the "coals of fire upon his head").

There is a potentially alarming thing about this passage: Paul seems to phrase his advice in such a way that the punishment of the enemy becomes the <u>motive</u> for his acts of kindness. If this were the case, <u>then</u> the Christian heeding Paul's advice (and Paul himself, in giving the advice) would offer a kind of ultimate example of sophisticated, duly sublimated aggression: actually wreaking vengeance upon enemies by showering them with kindness. It is as if a devil (to go back to our initial analogy) were to tempt his "charge" with the explicit intention of possibly increasing the virtue of his victim and making him more acceptable to

God. Surely Paul couldn't <u>mean</u> that Christians should try to incite their enemies with kindness and charity to responses of ultimate maliciousness and degradation. We may presume he meant something like, "be kind to your enemies: you may elicit a change of attitude in them, although, regrettably, there is always the chance that you will fail to change them." But the Pope, the Archbishop of Canterbury, and all of their confederates may also breathe a sigh of relief that this passage apparently escaped the notice of both Nietzsche and Freud.

2.   1 Cor. VI, 7: Why not
                     put up with injustice and
                     allow yourself to be
                     cheated?

    In this passage, Paul is directing his attention in particular to the practice prevalent among his converts at Corinth of pressing lawsuits against other members of their community, to obtain what they believed to be justice. Paul would have them desist from all lawsuits against fellow Christians, and be willing to put up with some injustice.
    The situation and Paul's consequent advice remind one of the question raised by Plato in one of his dialogues: is it better to do injustice, or to suffer injustice? Plato comes to the tentative conclusion that it is better to suffer injustice, since the man who does injustice defiles his soul, and loses his moral health and comeliness. But the question can be carried one step further: if the perpetuation of injustice is so degrading to the individual soul, should we not try to prevent individuals from performing their acts of injustice--out of our concern for their own moral well-being? One of the hardest things to understand about the final sufferings and death of Jesus Christ is why he did not use any of his well-known persuasive powers to at least try to dissuade his captors from defiling themselves by the atrocities they were about to commit. The martyr who is too eager to be martyred may prove an irresistable temptation to men of quite ordinary maliciousness who might conceivably be persuaded to think twice about their contemplated malicious acts.

But from the Christian point of view, it is of no great consequence whether a man with malicious intentions actually carries out his intentions or not. Everyone is judged precisely by their intentions--the thoughts which they harbor in their "heart." Could Jesus have persuaded any of his persecutors to repent from their <u>hate</u> and their <u>intention</u> to kill, by speaking up during those last hours? Perhaps not. Could Paul's converts at Corinth have elicited <u>repentance</u> from the cheaters in their community by suing them? Probably not. Jesus and Paul both seem to be telling us: be a willing victim of the malevolent person, and the chances are, he will be spurred to a reform of conscience when he sees the acute personal sufferings he is bringing about in his innocent victim. Or, with an extremely subtle and sophisticated degree of mysticism, they may be telling us: if you can suffer injustice completely willingly, you are no longer a "victim," because a victim is by definition unwilling, and you simultaneously may prevent your malefactor from incurring the <u>guilt</u> of violating your rights, since you voluntarily abdicate these rights.

3.   1 John II, 15: Anyone who
                       hates his brother is a
                       murderer.

In the gospels, Jesus admonishes his hearers that if a person even calls his neighbor a "fool" (perhaps in our day this would translate into "stupid bastard") he is guilty of "hellfire." The tenor of the passage cited above from John's first Epistle is quite similar: the fact that you have refrained from murdering someone out of fear of being caught is inconsequential. From the Christian point of view, the actual crime of murder is anticlimatic. Is there some individual (or group) whom you "can't stand," whom you consider almost completely worthless, whom you wish had never been born or would just disappear forever? If so, John categorizes you as a murderer.

These are hard words. It is difficult enough for some people, sometimes, to refrain from committing crimes such as murder; it is even more difficult to exert control over our likes and dislikes, our feelings of resentment and disapproval. But there is something sound in what John is saying, at least from a psychosocial and existential vantage point: a man's physical existence is not the main thing. In countless ways, all or most of which he is incognizant, he is in a very real way receiving existence from the recognition and empathy of others. If we look upon him with complete indifference, inspired by hate, and if he desires recognition from us at all, we are robbing him of his psychosocial existence, even if his physical well-being remains intact and unharmed. We can "murder" by our looks, or by not looking at all; and there are no doubt some men who have been "murdered" in this fashion countless times.

4.   Matt. V, 44: Love your enemies. . . This will prove that you are sons of your heavenly father, for his sun rises on the bad and the good.

With a little reflection, it can be seen that the very idea of loving one's enemies is a contradiction in terms. If we really love someone, he is no longer our enemy (although from his point of view, we may still be his enemy). Freud, in Civilization and its Discontents , tries to show how this command of "universal love" is psychologically unsound. If one were to take it literally, he observes, this indiscriminate dispersion of psychic energy would eventually take its toll: he would end up loving no one very efficiently. Was it perhaps a personal experience of the psychological difficulties involved that led John in the fourth gospel and the author of the "Epistles of John" to tone down the call to universal love in favor of the command to "love the brethren?" After communities of Christians had developed in a milieu of intermittent persecution, it certainly would seem sound advice to concentrate on strengthening intra-community bonds of love rather than wasting love on those who would most likely misunderstand it. But for Christians who are facing such problems concerning the "conservation of love," it may be important to advert to the example which Jesus gives of the Father, who "makes his sun shine" on everybody. Jesus is implying that the Father's "love" for his enemies consists precisely in allowing them to share in some of the benefits that are intended, of course, primarily for his friends, those who are "good." To imitate the Father in this regard would not be a very hard pill to swallow. But the problem is, we are told nothing about the <u>intentions</u> of the Father. Perhaps he not only "allows" the bad to share in benefits intended for the good, but explicitly intends to benefit the bad also. This is a "harder act to follow." To do likewise, we would have to perform good acts explicitly intended to benefit our enemies. Whichever way we interpret the intentions of the Father in making the sun shine, there are probably very good psychological grounds--Freud notwithstanding--for our continual efforts to "do good" to enemies as well as friends. For the attitude which gives rise to these efforts leads to the removal of all <u>subjective</u> impediments to friendship. It is tantamount to saying, "as far as in us lies, we will have no enemies."

5.   The Epistle of Paul to
                      Philemon

      In this extremely short Epistle, Paul notifies one of his converts, Philemon, that he is returning to him a slave by the name of Onesimus, who is another recent convert of Paul's.
      To us in the twentieth century it has to seem surprising that Paul would implicitly condone slavery by his act of returning the slave. True, in his Epistle he exhorts Philemon to receive Onesimus "no longer as a slave but as more than a slave, a beloved brother." But Paul still recognizes the prior right of Philemon over his "property," as he does for slaveowners in general in 1 Cor. VII, 21; and there is little doubt but that he expects Philemon to retain Onesimus in the condition of official servitude, but now as a better treated slave and a fellow Christian. And Paul is not alone in assuming this apparently tolerant attitude towards slavery. Jesus himself could not have failed to be aware of the condition of many slaves (slavery was rampant in Palestine at that time, as in many other parts of the world), and yet said nothing which would indicate he had any objection to this social institution.
      As an explanation for this silence on the part of both Jesus and Paul, we sometimes hear that they were

both so preoccupied with thoughts about the imminent coming of the end of the world that they would be unwilling to give priority to changing social structures which were bound to disappear soon, anyway. This is probably true, but it is still hard to believe that, if they saw slavery as a degrading and extremely immoral practice, they would not have spoken up about it anyway--as they did on other immoral practices.

There is a slight possibility that Paul (and perhaps Jesus also) saw slavery as a legal institution with which in their purely spiritual and non-political capacity they were unable to interfere--although they might have serious moral objections to the practices legally condoned. In this case, Paul's action in returning the slave to the slave-owner might be analogous in our day to the honest anti-voyeurist who returns a pile of stolen pornographic magazines to a pornography dealer, or the pro-life nurse who stands by helplessly as a living six-month old fetus is left to die after a legal abortion. In both examples, the respect of the individual for the law mitigates any personal moral objections they may have had to the practices they were observing.

It seems more likely , however, in view of their continuous silence on this matter, that neither Jesus nor Paul saw slavery as a serious moral problem in the ancient world. Politico-social institutions in their time, even among the Greeks (whose democratic city-state depended on slaves for its maintenance and success), had not evolved to the point at which the "individual's inalienable right of self-determination" or the "fundamental equality of all men"--concepts that are the cornerstone of contemporary liberal governments--were even vaguely apprehended. Slavery was such an integral and essential part of the economy in the world as a whole at that time, that to challenge it successfully would have almost certainly meant starting a revolution; and to abolish the institution peremptorily would have meant poverty, starvation and death for millions, especially the slaves who were emancipated. In view of this situation, perhaps the most "moral" thing for the evangelist to do was merely to recommend charity and understanding to both slave and slaveowner--which is what Paul does here.

If one accepts this latter explanation, he must also accept a certain relativity of morals in Christianity or in any other cultural and ideological system. But if there are certain things which seem

definitely immoral to us, but were "relatively" moral
to Paul, the obvious question suggests itself: what are
the areas in our own conduct now which seem tolerable
and moral, but which will be looked upon by some future
generation as intolerable and absolutely immoral?
Private property? Communism? Industrial pollution?
Underproduction? Large families? Or even the
"relativity of morals" itself (which might be shown, by
the wisdom of some later generation, to be relatively,
or even absolutely, false).

We, like Paul, won't know until hindsight comes
forth with the "obvious" solution.

H. Evangelization

1.

Acts II, 4-6: All the Apostles and disciples of Jesus were filled with the Holy Spirit. They began to express themselves in foreign tongues and make bold proclamation ' as the Spirit prompted them. Staying in Jerusalem at the time were devout Jews of every nation under heaven. They were much confused because each one heard these men speaking his own language.

The Pentecost experience described here bears some of the earmarks of the experience of glossalalia, or "speaking in tongues" mentioned by Paul in 1 Corinthians XIV and other places. This latter experience consists in being overcome by a religious ecstasy which enables one to utter foreign-sounding words and sentences which neither he himself nor his bystanders (unless they have the "gift of interpretation") understands. A considerable minority of Christians in our day claim to experience the same phenomenon, but unfortunately, testing by experts has so far been unable to give evidence of any praeternatural or supernatural knowledge of any foreign language among the charismatics. The "foreign-sounding words were shown to be either foreign to everybody or else snatches of foreign languages remaining as a residue in the memory of the charismatic subject, after some exposure to foreigners at some time in the past. Unfortunately also, the charismatics spoken of in Paul's Epistles were never subjected to any such initial scrutiny. However, in defense of all charismatics it should be mentioned that the absence of any miraculous knowledge of foreign languages does not necessarily prove that the experience is not worthwhile. It would be true to say that most charismatics, far from claiming any such miraculous knowledge, would simply claim that they feel caught up in something greater than themselves and don't know precisely what they are experiencing or uttering.

At any rate, it must be noted that the Pentecost experience described in the above passage from Acts, despite its obvious similarities to the "glossalalia," bears one striking difference: it does not result in <u>unintelligible</u> sounds (unless we are to assume that the Apostles all had the glossalalia and all their hearers had the "gift of interpretation"). In fact, the miraculous element here <u>seems</u> to be that all the bystanders are understanding what should be "foreign" language, and Luke (the author of Acts) in verses 9-11 gives a long list of the different nationalities represented in the audience, to corroborate that very impression. However, if one scrutinizes Luke's list carefully, he finds that either Greek or Aramaic was commonly spoken in all the nations and areas referred to; and since the Apostles and disciples would also be likely to know a smattering of Greek patois in addition to their native Aramaic, it is not necessarily marvelous or astonishing that their utterings had definite meaning for the onlookers. If there is any truly miraculous element in the phenomena reported here, it is precisely in the fact that the Apostles spoke with such sincerity, enthusiasm and power that the actual words used were probably an unimportant factor. The secret behind the mass conversions which resulted seemed to be not the propriety of the Apostle's words or even the fact that the hearers found themselves understanding languages to which they were unaccustomed, but the absolutely indubitable forcefulness and infectious conviction of the speakers.

2.   Luke IX, 5: When people will not receive you, leave that town and shake its dust from your feet as a testimony against them.

Just before he gave the above injunction, Jesus had instructed the Apostles (IX, 3) to go out without food or money or any visible means of support. This was no doubt much easier to do in a pre-industrial society, where hospitality was a tradition. In our day, as politicians as well as itinerant preachers have discovered, one almost needs an "advance agent" to make sure that the spontaneous invitations to hospitality

will be forthcoming. The important thing to notice in
Luke IX, 3 and IX, 5 is that the only "security" of the
Apostles would be the love and hospitality shown them
in the towns and villages they passed through.
Actually, as inhabitants of communes in present day
Israel have also discovered, this sort of security is
in many ways more reliable than the possession of
private property: it is almost impossible to be in
need, if one has many friends. But to one who is thus
dependent on friends, the converse also holds: don't
loiter any longer than necessary with those who seem to
be unfriendly.

What happens to the "love for enemies" which Jesus
also enjoins on his Apostles? If the Apostles really
practiced this love for enemies, shouldn't they be
willing to remain longer even in a hostile situation,
for the sake of contributing to the spiritual progress
and perhaps the conversion of some of the more
"difficult cases"? No. Here Jesus removes one
possible misconception about the meaning of love for
enemies: it doesn't mean lingering around enemies,
smiling and tolerating their behavior. It often means
overt criticism: in this case the act of shaking the
dust from their feet, a gesture which in our own
generation (which doesn't take hell too seriously)
might be roughly translated as, "the hell with you!"

3.   1 Cor. IX, 18: When
                      preaching I offer the
                      gospel free of charge and
                      do not make full use of
                      the authority the gospel
                      gives me.

This reference by Paul to his custom of financing
his preaching by plying a trade (tent-making) rather
than depending on donations offers much food for
thought. It is absolutely extraordinary that, while
the Pauline approach to evangelization has been widely
imitated in almost every respect--from his "rules of
thumb" about circumcision rituals and religious dietary
restrictions to his preference for a celibate
clergy--the conviction expressed here, and also
reiterated elsewhere in his Epistles, never caught on.
This is an understatement. The idea that the preacher
or minister, although having a moral right to receive

remuneration from his congregation, should in the interests of greater effectiveness earn his own living--has been almost completely ignored in mainstream Christianity. This conviction that the clergy should do manual work has been conspicuously ignored in Catholicism except in some of the stricter monastic communities such as the Trappist order, in which both priests and "lay brothers" do manual work and earn part or all of their subsistence by selling cheeses, fruitcakes, Christmas cards, religious articles, etc. to the general public. The attempts of the "worker priests" in France a few decades ago to return to the Pauline concept were eventually thwarted by the Vatican, and the considerable enthusiasm which the "new" idea generated was snuffed out. Some experiments in a "working ministry" are also at present being tried in the Lutheran church--but here again we are talking about splinter groups and nothing like a movement.

It would seem that in this regard the major Christian denominations, despite Paul's efforts to de-Hebraicize Christianity, have fostered their own variation on the old Testament Jewish tradition of supporting the priesthood by contributions from the "faithful." Nowadays, of course, the collection plate or a reasonable facsimile takes the place of the tithe in most Christian churches. But what churchgoer even in this era does not hear an occasional reference to tithing from the pulpit, with the observation, expressed or implied, that the "faithful" even in our own day should be offering a "tenth of their income" to their church (over and above what they give to charity and to the government through taxes, of course)?

It is hard to imagine what Christianity would be like now, had our notion of the clergy developed in that other, more Pauline, direction. Sociologically, would the presence of a "working" clergy in considerable numbers annul our present custom of looking upon the clergy in the major denominations as a kind of higher class of professionals, along with lawyers and physicians? or would we simply end up with lower, middle, and upper classes of clergy? Would the fact that the priest or minister is not dependent for sustenance upon contributions from his congregation perhaps bring about some subtle changes in his own attitude towards church membership and church attendance? We may never know unless the Maoist brand of communism (the only major movement in our day which

advocates some kind of regular manual work for
professional classes) overtakes the thinking of the
clergy. One hears a considerable amount of criticism
from inside and outside Christianity concerning the
extent to which Pauline ideas have "monopolized"
Christianity. But here at least is one area in which
the accusation would be far from the truth.

4.   2 John, 10: If anyone
                          comes to you who does not
                          bring this teaching, do
                          not receive him into your
                          house, do not even greet
                          him, for whoever greets
                          him shares in the evil he
                          does.

        Jesus had advised the evangelists not to darken
the door of the inhospitable (see H2 above), while John
here advises the evangelized not to extend hospitality
or even what might be considered common courtesies to
those of different religious persuasions. All this was
written, of course, before the more modern virtue of
"tolerance" was discovered. In our own day, from the
historical vantage point which adds up the countless
needless deaths and cruelties perpetrated in the name
of religious orthodoxy, we would tend to call such
behavior as John recommends "intolerant" and
"discriminatory."
        We would not be entirely justified, however, in
doing so. As the Wise Man in Ecclesiastes observes,
"there is a time for everything." At the time when
John wrote his Epistle, religious and political and
social convictions were more intimately intertwined;
and the Christian community, which was just gathering
momentum, might have suffered some irreversible
setbacks if they had not been careful to build up their
own distinctive body of beliefs and protect them from
heretical incursions. The "heretics" in question in
this instance were the docetists who believed in a kind
of phantom incarnation of Jesus and in related strains
of semi-gnosticism and antinomianism which denied man's
obligation to obey moral and religious laws. In our
own day, after benefitting from the combined efforts of
scientists, philosophers, theologians and Scripture
scholars, we are no longer quite so sure as our

ancestors about the precise mode of the Incarnation or even about the binding force of religious and moral laws. Also, there is no danger that Christianity will disappear and be forgotten overnight if we do the wrong thing. And so the upshot is--we can afford to be more tolerant.

In spite of our (hopefully) more advanced stage of moral and spiritual evolution, there is perhaps a lesson we can still learn from these ancient admonitions: If there were some principle of a moral, philosophical, or religious nature which we felt to be all-important for our survival and progress and for the survival and progress of our community, nation, or even the world as a whole, it would be wise for us to salvage that principle at the price of "intolerance," if we were faced with a clear choice beteen intolerance and an inevitable watering-down of the principle in question. It is not inconceivable that "Christian love" could be used as a mere excuse for avoiding the hard and sometimes dangerous duty of criticism of the status quo. A little Christian intolerance in Europe in the 30's would have perhaps prevented the Nazi debacle. A similar intolerance may be called for now, if we are to avoid destruction a few decades from now, from political totalitarianism or social conformism or economic laissez faire.

5.   Luke XXII, 35: He asked them [at the Last Supper], "when I sent you on mission without purse or traveling bag or sandals, were you in need of anything?" "Not a thing," they replied. He said to them, "Now, however, the man who has a purse must carry it: the same with the traveling bag. And the man without a sword must sell his coat and buy one.". . .They said, Lord, here are two swords! He answered, "Enough."

This passage is difficult to understand because 1) the injunction to take money (purse) and food (traveling bag) with them contradicts not only the earlier instructions (which he refers to also here) but also his previous injunctions to "sell everything they possessed," and be completely dependent on God's providence, etc. (were those just temporary counsels?); and 2) the recommendation to carry a sword seems to contradict earlier recommendations to passivity in the face of violence, e.g. "turning the left cheek" to the man who strikes us on the right. The reason why Jesus gives this advice seems clear: he is now facing the possibility of execution as a criminal, after which, of course, his own ignominy would redound to his disciples. But he makes no attempt to clear up the contradiction, or apparent contradiction, emerging from his earlier statements.

In regard to the first contradiction, which seems to amount to a complete reversal in tactics, we will simply observe that the work-and-preach modus operandi adopted by Paul (see section H3 above) seems to be a perfect means for making sure that the purse and the traveling bag one carries around are not empty. (Whether or not Jesus would like Paul's approach to be adopted universally and persistently is another question.)

The second contradiction is the one that has caused the most problems in Scripture interpretation. If one reads some of the patristic and Medieval Scripture commentaries on this passage, he can almost feel the emotional upset of the exegetes in handling the question of the "sword": St. John Chrysostom suggests that "sword" was not meant to be taken literally, but was to be taken as a symbol of coming difficulties and persecutions. Basil, on the other hand, believes there was a mistake in grammar--Jesus must have said his disciples "will. . . buy" a sword, not "must. . . buy" (that is, he was predicting something they would do in the future, not approving a certain course of action for the present). Ambrose makes the interesting suggestion that Jesus simply was telling his disciples to take along the sword to scare off would-be attackers (as we in our day might carry an unloaded gun for the same purpose). Theophylactus, showing some fine subtlety, goes so far as to say that when Jesus, hearing about the two swords, said "That's enough" he really means "That's enough for all the killing you'll have to do (namely, no killing at all)!"

Pope Boniface VIII, on the other hand, showing no
embarrassment at all about the "two swords" statement,
used it in writing the Bull <u>Unam Sanctam</u> to prove that
the Church should have secular power and authority as
well as spiritual jurisdiction over men. The tendency
in contemporary Scripture interpretation is to take the
reference to the sword rather literally, as a simple
exhortation to be prepared for self-defense. On
reflection, it seems this passage, on this latter
interpretation, is not really inconsistent with those
other sayings of Jesus which seem to inculcate
nonviolence: it is one thing to turn the cheek and
allow someone to strike you, but quite another to
voluntarily look the other way when someone is about to
run a sword through you.

6.   1 Tim. V, 17: Presbyters
                      who do well as leaders
                      deserve to be paid
                      double, especially those
                      whose work is preaching
                      and teaching.

     There are shades of capitalism, free enterprise
and the merit system in this advice given by Paul to
Timothy, a bishop with quite a few presbyters under
his jurisdiction. The practice recommended here
contrasts perhaps most sharply with the present-day
practice in the Catholic Church, in which priests not
only may not marry (unlike the presbyters in Timothy's
time) but also are in most situations given only a
relatively small fixed income. If an efficiency expert
were to do a thorough examination throughout all the
corners and edges of the Catholic hierarchical
structure now, one of the first things he might
recommend to infuse greater vitality into it would be
something like what Paul recomends above. The
immediate reaction to this in the higher echelons of
the Church hierarchy would be, of course, something
like the following: "How could greater financial
rewards and material incentives make for greater
productivity in the spiritual realm? Is it conceivable
that an increase in material benefits for the clergy
would result in an increase in spiritual benefits for
those they are dealing with?" This question, however,
in its very formulation shows a rather rigid

distinction being made between the spiritual and the
material--a distinction which has rather tenuous
philosophical foundations, and, at any rate, seems to
be rejected by Paul, if we were to judge from the
practical advice which he offers here.

I. Mystical body

1.

Luke II, 35: You yourself
[Mary] shall be pierced
with a sword--so that the
thoughts of many hearts
may be laid bare.

Since Mary, the mother of Jesus, as far as we
know, never endured any physical violence of the sort
described here, we may presume that the "piercing with
a sword" refers to her vicarious sufferings especially
at the time of Jesus' crucifixion. If, then, we were
to take this whole verse literally (and if it is
authentic), a causal connection is implied between
Mary's vicarious sufferings and the "laying bare of
thoughts" in many hearts. The tendency in Scripture
interpretation from the past to the present has been
to either downplay the implied causal connection ("so
that. . .") or to refer it to the immediately preceding
verse, which prophesies Jesus' ignominy and perhaps his
death on the cross. This tendency is understandable,
because it is not clear how there could be any causal
connection between the purely personal, emotional
sufferings endured by Mary and the fact that the
thoughts (we don't know whether good thoughts or bad
thoughts are being referred to) of many would be laid
bare. However, a causal connection would <u>not</u> be
inappropriate, in the light of some of the basic tenets
of Christianity. According to these tenets the life
and sufferings of Jesus were responsible for the
salvation and illumination of men; and, in general,
personal sufferings endured by individual Christians
can have an expiatory effect, releasing others from
their sins, procuring grace and illumination for them.
It is as if there were some kind of a super soul, whose
links are invisible to us, which brings it about that
my own seemingly personal experiences are intimately
connected at base, in varying degrees, with the
spiritual condition of others (though I may never have
met, or had any observable effect on, those others).
This "hypothesis of Christianity" is similar in major
respects to theories elaborated by Avicenna, Spinoza,
Bergson, Chardin and other philosophers; and if applied
specifically to the case of Mary's sufferings described
here, would imply that these very personal sufferings
could be causally related to the illumination and
salvation of many ("good thoughts" being revealed).

2.   1 Corinthians XII, 26-27:
            You. . .are the body of
            Christ. Every one of you
            is a member of it. . .
            If one member suffers,
            all the members suffer
            with it. . .

    Paul in this Epistle is expounding on the same
"hypothesis of Christianity" which was discussed in the
immediately preceding section. In doing this, he
utilizes the analogy of the Mystical Body, the idea of
a quasi-organic community of Christians joined together
by the Holy Spirit under Christ as their head, and
sharing the same inner spiritual experience as well as
the same fate or fortune. Paul uses this same analogy
in Romans, Colossians and Ephesians. Peter in his
first Epistle dwells on substantially the same theme,
but prefers to use the analogy of a temple built up
from "living stones," with Christ as the chief
cornerstone. Peter also speaks (in 1 Peter, V, 9)
about suffering shared by different Christians in
different parts of the world. But Paul's imagery is
more graphic and pointed.
    Does he really mean to say that there is some sort
of mysterious sharing of suffering among Christians, no
matter how widely separated from one another? If so,
then it would seem that a Christian in the United
States should be intimately affected by the sufferings
of any "fellow members" he may be related to in
Bangladesh, Laos, or Nigeria. But we must not carry
the analogy too far. If my ear is in pain because of
an infection, this does not mean that my mouth or hand
will also be in pain in the same way (unless the
infection spreads to these other organs); the only
sense in which the suffering is ordinarily shared is
the sense in which the mouth or the hand, because they
belong to the same ego which has an earache, are no
longer able to enjoy their wonted pleasures, or engage
in the usual range of their activities, with the same
gusto as before. Following up on the analogy, I would
experience the external sufferings of different and
distant members of the "Mystical Body" only in an
indirect way, and in proportion to the degree that I
identified with these other members emotionally.

If there were any more direct sharing of suffering, it would no doubt be in respect to inner, emotional suffering. A case in point may be the deep spiritual distress and feeling of irrelevance of religion which gave new impetus to the "death of God" movement in the Sixties and still, from all indications, lingers with us as a kind of common worldwide experience. All of this may add up to the final death pangs of religion that the atheists and skeptics have been predicting all along; but, short of death, the still lingering alienation and disillusionment may also be simply symptoms of a negative spiritual experience still being endured and shared through something like empathy, by many members of the "body."

J. End of the world

1.

Mark XIII, 32: As to the
exact day or hour [of the
"Last Judgment" and the
final coming of Christ],
no one knows it, neither
the Angels in heaven nor
even the Son, but only
the Father.

Up until not too long ago, when Christians were
more intent on emphasizing the divinity of Jesus, this
particular passage characteristically always caused
trouble. It definitely seems to say that Jesus does
not have any precise knowledge of the End of the World.
It is interesting to read the elaborate and sometimes
ingenious explanations of this passage which used to be
given by exegetes, in order to make it jibe with the
supposed omniscience and omnipotence of Jesus.

One could strive for subtlety here and point out
that, if the sun and the moon were to gradually or even
suddenly cease to give their light (a prophecy of Jesus
appearing just prior to this passage), there would in
a very real sense be no exact days or hours left--a
fact which would exonerate even God from imperfection
for not knowing them.

But this is no doubt unnecessarily subtle. In
order to capture the spirit of what Jesus is saying, it
would probably be best to follow the mainstream of
contemporary Scripture scholars who read this passage
quite literally: Jesus really didn't know all the facts
and details about the final days and his own
"Parousia." He was a man, limited in knowledge, just
like us. Theologically speaking, they tell us, those
who have difficulty with this passage probably do not
have a serious enough appreciation of the definite and
limiting humanity of Jesus.

Nevertheless, the Scripture scholars have not
succeeded in dispelling all the lingering doubts and
ambiguities. It is still hard for anybody to
understand how Jesus, who not only supposedly predicted
the time of his own death and the destruction of
Jerusalem, but also claimed to have known Abraham
before Abraham was even born, and to be equal with the
Father and share all things with Him, could have this
single flaw in knowledge because the Father had failed

to reveal it to him. And yet this is the slightly
flawed picture which the somewhat complex mosaic of the
four gospels presents to us.

We should take this opportunity to ask ourselves,
however, what it would be like if God really became
man? No doubt he would be subject to some rather
embarrassing ambiguities, including some inexplicable
lacunae or "blind spots" in knowledge--otherwise we
(and he himself as well) would have to take his
supposed "humanity" with a grain of salt. The Medieval
mystic, Meister Eckhart, in an exuberant moment once
proclaimed that his own true ego was basically
identical with God. He was "called on the carpet" by
the Pope, and recanted, no doubt with considerable
embarrassment and confusion (since it really seemed to
him that this divine element did constitute a major
part of his personality). Perhaps if someone had been
bold enough, after Jesus had made his apocalyptic
statements but disclaimed any precise information as to
the time of the apocalyptic events, to challenge him
concerning this apparent deficiency in his otherwise
cosmic expanse of knowledge, Jesus might have felt a
similar sort of embarrassment and ambiguity. Or he
might have said, "that's not the only thing I don't
know." But no one ever asked him.

2.   James V, 7-8: Be patient,
                      my brothers, until the
                      coming of the Lord. . .
                      . Steady your hearts,
                      because the coming of the
                      Lord is at hand.

James, along with the rest of the Apostolic
community, seemed to expect the imminent reappearance
of Jesus bringing an end to the present state of the
world. Such an expectation was bound to have some
practical effects on the behavior of those who took it
seriously. They would be discouraged from undertaking
any extremely long-range plans or making any very
long-term investments. There would be little incentive
to instigate major changes in social structure or roles
(witness Paul's advice concerning slavery and the role
of women). In the present Epistle, James condemns
employers for exploiting workers, but does not

recommend any time-consuming improvement of working conditions, or even patience on the part of the worker in obtaining "better conditions." Rather, he recommends patience in waiting for the coming of the Lord, who will appear imminently and make short shrift of any employer who has exploited workers.

Compare our situation now, a situation which can be characterized as doubly ironical:

First of all, it is ironical that all the massive scholarly scepticism about the imminent end of the world has reached its zenith precisely at a time when (in the wake of a nuclear attack or a nuclear accident) a worldwide holocaust could quite conceivably and easily take place! Is there any era other than our own in which all the impassioned Jeremian warnings of Christian preachers of the past seem more appropriate? But now no respectable preacher dares to preach the End of the World and the imminent coming of the Kingdom of God -- because, after all, that message, repeated so often during the last two thousand years, has finally become discredited (like the message of the unfortunate little boy who cried, "Wolf! Wolf!" one too many times).

But secondly, it is also conceivable that the Christian's downplaying of these traditional eschatological predictions may actually pave the way for the actualization of those predictions. The very lack of urgency we feel about "the end of the world" now, may release the Christian to undertake some broad-ranging changes of political, social, economic and environmental structures--changes that may take hundreds of years to be completed. And it may change the Christian perspective on social injustice as something that should be "patiently endured" or a situation that will be remedied very soon when the rewards and punishments are distributed in the afterlife. If we do not depend on "the Lord" to come any day now and dispel injustices, we may just have to take the initiative ourselves. And ironically--if Teilhard de Chardin and others, who interpret the "coming of God's kingdom" as an evolutionary development rather than a merely cataclysmic event, are correct--this sort of initiative and dedication to long-range and systematic social change may be precisely what is necessary to accelerate (or even bring about) the long expected and long-deferred Parousia.

CHAPTER IV

THE REVOLUTION VERSUS THE AFTERLIFE: A CHRISTIAN REVOLUTIONARY BUTTONHOLES A REVOLUTIONARY THEORETICIAN

CHRISTIAN REVOLUTIONARY: I don't think you should continue theorizing without giving some very close attention to the relationship of Christianity to current revolutionary movements.

REVOLUTIONARY THEORETICIAN: You mean, Christianity as a _positive_ revolutionary force? I have so many important things to do. . . .

CHRISTIAN REVOLUTIONARY: Surely you're not going to maintain that the fundamental changes going on within Christianity have no relationship to socio-political changes?

REVOLUTIONARY THEORETICIAN: We in the Western world have inherited so much from the Greek and Roman traditions and other sources, that I would find it hard to point to any _distinctive_ contributions of the Christian religion in bringing about socio-political changes or even changes in secular ideology. Perhaps you could enlighten me.

CHRISTIAN REVOLUTIONARY: I would simply point to some of the seminal ideas in Christianity that everyone knows about but very few people take seriously enough--the obligation of the rich to share what they have with the poor, the command to extend the horizons of love, the importance of the individual conscience and self-transcendence, the paradoxical notion that the leader should be the servant of those he leads, the exhortation to build up an organically concatenated community in which a broad diversity of opposites would be drawn into spiritual reconciliation and harmony. Admittedly, these are not ideas that have been worked out with philosophical precision or in detail. But they are certainly there in Christianity, from the beginning. And you would have to be intellectually blind to claim that these ideas are unrelated to the fundamental socio-political changes envisaged by revolutionary movements.

REVOLUTIONARY THEORETICIAN: First of all, I'm not so sure that the "seminal" ideas you mentioned are strictly Christian in origin. Some of them seem to be derived from the Judaic tradition. And even if we could classify a few of them as distinctively Christian, there is always the problem of wide differences among Christians themselves as to the meaning or importance of these ideas. There is the Petrine interpretation of Christianity, the Pauline interpretation, the Catholic and Protestant interpretations, etc.

CHRISTIAN REVOLUTIONARY: I would hope that we might focus on the historical Jesus himself, and the basic reinterpretation and redirection he gave to the Jewish religion. We will, of course, have to discountenance any distortions of, or interpolations in, his essential message, by zealous but opinionated disciples.

REVOLUTIONARY THEORETICIAN: I'm sure you realize the difficulty in distilling the "historical Jesus"--free from distortion--even out of Matthew, Mark, Luke, and John. But even if this could be done, and if you found the seminal working concepts for revolution--I doubt if you would enhance the intelligibility of the latter. You would end up with an eclectic melange. An isolated insight here, a moment of inspired thought there; put them together and you have merely a collection of all the possible "revolutionary" tendencies in Christianity. You might do the same thing with Buddhism: select the appropriate ideas and label them "seminal revolutionary concepts" when you are finished.

CHRISTIAN REVOLUTIONARY: You are implying that I am focusing on some of the lesser, esoteric insights of Christianity. That's not true. I think I could show that these "revolutionary" ideas supply the life blood, so to speak, of the mainstream of Christian thought.

REVOLUTIONARY THEORETICIAN: Perhaps you could prove this to me. I might even agree with you that Christianity at its very inception, before it became institutionalized, operated as a revolutionary force among certain groups of people. The question is, is Christianity anything like a revolutionary force now? I am referring to Christianity unmixed with Marxism or any other contemporary revolutionary movement. Pure Christianity. A revolutionary force? Not strictly speaking.

CHRISTIAN REVOLUTIONARY: That may be so. But it is a great potential force, and could be the deciding factor in assuring the success of many revolutionary endeavors. That is all I'm trying to prove.

REVOLUTIONARY THEORETICIAN: That's not enough. Potentialities can be either real, viable potentialities or remote, unreal potentialities--bare possibilities. I can't conceive of Christianity having a revolutionary potential in the former sense. In fact, in all candor, I think we would have to admit that Christianity seems to take on the aspect of a counter-revolutionary force as we peruse the murky tableaux of Western history: I am thinking of the continually recurring alliances of Christianity with the propertied and ruling classes; the preoccupation with an afterlife to the detriment of ordinary human fulfillment in this life; the exhortation of the masses to be obedient to corrupt oppressors; the hierarchical elitism (overt and blatant in Catholicism, more subtle and oblique in some forms of Protestantism): and so forth. I'm sure you've heard this litany before. Many others have pointed out these unmistakably counter-revolutionary tendencies.

CHRISTIAN REVOLUTIONARY: If I may be allowed to borrow a Kierkegaardian term--you're speaking about Christendom, not Christianity. Christianity is that other element--the one that is so frequently ignored by critics--the one that has been concerned and is concerned with the education of the masses, helping the poor and the weak, bringing about justice--Christianity, the instrument of healing and reconciliation.

REVOLUTIONARY THEORETICIAN: I am not unaware of those other aspects. But still the whole history of Christianity or "Christendom" is such a motley pattern of up and down, good and bad, that you could not expect me to point to it as a prime meta-revolutionary force, so to speak. I will grant, it might have become a viable force in revolution. But something happened.

CHRISTIAN REVOLUTIONARY: I can tell you what happened. The Church became too involved in dogmatic and sectarian squabbles, utilizing all its energy in defending or attacking positions concerning the Immaculate Conception, the Apostolic Succession, the Real Presence, Predestination, Salvation by Faith Alone, the Liberal vs. the Fundamentalist interpretation of the Bible, and so on ad infinitum. So much energy was wasted on these cerebral contests that little of the socio-political message of Christianity was allowed to emerge. The transmission of this message was also impeded by the Church's involvement in politics and war.

REVOLUTIONARY THEORETICIAN: You speak of the
quibbling intolerance, dogmatic cerebration, political
intrigue and warmongering, as if it were a thing of the
past. After the separation of Church and state in many
countries, the aforementioned predilections in the
Church became (had to become) more subtle or
"low-keyed"; but I haven't heard of any stark reversal
of emphasis in the Christian Church. To my knowledge,
"Christendom" still prevails over "Christianity."
      CHRISTIAN REVOLUTIONARY: There has been no
reversal yet. Christianity is in the state of crisis
at present.
      REVOLUTIONARY THEORETICIAN: The crisis seems to me
to be the result of that dogmatism that you have
alluded to. The Church has gradually been overwhelmed
by the realization that it is getting harder to
maintain strict theological positions on anything, in a
world devoted much more to science than theology.
      CHRISTIAN REVOLUTIONARY: It is not competition
with science but amalgamation with science that seems
to have brought on the dogmatically-engendered crisis
you are referring to. By "science," I mean here the
scientific study of the Scriptures. In the wake of
meticulous historical, linguistic, anthropological and
cultural studies of the Gospels, one hardly finds it
possible anymore to be dogmatic about the Virgin Birth,
the genealogy of Jesus, his birth in Bethlehem, even
his resurrection. One becomes aware of a plethora of
myth, out of which it is hard to extract the historical
Jesus.
      REVOLUTIONARY THEORETICIAN: I seem to recall you
saying something in the beginning about the necessity
of going back to the historical Jesus to discern the
true spirit of Christianity and its potential as a
revolutionary force. But in view of the difficulties
you mention, I should think that skepticism would be a
more likely result than an understanding of the "true
spirit of Christianity."
      CHRISTIAN REVOLUTIONARY: Not at all. When the
mass of superfluous beliefs have finally been exposed,
the way will be clear for a concentration on the
essential kernel of Christian faith, the things that
Jesus really stood for: universal love, a concern for
the less-fortunate and the suffering, freedom of
conscience from external control, personal virtue, a
disposition for reconciliation--all of the elements
that were there from the beginning, exemplified in the

historical Jesus, but misunderstood or de-emphasized
because of a misdirected, bureaucratizing,
mythologizing faith.

REVOLUTIONARY THEORETICIAN: Even if these
"essential elements" become newly emphasized in
Christianity, I fear that the resemblance of Christian
objectives to revolutionary objectives would be
superficial, at best. In Christianity there is an
intermingling of foreign motives. For example, a
Christian saint like Francis of Asissi gives all his
possessions to the poor. Does he do this out of a
human compassion for the poor, a desire to share what
he has? Far from it. He does it purely and simply to
gain a higher degree of merit in the eyes of his God;
he divests himself of worldly goods so that he can lay
hold on heavenly treasures and outrank other mortals in
his degree of perfection. He is not even thinking
seriously of helping others. If he were, he would no
doubt have tried to devise some more stable and
permanent means of helping the needy than throwing off
his clothes and giving away his money in a classic
emotional Italian gesture.

CHRISTIAN REVOLUTIONARY: You're somewhat selective
in your examples. I don't think there is any doubt but
that Jesus taught a genuine concern for others in his
words and actions.

REVOLUTIONARY THEORETICIAN: But a concern
motivated by a desire for a heavenly _reward_ and
advancement in _virtue_. That's the point.

CHRISTIAN REVOLUTIONARY: That's a distortion.
Jesus does speak in a couple of places about a reward
in heaven to be given to those who practice his kind of
"philanthropy." But those are isolated texts. The
total thrust of his teaching is a recommendation to
share what one has with others, without any "extrinsic"
motives. I can think of a graphic example of this: the
parable of Lazarus and Dives (Luke XVI, 22ff.). In this
parable Dives, the rich man, finds himself in hell
precisely because he wouldn't share his wealth with the
pauper, Lazarus. There is no mention of Dives'
motives, his lack of virtue, his lack of faith. There
is only one important consideration: Dives did not
have enough concern for his fellow man to share his
wealth with him. That's his crime.

REVOLUTIONARY THEORETICIAN: Dives almost sounds
like a pre-Marxist version of Monsieur Kapital. . . .
You're forgetting one thing about that parable,

however: if a man like Dives were to have been
converted, his conversion would almost certainly have
been instigated by a desire to avoid "hellfire." In
other words, his consequent flings at benefaction and
philanthropy would be, for all practical purposes, the
mere nervous twitchings or ritualistic purifications of
a superstitious man who is trying to avoid certain
punishment. His "concern for his fellow man" would be
a put-on. The thought of the afterlife becomes the
main motive here; and an extrinsic motive, to be sure.

CHRISTIAN REVOLUTIONARY: In the long run the
thought of the afterlife may be the most effective, and
the only truly voluntary means for making insensitive
rich people more sensitive to the needs of the less
fortunate. Does a Marxist revolutionary have any hope
of converting the wily capitalist? Voluntary change of
disposition due to the intrinsic attractions of Marxism
is almost out of the question. He must resort to some
species of force (which may be called "re-education").
And force has its own drawbacks, in a world in which
the importance of freedom is becoming more and more
paramount. Perhaps it would be wiser and more
efficient for them to reinstate the afterlife as a
viable motive.

REVOLUTIONARY THEORETICIAN: I presume you are
merely suffering a momentary loss of sanity, a
transient loss of historical perspective. You got so
carried away by argument for argument's sake, that you
forgot all the facts--the unending array of repressive
regimes and institutionalized injustices that were
borne by the common people at the bidding of their
priests and ministers--in the hope of meriting an
"afterlife." There has been perhaps no belief so
inimical to progressive social change as that single
belief. Armed with this fiction, the Church became the
spiritual right hand of the Establishment. In the
latter stages of the "Christian era," revolutionaries
began to sense this conjunction of Church and
Establishment; and it is not without reason that every
major revolution since the 17th century has had to
attack established Church as well as established
political regime.

CHRISTIAN REVOLUTIONARY: I suppose this must seem
an irresponsible and pragmatic response to you: but. .
.really, do we do any harm to people by opening up to
them vistas of an afterlife, especially when they have
no hope of attaining justice or happiness in this life?

You seem to suppose that it would be possible to achieve justice for everyone, if only we could use blinders on them and re-educate them to direct all their energies towards this present life. But you know that is not true. There will always be the countless victim cases; the slow, the weak, the intemperate, the "they's" whom the "we's" forget or ignore.

REVOLUTIONARY THEORETICIAN: You can conscientiously offer them a better world in the future; that is attainable. But not an afterlife; that is an illusory goal.

CHRISTIAN REVOLUTIONARY: You can't prove that statement, you know. In fact, I've heard some good philosophical arguments to the effect that one can't even understand the meaning of the phrase, "life after death." It goes so completely beyond our experience that it is unintelligible. When we try to imagine an afterlife, we think of indefinite continuance in time. But, to continue in time, one would have to exist in time, which presupposes life. In order to have an afterlife of this sort, one would have to never die.

REVOLUTIONARY THEORETICIAN: You've stolen my line of thought. That's my argument; or it should have been. You put it very nicely. You must have been sent by the "Death of God" theologians.

CHRISTIAN REVOLUTIONARY: I am just emphasizing the fact that nothing can be known about the afterlife, one way or another. It's a matter of faith. Faith never emerges except in cases of absurdity and/or ambiguity. It's only where the embers of knowledge begin to fade and die out that faith begins to appear as a light (not as a purely negative boundary, "The things we don't know," the mysteries).

If we know anything with certainty, it becomes a part of our experience and life, this life. "Knowledge" of the future (any future) can never be knowledge in the strict sense. This applies especially to knowledge of the ultimate or absolute future (which would have to be beyond all time experience).

REVOLUTIONARY THEORETICIAN: By your own admission, the belief in an afterlife is a pure belief (possibly an absurd belief). This belief has always had a quite definite counter-revolutionary effect in the past. Why go on any further? For anyone who believes in the future of revolution, such religious notions must be eschewed.

CHRISTIAN REVOLUTIONARY: Did I hear you utter that forbidden word, "believe"? You can't avoid it, because you are concerned with the evasive ambiguities of the future, too.

One thing you don't seem to realize about the Christian idea of the afterlife, however: Whatever it is, it doesn't begin at death. "The kingdom of heaven is within you." Jesus makes it quite clear in many of his sayings and parables that the divine or eternal life begins even now, within the souls of living individuals. In fact, the phrase, "entering into eternal life," involves a paradox: only those who already have eternal life will be able to "enter into it" at death.

REVOLUTIONARY THEORETICIAN: This is getting abstruse and a little lofty for me. I can perceive the direction of your reasoning well enough to realize that you are trying to relocate the "afterlife" in the deep interior of man. But this doesn't satisfy my objections to the concept. Whether you relegate the afterlife to heaven after death or to some secret soul of man during life--the effect is the same: withdrawal. The timid and oppressed individual harks to his haven of salvation, and is loathe to change any of the oppressive circumstances which are hastening his entrance into that haven (whether it is thought to be above the skies or inside the soul).

CHRISTIAN REVOLUTIONARY: You are apparently unfamiliar with what I might call the "pragmatic criterion" in the original teachings of Jesus: "By their fruits you shall know them," he insists. He applies that criterion rigidly to everyone he encounters, whether Apostle or Pharisee. In regard to the afterlife, the criterion necessarily implies that it would be worthless and senseless to talk of having the "new life" unless there were corresponding and unmistakable changes in external behavior. A new internal state that did not <u>appear</u> externally and practically would be an empty abstraction.

REVOLUTIONARY THEORETICIAN: I suppose I would have to be privileged with special interior powers myself to perceive the presence of this new life permeating the activities of the reborn, authentic Christians.

CHRISTIAN REVOLUTIONARY: Not at all. It should be an unmistakable phenomenon--even for those with quite ordinary powers of perception. The activities and the external relationships and interrelationships of

Christians should give definite proof of the existence of that "life." In fact, a Christian cannot even know he has that life himself, unless he sees the proof of this in his external activities.

REVOLUTIONARY THEORETICIAN: What would be the nature of these "external activities"?

CHRISTIAN REVOLUTIONARY: The sort of activities that Jesus himself was engaged in--reconciling the sick and the healthy, the rich and the poor, the advantaged and the disadvantaged, servants and masters, Jews and gentiles; doing away with natural enmities and rivalries, this is what it means to bring about the "kingdom of God" on earth: offering all men an example of creative and productive life and the existence of human excellence (i.e. the "divine").

REVOLUTIONARY THEORETICIAN: If these are the external signs that you want me to look for, then I must sadly reach the same conclusion that I suppose many honest Christians have already reached about themselves--namely, that judging from the results, they must have no special interior qualities or virtues that would serve to differentiate them from the unconverted masses.

CHRISTIAN REVOLUTIONARY: Mind you, I am not implying that these external efforts have to be successful. Jesus himself was a failure; but he was signalized by the unflagging efforts which he made to bring about the "kingdom of God." Do you mean to tell me that, looking around you, you can see no one engaged in these tasks--at least striving and struggling to improve their life and the world about them?

REVOLUTIONARY THEORETICIAN: Yes, I do. But those I see doing this are not chiefly or even generally Christians. In fact, many of them are unmistakably anti-Christians. And I'm sure that most of them would not lay claim on any extraordinary "inner life" as the source of their labors. Interiorly, they are only conscious of a gnawing unrest and disquietude that motivates them to continue to try to make some very difficult but necessary re-routings and interconnections out of almost unmalleable masses of human protoplasm.

CHRISTIAN REVOLUTIONARY: Then, by whatever criterion we have set up, these are our "Christians"--whatever they choose to call themselves, even if they be overtly anti-Christian.

REVOLUTIONARY THEORETICIAN: Are you sure you are satisfied with a "kingdom of God on earth" of this sort--the restless and unremitting efforts and conflict? What happened to the kingdom of peace, love, and reconciliation?

CHRISTIAN REVOLUTIONARY: Jesus had something to say about that:

> Do not suppose that I have come to bring peace to the earth; it is not peace I have come to bring, but a sword. For I have come to set a man against his father, a daughter against her mother, a daughter-in-law against her mother-in-law. A man's enemies will be those of his own household. (Matthew X, 34)

These words give us an indication of the kind of price we are going to have to pay for bringing about the extension of the kingdom of love. After all, some of the reconciliations (that love is trying to bring about) are between traditionally antagonistic or naturally opposed forces--the rich and the poor, slaves and master, etc. When one begins to work for such reconciliation, the sum-total of his "love-energy" (to use an analogy from physics) will be differently distributed than it was before, with the result that there will be a consequent diminution in the manifestations of love to those who previously received it. "Alienation" will result. On the local level, this means there will be a diremption, often violent, from one's kinfolk and friends. In a more universal sense, it implies that every serious attempt to bridge gaps, reduce inequalities and extend understanding, will be met with an "equal and opposite reaction"--a proportionally strong effort on the part of natural affinities and prior relationships to reassert themselves and re-establish their dominance. Those who try to extend the horizons of peace will necessarily offend those who want to keep the benefits of peace "within the family," and, moreover, are certain to lose something (property, personal affection, or an established way of life) because of such further extensions. Thus these efforts will indirectly result in "the sword"--wars, civil wars, revolutions, familial discords: traditional, time-honored, and "natural" affinities cannot be challenged and threatened with impunity.

REVOLUTIONARY THEORETICIAN: Then you must be expecting countless outbreaks of violence or "the sword," since the "extension of love" involves the reconciliation of so many "odd bedfellows" and the sacrifice of so many "natural" attractions?

CHRISTIAN REVOLUTIONARY: You make the whole thing sound like a world-wide establishment of endemic "unnaturalness". But I'm sure I need not remind you that "natural attraction" is something quite relative. It depends on background and habitual associations, on one's state of development and his openness to new associations and new ways of doing things. Through education or revolution natural attractions can become completely different from what they used to be. What was once unnatural will become second nature. Peace will return.

REVOLUTIONARY THEORETICIAN: You talk about education or revolution as an instrument for changing the character of natural attractions. What about conversion? I find it strange that you don't refer to conversion in this connection. You don't seem to be talking like a Christian, or how I think a Christian should talk. Haven't Christians always claimed to offer an inner force--divine "grace" or the "power of faith"--to help in the accomplishment of tasks that would otherwise exceed the limits of one's "natural attractions"? Education, revolution. . . No one needs Christianity to offer these instruments of change. But if Christianity could offer the possibility of a real, concrete increase of inner strength for bringing about the fullest possible extensions of love--this would seem to be more "in character." This would also amount to a distinctive contribution--Christianity offering not just another theory, not just ideas, inspirations, allies and/or leadership, but an inner power and an inner peace anticipating and facilitating the establishment of "Peace on Earth."

CHRISTIAN REVOLUTIONARY: Religions from time immemorial -- and not just Christianity -- have offered the possibility of inner peace and the experience of "transcendence." But the state of consciousness that I am referring to is not esoteric or mystical. It is simply the satisfaction that results amid one's struggles to affirm love; the experience of peace that results on occasions when one is successful, or at least knows he is trying; the sense of freedom that results from escaping subservience to the idols

which happen to be current and prevalent in one's own
historial era; the "transcendence" that comes from
constant progress and forgetfulness of self. Some
highly emotional Christians have tried to give the
impression that they were receiving some superhuman
strength from "on high," like modern Sampsons. But
they are only deluding themselves. They have to learn
to de-emphasize the importance of the emotional fervor
or psychological satisfaction they may feel--feelings
which may be due to temperament, auto-suggestion,
imagination or even subconscious sexual
need-fulfillment. The man of faith does not derive his
strength from such experiences. The experiences are
just side-effects, epiphenomena.

REVOLUTIONARY THEORETICIAN: I seem to recall a
story about the Holy Spirit descending upon the
disciples on Pentecost to imbue them with power and
wisdom. Would you as a Christian consider this just a
"side-effect" of something the disciples were doing?

CHRISTIAN REVOLUTIONARY: The manifestation of the
"Holy Ghost" is just an example of the sort of legends
that result from an age of myth and miracle. This is
just their way of saying that the disciples of Jesus
united in a community of faith to foster and perpetuate
the teachings and spirit of their master. A mature
Christian doesn't require such supernatural phenomena
to bolster his faith.

REVOLUTIONARY THEORETICIAN: I wasn't really opting
for anything supernatural. I was simply adumbrating
the possibility that there might be latent, natural
human forces as yet untapped, forces that Christianity
(or some other religion) might help to unleash in the
service of progressive change.

CHRISTIAN REVOLUTIONARY: I am gratified by your
solicitous and magnanimous efforts to make a
distinctive "place" for religion in your theoretical
constructs. But I don't think you realize what this
concern for "untapped" human forces could lead to. The
end result would be a reversion of Christianity to the
withdrawn, introspective, uninvolved role of mysticism
and self-realization that it has played so frequently
in the past. You would apparently like to refurbish in
modern dress the figure of the hermit-pathfinder of the
interior life, who by his "fastings and watchings" will
somehow unleash latent forces of peace and love in
mankind.

REVOLUTIONARY THEORETICIAN: I was actually thinking of something more practical: the possibility that certain Christian rituals or activities might offer man a practical instrument for activating powers that are lying obstructed or dormant within his troubled psyche.

CHRISTIAN REVOLUTIONARY: You are confusing Christianity with Yoga or perhaps with psychoanalysis--both of which have a rather poor record for activating within the individual a consciousness of the need for social change.

It is precisely ideas such as this that have obscured the social and humanistic message of Jesus for centuries. There may be some need for "self-cultivation"--but its importance has been unduly emphasized or distorted in Christianity and elsewhere. As Christians become involved in human progress, many of their imagined personal weaknesses or impediments will disappear.

REVOLUTIONARY THEORETICIAN: Fine. I am in favor of "involved" Christians. But I must repeat: if they become involved in revolutionary activity, they would still make no distinctive contribution to revolutionary perspectives or ideology by being Christian. I think your own defense of the revolutionary nature of Christianity makes that clear. According to your own account, when you clear away the dross, you will find many points of convergence where the "Christian Spirit" joins with this or that revolutionary spirit. But granted that this convergence does take place, I would be inclined to doubt that the convergence has been initiated, prepared, or brought to a conclusion by Christianity itself. It seems much more probable to me that we--both of us--are simply finding that a revolutionary movement, here or there, has overtaken Christianity (in the same way that it overtakes and transforms "secular" institutions or ideologies).

CHRISTIAN REVOLUTIONARY: Christianity has been compared to a mustard seed or a pinch of leavening--something hardly noticeable at first which nevertheless has the power to generate impressive results. I think the reason you have been unable to discern anything "distinctive" about it is that it is not readily identifiable with any particular revolutionary movement. You miss the point that it is adaptable and versatile enough to be able to contribute to progressive movements at all times and in

all places. Such universal adaptibility is itself
something quite remarkable and distinctive.

REVOLUTIONARY THEORETICIAN: Here you seem to run
into a contradiction: Just a short while ago you
offered a "pragmatic" criterion for gauging the
intensity of the inner spirituality of Christians: "By
their fruits you shall know them." I take this to mean
that you think Christian commitment should issue in
some very concrete, particular and recognizable
results. But now you say that the basic genius of the
Christian spirit is that it is able to adapt itself to
progressive movements of all types--in other words, the
"specific" contribution of Christianity is that it is
"general" enough to further "progressivism" everywhere
without becoming identified with any particular
movement. You want to have your cake and eat it
too--to keep Christianity strictly general, and
embellish it with concrete results as well.

CHRISTIAN REVOLUTIONARY: It would be a
contradiction if I were saying that the fundamental
Christian characteristic is some general <u>tendency</u> of
adaptability. But I'm not saying that. You
misunderstand my meaning. I'm talking about the
<u>Church</u>, which as a superstructure with social
ramifications is something "general," and maintains an
identity and stability of its own; but also is quite
visible and eminently progressive in its particular
effects. In the earliest days of the Church, its
revolutionary genius was manifested in the almost
unprecedented phenomenon of communistic groupings
which, if we may believe the Acts of the Apostles, seem
to have been very widespread throughout the then
burgeoning Christian world. As socio-economic forms
became more and more complex, however, Christian
communism became more specialized--relegated to
communities of professional religious engaged in
farming, preaching, teaching, medical ministrations,
and so forth--the so-called "religious orders," which
were as radical and as revolutionary innovations in
their own day as the Israeli kibbutz was a few decades
ago.

REVOLUTIONARY THEORETICIAN: By talking about these
organizations as forms of "Christian communism," you
make them sound very egalitarian. But you know as well
as I that, for example, most of the religious orders
turned out very elitist--coteries of privileged
professionals enjoying a moral and often real political
supremacy over the lowly laity.

CHRISTIAN REVOLUTIONARY: There were imperfections, of course. But I think the main thing you are calling attention to is that political society in a larger sense was not ready during the heyday of the religious orders for egalitarianism or Christian communism on a larger scale. It <u>had</u> to be something esoteric and privileged then.

REVOLUTIONARY THEORETICIAN: But are we now ready for egalitarianism "on a larger scale"? I get the impression that you would like to paint the current exponent of revolutionary Christianity in Marxist colors.

CHRISTIAN REVOLUTIONARY: Not necessarily. I think that the various non-Marxist "Christian socialist" movements in certain European countries today would be a better example of what I have in mind.

REVOLUTIONARY THEORETICIAN: Would you interpret the attempts of Christian theologians in Czechoslovakia to arrive at intellectual detente with Marxist theoreticians, and the "liberation theology" movement in certain Latin American countries--as thrusts in the same general direction?

CHRISTIAN REVOLUTIONARY: Since the Czechoslovakian experiment was cut short by the Soviet invasion in 1968, and the practical alliances of Christian and non-Christian Marxists have been obstructed by violent political events, for example in Chile in 1972--we can speculate here only about "what might have been." This, of course, is unsatisfactory to the doubter. I think a better current example of the revolutionary operation of the Church in a Marxist context is to be found in Poland.

REVOLUTIONARY THEORETICIAN: I'm sure the communist authorities in Poland would see the Church more as an adversary than as any ally in the attainment of revolutionary objectives.

CHRISTIAN REVOLUTIONARY: They would be wrong. The Polish Church is now resigned to the basic socialistic objectives of their government: the cooperation of the Church towards the attainment of these objectives is qualified, however, by certain conditions -- that the socialist solution be pursued spontaneously, that human rights be studiously protected, and that social democracy be introduced into the industrial and agricultural sectors of society.

REVOLUTIONARY THEORETICIAN: A little while ago you were portraying the revolutionary message of

Christianity as a kind of egalitarianism, but now it sounds like Christianity is making a clarion call for individual rights.

CHRISTIAN REVOLUTIONARY: Equality and personal freedom need not be in mutual contradiction. They are both equally important and equally revolutionary values, expounded unambiguously in the New Testament. The special significance of the experience of the Polish Church is that it offers the example of a long-sustained and serious effort to make sure that the "revolutionary" objectives of a single government will be pursued with minimum loss of individual freedom.

REVOLUTIONARY THEORETICIAN: I think it is a mistake to talk about the "Polish Government" as if it were an independent, sovereign state like any European state. It is controlled by the Soviet regime. And so the Church in its "revolutionary" role there is not really interacting with the real government at all, but Soviet pawns.

CHRISTIAN REVOLUTIONARY: No. The function of the Church there is precisely to insure an authentic non-Soviet Marxist revolution, i.e. to keep their government officials from being pawns. And I think the officials themselves, in their finer moments, have an intimation that the degree of independence they enjoy in the pursuit of revolutionary objectives is due, in large measure, to the Church. And if the Church in Poland is allowed to pursue its objectives and continue its contributions, you will see established there the ultimate social paradox: the true Marxist ideal of mutual solidarity and emancipation of workers, attained not through Leninist power- politics but through grass-roots Christian action.

REVOLUTIONARY THEORETICIAN: A little while ago you were speaking about the "Kingdom of God" as an interior state that begins in the soul now and can be conceived as perduring into some future life. But now you are speaking of it as a quite external and visible millenarian organization which may be able to find sympathetic reverberations in, and even contribute to, Marxist utopianism. It seems to me that you exemplify the constant vacillation among Christians as to how the "Kingdom of God" is to be interpreted. Christians are at a crossroads where their whole future depends on just how those references to the "Kingdom of God," which are so hard even now for Scripture scholars to interpret, are to be taken.

CHRISTIAN REVOLUTIONARY: I agree. But we can't wait for the Scripture scholars to make up their minds. I submit that the two senses--the "inner" and "outer" kingdom--are not mutually contradictory or incompatible. We should try to establish <u>both</u> of them.

REVOLUTIONARY THEORETICIAN: Obviously you don't believe in the separation of Church and state.

CHRISTIAN REVOLUTIONARY: I don't believe that the separation of Church from state means that the Church must be a-political. For the Church to separate itself from politics would be for it to separate itself from life. This would be a peculiar version of stoicism. It would not be Christianity.

REVOLUTIONARY THEORETICIAN: You are ignoring the experience of centuries. The Church that interferes in politics leaves itself prey to state interference in religion.

CHRISTIAN REVOLUTIONARY: I don't have "interference" in mind, but participation--participation of the Church in politics, and of the state in religion.

REVOLUTIONARY THEORETICIAN: "Participation without interference." That's been the goal of Western Christendom for so many centuries. What hope is there of your attaining that goal when so many of your forefathers have failed?

CHRISTIAN REVOLUTIONARY: With God's help, and perhaps a little moral support from the a-political Christians, we will.

CHAPTER V

AN ECCLESIASTICAL COMEDY

After reading Castaneda's The Teachings of Don Juan and hearing accounts from a friend concerning the extraordinary and apparently beneficial effects of his experiment with LSD, I was attracted to the idea of experimenting with drugs--not, I think, for the purpose of achieving some psychic escape or release of neurotic tension, but rather on the belief that somehow I might be able to unlock and temporarily intensify basic creative forces in my own imagination, by using admittedly artificial stimuli for awakening the unconscious levels of the mind. However, I was also acutely afraid of having a drug-induced "bad trip." And so, rather than purchasing some LSD on the streets and "tripping" at a summer cabin (which was the wont of my friend), I approached another friend, a psychiatrist,, whom I shall call "Walter," who had engaged in some clinical research on the effects of LSD on terminally ill patients, and I asked if we might arrange a very controlled experiment, with carefully calculated dosages and complete with antidotes (in case anything went wrong.) All these precautions would, of course, be anathema to the true "acid head," but my intentions were more cerebral than simply "freaking out." I told Walter I would like to start out with minimal dosages and work up gradually to the point where my imagination would be freed, without ever losing control of my reason or becoming subject to whatever hallucinations resulted. Walter was amenable to the suggestion and agreed to serve as guardian for such an experiment when we both took our annual vacation in June. We planned to take a three week camping trip, but we would remain in the city for a few extra days before leaving, to conduct our "experiment." No problem, he assured me. In fact, he would be quite interested in the results, although he would not be able to publish them in any medical journal, or even mention them to colleagues, for fear of reprimand or censure.

We went about our experiment in our conservative
fashion on three consecutive evenings. On the first
couple of tries, the dosage was obviously below
whatever threshold was required, if one were to go
beyond a state of titillation or euphoria to
unequivocal fantasizing. It was not an unejoyable
experience, however. My companion indulged himself in
dry martinis while I occasionally imagined that I was
imagining things, and we both spent our time listening
to several symphonies by Mahler and, on television,
some talk shows and the late movie. On the third
night, much the same pattern ensued. A little more
euphoria and a little difficulty concentrating on the
late movie, but that is all. We obviously were being
too conservative. I went to sleep on the floor, bored
with the whole experiment and ready to get on with the
camping trip at last.

I woke about 9:30 a.m. and decided to go out for
breakfast and then head out for my place to begin
packing. I crept out the door without waking Walter,
and began looking for my car in the parking lot next to
the high-rise city condominium where Walter lived. The
lot was by this time a jumbled jungle of automobiles
because of the Wednesday morning influx of suburbanite
white-collar workers to the city. I had difficulty in
locating my car. I wandered about the lot rather
aimlessly, and began to get irritated at the fact that
I couldn't even remember which of the two entrances I
had used or which side I had parked on. I thought to
myself with a shudder that perhaps deterioration of
memory was one of the side effects of using psychedelic
drugs, even small dosages. I was about to curse my
recent intussusception of suspect artificial
substances, when I was approached by a gentleman who
was dressed in medieval garb and seemed to look like
Dante. Not knowing of any theater companies nearby
whose actors might be in period costume, and feeling a
vague sense of unreality, I concluded uneasily that in
spite of the uncongenial environment, here, belatedly,
and as a delayed reaction, must be the experience that
I had been trying to conjure up these last few days.
My first impulse was to yell for Walter, but I got
control of my feelings when I realized that there was
nothing intrinsically fearful about meeting a strange
figure in strange garb somewhere in a parking lot which
I knew was real.

"Excuse me," I said, "but you look like pictures I've seen of the poet Dante Allighieri."

"That is my name," he replied. "You are looking at me as if I were some figment of your imagination."

"Perhaps so, but I'm not used to seeing my mind's images in the flesh, so to speak."

"You speak as if the productions of the imagination were somehow inferior in degree to the rather prosaic externalities you see around you." He gestured towards the cars, the parking lot and surrounding buildings. "If you're consistent, I suppose the figures of 'Luther' and 'Christianus Radicalis' which you created with your imagination are some sort of second or third-rate realities."

"You know about that, then?"

Yes, and I have something of an interest in the ecclesiastical subject-matter, as you may know."

I was beginning to feel more relaxed about this encounter. I have even found a category for it. It reminded me of dreams I have had in the past--dream researchers call them "vivid dreams"--in which I suddenly realized that I was dreaming and began to manipulate or distort my dream-images at will, with subliminal consciousness of what I was doing. Only, in the present experience, consciousness seemed much more acute. I heard street noises, saw people walking about, etc. I gathered my wits and decided to play along with "reality" as it presented itself to me now, to see where it would lead. I started with something simple:

"My friend, Dante--since you spent so much time writing the Inferno, Purgatorio and Paradiso, you may be disappointed in knowing that these notions of the afterlife are no longer viable notions in our day. Even theologians do not find them of great interest."

"Viable?" he asked. "I suppose you mean 'useful.' After all, you're living in a more practical age. . .No, I'm not disappointed. In fact, I don't think even I would be as successful speculating about the themes of my Divina Comedia in your day and age. The world seems to be getting very complicated, with space-time, relativity, evolution, quantum theory, the indeterminacy principle and all the rest. Heaven, hell and purgatory were much easier to visualize in the old days."

I was delighted with his answer, which I took to
be just a sort of projection and clarification of my
own thought. If this was a semi-hallucinatory
experience, it was nice, even intriguing, to be able to
carry on what seemed to be a lucid thought process
through its means (and not merely in spite of it). But
in addition to being this consciousness which enabled
me to de-mystify what I witnessed, the "person" I saw
and heard also seemed to have a certain independence of
his own, and I decided to capitalize on this. If I
could "make" a personage, why not make him independent?

"Knowing what you now know from the standpoint of
our present," I asked, "does all your effort still seem
worthwhile? Or do you see it as inconsequential
speculation seriously infected with a defective and
unscientific view of the cosmos?"

"Is it so bad to be unscientific? There was a
different notion of unorthodoxy prevalent at the time I
wrote the Divina Comedia. . .But even from your
orthodox utilitarian point of view, it was not a waste
of time. In peopling heaven, hell and purgatory with
figures out of my own culture I gave to these rogues
and heroes a universal significance and valuation which
they would not have had otherwise; and, by the way, I
also helped defuse some of the alienation with which
ideas about the 'afterlife' affected people then. The
afterlife is not such a regressive notion when people
from your world and your era are immersed in it and
evaluated according to its gradations and degrees."

"Please don't misunderstand me. I would never
allege or even think that your efforts were a 'waste of
time,' any more than my own more pedestrian enterprise,
which as you know, has been concerned more with the
'Church Militant' here and now, than with the future
'Church Triumphant' or any of the more extramundane
categories of ecclesiastical existence or
non-existence."

"If you are going to see any deeper into the
present situation of the Church in the world, you need
a guide. Let me take you on some visits."

By this time, any sense of apprehension I may have
had in the beginning had disappeared, and the "figment
of my imagination" was beginning to show just enough
independence from my own control and will to challenge
and intrigue me. I offered no resistance to the trip

he proposed. And it began, as one might expect with Dante as a guide, with some of the lower levels of religious and ecclesiastical existence.

A. Via Purgativa

1. The ex-priest

I looked around curiously as we made our way through some parts of the city unfamiliar to me. As I noticed that we passed through material objects easily, I suffered a temporary loss of nerve and was almost prepared to try to wake myself up; but curiosity and the spirit of adventure reasserted their attractions and I renewed the focus of my concentration on what was going on.

We found ourselves in the living room of a flat, apparently part of an older house of the kind that are found in the center of our city. The room was cluttered with toys, books and magazines, letters opened and unopened, screws, bolts, hats, a sweater, and a can of furniture polish. Two little boys, both toddlers, were fighting for possession of a toy truck, and the younger one was howling as the older caught him in a vise-like grip and took an unfaltering and decisive bite into his brother's shoulder. A fortyish man sitting on a sofa nearby looked up from his evening paper at the children. (Since he took no notice of our presence, I concluded that whatever the status of this gentleman's own reality, we were invisible to him.) He reprimanded the older boy for biting again. His wife came charging out of the kitchen. "Goddammit, can't you play with those kids or something? Do you have to keep your nose buried in the newspaper like some kind of stupid ostrich?"

"O.K., O.K.," our man on the couch replied. "Look. I just want to take a look through the headlines and read Doonesbury and Spiderman. It's been a rough day. Give me a few minutes to relax."

"Just watch the kids, will you? How can I keep an eye on them when I'm in the kitchen?" She started to head back towards the kitchen.

Our man ruminated for a moment and then called out after her. "They're obviously hungry, and I am, too. Do you want me to go to McDonald's again and pick up some hamburgers?"

"I'm cooking something, you idiot!"

"Do you always have to wait until everyone is having pangs of starvation before you begin to think about cooking?

"Fuck you, you asshole. If you don't like it, do the cooking yourself. You leave me taking care of the kids every day and you come home expecting everything to be done for you."

"How am I supposed to take care of the kids and work full time, will you tell me that? You go to work and bring in enough money to support this family and I'll take care of them and the house and have a hell of a lot of time left over. That's a standing offer."

"Big hot-shot stud male. Super-organizer. Proud of yourself, aren't you. I'm sick of you." As she returned into the kitchen, her husband laid his newspaper down and stared out into the distance with an exasperated expression.

My friend Dante made a Florentine gesture which was apparently calculated to indicate that he was summing up the situation. "This man's name is Charles. He left the Catholic priesthood some years ago to get married. Like many priests, he had been doing some reading in psychology and sociology and avant-garde theology, and come to the conclusion that communication and interaction with the opposite sex was necessary for a total human existence. At first he resolutely decided that he must simply sacrifice the opportunity for such 'total human existence' to attain a correspondingly higher degree of pure spiritual perfection. In accord with his habitual altruism, he busied himself in his pastoral work, doing all he could to introduce others to the "right" member of the opposite sex. He took graduate courses in counseling and testing, and began to use some of the more reliable personality and compatibility tests on his counselees. He was quite successful, and became known colloquially as the 'matchmaker.' But then his idealism came to the fore. He passed from the rather abstract ideal of the perfect marriage to imagining himself in that state and, of course, idealizing his perfect mate." Dante shook his head in disbelief and seemed almost unable to go on. "Tell me, how is it possible for a man to be so cool and calculating about love? to fall so wide of the mark, missing all the spontaneity and natural beauty of love?"

"Dante," I said reassuringly, "love still
flourishes in our day in all its spontaneity. But in
certain types of people personality or background
sometimes inculcates a species of impractical idealism,
and the attitude of men like Charles is the occasional
result."

"The poor man!" Dante seemed genuinely affected
with sympathy, as only one who had known romantic love
in its splendor could be affected. "At any rate, you
can probably guess the rest of the story," he
continued. "Charles left the priesthood and married.
He suffered some opprobrium from ecclesiastical circles
and conservative layfolk, as you might imagine. But he
was not a pathfinder. There were others before him.
So there were no emblazoned headlines in newspapers
about his resignation from the priesthood or his
marriage. There was really no persecution involved,
since he was neither a famous cleric making a major and
spectacular transition nor a sufficiently sinful cleric
flouting conventional morals (people by this time were
beginning to yawn, when they heard news of 'another'
priest getting married).

We watched Charles and his family at their
evening meal. There was almost total silence except
for the jabbering of the children, the efforts of
Charles' wife to get the older boy to eat, and Charles
himself chiding the younger boy for throwing his stray
particles of food. I turned to my mentor and
philosophized: "Married life, like every other form of
life, has its agonies as well as its ecstasies. I'm
sure we must be 'tuning in' on Charles in one of his
troughs or slump periods so to speak."

"That's true, this is one of the more
negative moments," answered Dante. "But there are many
of them, so the scene you saw is not an atypical slice
of his life. . .I should perhaps let you in on
something further: there is hardly any physical
expression of sexual love between these two people at
this point. Feelings of animosity and resentment have
grown to such a degree that it has become repugnant, or
at least a humiliating sign of weakness, for one to
make sexual overtures to the other: it is ironical that
Charles at this time is living almost as celibate a
life as he was living just before he was secularized.

I found this easy to believe, although they both seemed reasonably attractive and neither one of them appeared to be deteriorating physically, since the psychological wall between them was so real as to be almost tangible. I mentioned to Dante that, even if the living tableau in this case seemed to have such negative features, I felt sure that it was not typical of ex-priests who marry.

"No, not particularly typical of them," he agreed. "But typical of a melancholy brood of cerebral Christians who never learn to synthesize their own natural feelings with their ideals or aspirations, who are always doomed to project an artificial appearance because they have brought about a divorce of feeling from religious or philosophical ideals in making major decisions in life. "

I was saddened at these reflections. "This seems to be one of the lower levels of ecclesiastical existence. Are we to encounter higher levels as we proceed from here?"

Dante responded with a cryptic paradox. "Do you mean 'higher levels' in terms of human happiness and fulfillment? or spiritually? In the Church Militant, the highest is often the lowest, and vice versa. Some men have a longer way to their goal, but this may be due as much to the fact that their goal is higher as to the circumstance that their starting point is lower or further away."

I took this as being just another way of saying that spiritual perfection is not independent of the physical and emotional--a thesis that I had no particular difficulty in accepting. But I couldn't help giving vent to some final puzzlement. I cleared my throat and felt a little strain in introducing this topic. "Coming from an era and culture with much stricter marriage customs, you may feel differently about divorce--but I have to say in all honesty, if the inner feelings of Charles are anything like the look of utter degradation that I saw in his face, I can't understand why he doesn't get a divorce, or at least a separation."

"Here again there is another ironical development," said Dante, who did not seem to be offended at my suggestion. "Charles as a priest came to value the title,'Father,' more than any other

title.   His commitment to paternity in a deep personal
sense was one of the overriding characteristics of his
period   as   a   priest,   and   still   predominates in his
'personality profile,' as you might call it.   If he
were to get a divorce or a separation, he would want to
retain   custody   of   the   children.   And   you know how
difficult that is for male parents in your society.
And besides, he would not want to deprive the children
of companionship with their mother." As we   left
Charles' place, I saw the father enthusiastically
playing with his two sons amidst the clutter of toys on
the floor--and this new perspective made me realize
that my question about divorce had been the premature
reaction of a bachelor who is not cognizant of some of
the more subtle satisfactions of even a relatively
unhappy marriage.

2. The missionary

"Lest you get the impression that it is only
ex-priests   who   find   themselves   in   purgatorial
circumstances," said Dante, "take a look at another
quite different case."
"We moved away from the city and its traffic and
through some suburban areas until we arrived at a
wooded and nicely landscaped piece of property. There
was a sign in front which announced, "Seraphic Fathers
Missionaries, Provincial Novitiate." We made our way
into the grounds, passing an older building which
looked like it might have been the original novitiate,
and arrived at a complex of modern stucco buildings
grouped amid parking lots, tennis courts and basketball
courts and a conspicuous chapel. Dante stopped at the
entrance to one building, which looked more or less
like all the rest, and indicated with a nod of the head
that I should follow him up its steps. We entered into
a smallish office in which three large desks, with
matronly women sitting at two of them, were neatly
arranged to get the maximum amount of illumination
from the fluorescent lights in the ceiling overhead.
One of the women was stuffing materials into envelopes,
while the other was cutting out address labels and
pasting them on the envelopes.   A third was in the

corner of the office, operating a mimeograph machine.
On a long table, various blurbs, leaflets and
mimeographed materials were stacked side by side. One
leaflet featured a photo of what appeared to be a
happy, retired couple and was captioned, "Why not think
of Seraphic Fathers when you make your last will and
testament." Another bore the caption, "What your
dollars are doing in Transoceania" over pictures of
teenage native boys sitting attentively in a classroom
in which a white-robed missionary was pointing to some
algebraic formulas on a blackboard. On the side of the
long table I noticed boxes of plastic statues of Jesus,
Mary and Joseph; combination
Miraculous-Medals-and-key-chains, and Mass cards next
to an announcement beginning, "Remember your departed
relatives and friends in our annual Novena of masses."

In a smaller office to the rear of this room,
there was sitting a lean, balding, bespectacled,
bearded white-robed missionary doodling meditatively as
he was speaking to a portly companion in clerical suit
and Roman collar, who was holding the last remnants of
a burning cigarette and seemed unwilling to extinguish
it until it burnt exactly to his fingers.

The portly cleric raised the palm of his hand as
if to halt the missionary's line of thought, and said
in a confident tone, "Jack, bingo's a healthy, harmless
game. It's one of the best fund-raisers that the Order
of St. Stephen has got. Two or three games spaced
between card parties, teas and art exhibitions bring in
more for us than ten or fifteen guest sermons given by
our missionaries on the parish church circuit. I'd
suggest your order try it too."

The other uncrossed his legs under his robe and
pursed his lips seriously. "I don't know. Sometimes I
wonder if this is why we become missionaries. The
other day our Provincial suggested that I should go to
more cocktail parties and golfing dates--"spread myself
around more," as he puts it--so I can be
Jack-on-the-spot to explain our needs to wealthy ladies
and gentlemen, and, of course, also point out some of
the tax and inheritance shelters and deductions and
loopholes applicable to those who are interested in
including us in their wills. This stuff seems so far
removed from what I used to visualize myself doing as a
missionary, when I was a seminarian."

"Jack, let's face it. We're conduits of money from the rich to the poor. 'God's conduit--Fr. Anthony Pastore': that's my self-image." He jumped a little as his cigarette began to burn into his fingers, and quickly extinguished it. "I'm here to help 'relieve' those who are burdened down with this world's goods and cares, of some of their burdens. It's not the most glamorous religious function to perform, but it's a necessary one. Without you and me, a lot of people on the other side of the globe. . ."

Dante interrupted and gestured towards the lean man. "He was a zealous missionary in Transoceania after he was ordained. But within a very few years he ran down his health from overwork and suffered a nervous collapse. His order transferred him back to the states and put him in a sanatorium. He recovered very slowly. When his health improved sufficiently, they gave him a job teaching at the seminary. When he expressed his dislike for this job, they made him a kind of apprentice to the Order's chief fund-raiser. The fund-raiser passed away a few weeks ago, and now this man is the heir-apparent to the job. As you can see, he is subject to some doubts and self-searching about his present functions."

I observed an ornate poster above the missionary's desk, reading, "Make ye friends of the Mammon of iniquity, so that they will receive ye into heavenly habitations." An analogy occurred to me: "This man seems to be a sort of ecclesiastical Robin Hood, taking from the rich to give to the poor. Only without violence, of course."

Dante corrected me. "Your analogy is only partially true. The missions for which they are collecting funds are not primarily concerned with benefitting the poor in Transoceania. The schools and hospitals which they have established are patronized primarily by those who are better off in that country (although many are still relatively poor by your American standards). This is not an accident, but the result of a policy decision that was made several decades ago by the missionary bishops. They reasoned, partly on the basis of past experience, that to attend primarily to the lowest classes would put the order in disrepute-by-association. On the other hand, if the upper classes accepted Christianity, and it became the

'in' thing, the lower classes would follow suit, since
trends are set by the upper classes. And thus, as a
consequence, their schools have been concerned mostly
with educating the scions of the 'better' native
families, although they are also committed to accepting
quite a few 'charity' cases every year."

"That sounds like a pragmatic decision to me," I
observed. "I guess, if success and results are
important, churchmen can't afford to be any more
idealistic than politicians. Was it any better in your
day?"

Dante looked pensive for a moment, as if
re-examining old memories. "Not at all. It was
worse."

As we prepared to leave, the portly cleric arose
with a final comment. "Jack, neither your order nor
mine is equipped to make cheese for a living like the
Trappists. There are only certain things that are
'marketable' in our lives, and we must concentrate on
these. Besides, I've tried that Trappist cheese, and I
don't recommend it at all."

They both laughed.

3. The theologian

Dante next whisked me to a motley group of large
old and new buildings situated by the side of streams
of city traffic and wafted occasionally with the breeze
of industrial pollution. A bell rang as we arrived,
and I saw flocks of students exit from the various
buildings. I realized we must be at a large city
university. We made our way to an older building at
the edge of what might be called the "campus," and as
we entered I noticed that "Administration" in fancy
lettering was embossed over the doorway.

Fr. Adams walked into the Dean's office and began
looking for the coat rack. Mrs. Sanders, the Dean's
matronly secretary, pointed to the corner. "It's over
there next to the filing cabinet," she said. "You're a
little early. It'll probably be five or ten minutes
before Fr. Weber gets here." Fr. Adams assured the
secretary that he was in no hurry and made a few

observations about the terrible weather, which drew
instant agreement from the secretary. He sat in one of
the two chairs just outside the Dean's office and began
thumbing through The College Adminstrator's Quarterly,
which proved to be full of advertisements and
thoroughly boring. Besides, his thoughts were
elsewhere. He was more than mildly curious as to why
the Dean should have summoned him to the office. In a
large Jesuit institution such as Suarez University,
individual professors did not usually meet directly
with the Dean unless they happened to be department
chairmen or heads of committees. Fr. Adams fantasized
that perhaps the Dean was going to offer him some
administrative post, but quickly dismissed that thought
as being thoroughly unrealistic, since he had only been
at Suarez for three years and had been prevented by his
chairman from performing any duties that would display
administrative talent, anyway. (The Chairman had
apparently categorized him as the "scholarly" type who
would be sure to fumble any sort of practical duties
meted out to him.) Having dismissed the
administration-possibility, another possibility entered
Adams' mind with some suddenness and unnerved him: he
had recently given a talk on "The Gay Christian" to a
group of homosexual men and women. Was he to be
"called on the carpet" for this? Did the Dean suspect
that he was a homosexual? But why would the Dean call
him in for something like that, especially since he had
never encouraged overt homosexual activities? No,
these days even middle-aged Jesuits were becoming more
tolerant, less dogmatic. It was the climate of the
times. The hierarchical Church was still there, but
was being gradually democratized in spite of itself.
At least, one could be a "liberal" now without fearing
excommunication.

The Dean entered the outer office, greeted Adams
and promised he would be with him shortly. He entered
his own office, brought some notes and papers to his
secretary, and, after giving some instructions to her,
beckoned Adams to come in. This was their first
face-to-face meeting. The Dean shook hands with Adams,
and invited him to sit down. "I'll come right to the
point," he said. The smile had suddenly vanished
from his face and he was the picture of resolution and
firmness. Adams felt his own internal barometer fall

in a proportionately swift manner, and he steeled himself for the worst. The Dean pointed to two or three letters on his desk. "Some of your colleagues have brought it to my attention that you've been propounding some rather strange theories lately. . ." He picked up the letters and began flipping pages: "For example, that God, in the book of Genesis, commanding Adam and Eve not to eat the 'forbidden fruit,' was really hoping they would sin, so that they would become 'free.'" "Yes, I think I can explain that," said Fr. Adams.

The Dean continued perusing the letters. "Now here's something that I find just a little incredible: Christ's references to 'Hell' in the Gospels are just a sort of 'white lie,' calculated to keep people in line, since 'the only language some people understand is the language of force and punishment.'" The Dean looked up with a quizzical look. The theologian began to speak, but the Dean turned to another letter. ". . . And here I have a newspaper clipping about your address to the. . . 'Self-Realization Fellowship'"--the Dean shook his head--"to the effect that all religions are equal since they are all based on a certain common denominator of mystical experience which can be interpreted in different ways."

"I didn't say they were equal but that they all had a common source," Assistant Professor Adams objected. "And those other points you mentioned have to be taken in context. God's 'white lie' is only a 'lie' from our point of view, since God. . ."

"I'm sure there are some very intricate and even plausibly consistent explanations for these positions," interrupted the Dean. "Now, I've been very busy these last few years and haven't been able to keep up with all the latest developments in theology, so I'm not going to debate these issues with you today. However, I think it is my duty to inform you that you can hardly expect this university with its traditions, and--if I may say so--its international repuation in theology, to offer itself as a kind of sounding-board for maverick opinions like this."

"Maverick? Professor Ludwig at Tübingen agrees with me on that 'hell' thing, and I could support my interpretation of the Genesis passage by citing a whole slew of. . ."

"As I said, I have not been following all the currents of avant-garde theology lately. My job is to maintain the integrity and standards of this university. Now, I've always believed in democracy, and if you can argue these ideas with the respectable theologians in your own department and win their support, I'll listen to them and you. But short of that. . . Yes, you have complete academic freedom here, and no one is going to tell you what you can or cannot teach. However, there are some very practical considerations that you should be aware of at this stage of your career: if you keep this up, your colleagues are certainly not going to recommend you for tenure a few years hence. And even if you became tenured and the university judged that your opinions continually bordered on 'heresy,' we would risk general secular opprobrium and censure from the American Association of University Professors in dismissing you. We have our scale of values, after all, and theological integrity is just about at the top. So--once more--you can't expect us to provide you a forum for opinions we find unconscionable." The Dean mitigated the sternness of his look and spoke in a more fatherly fashion: "Be sensible, Father Adams. If you separate yourself from us, you are just a John Doe theologian. If you want to remain here, there are certain responsibilities and reciprocities entailed. It's as simple as that."

The theologian seemed still unpacified. "I'm not sure if you and I mean the same thing by 'academic freedom.' I have insights, and I have a deep and overriding responsibility to follow them up--wherever they may lead me. My research has led me to certain tentative conclusions, which some of my colleagues apparently find objectionable. But I can't help--"

The Dean interrupted. "Fine. We don't want to discourage or quash your research. But--can I offer a suggestion?--stop looking for the outlandish and the sensational. Work on some of the more humdrum problems and establish your reputation before you begin getting into all these. . . exotic issues--and then maybe you'll find that you don't have to flout tradition to be 'original.'"

I had almost forgotten I was with Dante. He resumed his role as guide and observed, "This

theologian is an interesting psychological case. He
was bright as a youngster, but was never accepted very
thoroughly by his peers in or out of school. He still
is a loner, even though he tries to think of himself as
a member of the 'academic community' and a 'colleague.'
He's quite convinced about his insights and even has
passing suspicions that he is charismatic. And he may
be. Who knows? But he lacks humility--a feeling of
common humanity with others. And he is discovering in
a very practical and concrete way that 'charismatic
personages' are made, at least in part, by their
generation."
  "Are you saying he should compromise?" I asked.
"Isn't it important for anyone--charismatic or not--to
remain faithful to his insights?"
  "Yes," answered Dante, "but insights are in a
certain sense wasted unless one finds a way to express
these insights in conventional ways, and to an
impartial audience. However, very few people can
cultivate an audience by despising them and the
'ordinary' insights that they have."
  Dante seemed to have an absolute conviction about
this matter, and I told him that there was a
"conservative" strain in his character that I had not
noticed before.

  The Dean replaced the letters concerning Fr. Adams
in a manila folder and began clearing his desk
mechanically. Fr. Adams heard the secretary speaking
to someone in the outer office. Probably another
appointment. "Dean Weber, why don't you appoint a
committee to hear my explanations. I'm sure that if I
have a chance to clarify. . ."
  The Dean rose to accompany the theologian to the
door. He seemed in a friendlier mood. "I don't know
whether that would do any good. It might hurt you.
Why make a big thing out of this? Look, Father, no one
is going to call for your dismissal right now, and if
they did, I wouldn't listen to them. But your
department chairman felt that somehow you weren't
getting the 'signals' that you should be getting, and
asked me to advise you about your situation. Look upon
this as a kind of 'early warning system' that will
probably prevent problems from emerging later on. I
understand that everyone in your department likes you,

basically.   Listen   to   them a little more.   Isn't community, and community spirit, a Christian concept, too?
     "Yes, and a very important concept. I think I see   what   you mean,"   said Father Adams as he entered the outer office and tried to remember where the coat rack was.

B. Via Illuminativa

4. The journalist

Our next stop was at a large modern office
building which seemed to be situated in the middle of
nowhere, presumably in some low-tax area. (I had by
now completely lost track of what town or city or state
we were in, but for some reason or other this was no
matter of great concern to me, and I felt a certain
unshakeable confidence in my guide, although, if I had
reflected on the matter, I'm sure I could have come up
with no rational grounds for such confidence.) The
building had a sign in front which announced the
presence of the offices and plant of <u>The National
Catholic Herald</u>.

We followed a tall, well-built, middle-aged and
graying cleric into the large, well-lighted editorial
offices. He stopped at one of the desks to ask for
directions, then headed in the direction of one of the
rear offices. Hardly any of the typists, copywriters
or junior editors looked up as the cleric passed the
rows after rows of desks and cabinets. He strode into
the outer office of George Hoyle, Editor-in-Chief, and
announced himself; but before the secretary had a
chance to ring the editor, Hoyle came out from behind
his door and offered his hand. "Hello, Bishop Bradley,
I'm glad you could stop by. To what do I owe the
pleasure of this visit? Come on in."

As they entered Hoyle's office, the Bishop
remarked that this visit might not be an occasion for
unadulterated pleasure. Hoyle laughed and offered one
of the cigars in his pocket to the Bishop. The Bishop
declined and seated himself. As Hoyle eased his soft
and flaccid bulk into his chair, the Bishop twirled his
ring pensively, and Hoyle seemed to be hypnotized by
its sparkle.

"I guess you know why I'm here," said the Bishop.
"I'd like to think it was to give me a news leak,"
joked Hoyle. "But I suppose that would be too much to
hope for. What can I do for you?"

The Bishop took a folder out of the small leather
satchel he had brought with him. "I've been collecting
newspaper headlines lately from your paper." He opened
the folder and rummaged through some of the clippings.

"Here's an interesting one from last week: 'Diary of a Female Priest, Part I.'"

"Yes, that's a series on an Episcopalian woman who was recently ordained. We intend to run it for the next five issues," said Hoyle. "You know, of course, that we don't take sides on this issue of the ordination of women. We present both the pros and the cons."

"Of course," murmured the Bishop. He brought out another large clipping. "Now I believe this article is supposed to be a sort of, um, survey of the sins most commonly brought up in confession?" The Bishop cleared his throat.

"Yes. Of course, I'm sure you realize that the anonymity of the penitents was carefully guarded in every respect in this survey."

"I realize that. I'm wondering if the identity of the confessors who supplied this information is just as carefully guarded. I personally would like to know who they were." The Bishop was beginning to show some irritation.

"I'm sure you would," laughed the Editor. "But obviously we couldn't present such information ethically unless we made certain that the anonymity of our sources was absolutely protected. I'm sure you realize that, Bishop Bradley."

"I'm not sure how 'ethical' this survey is," said the Bishop, "but I do realize the information would never have been offered if your sources thought they would be identified. They would have been ashamed to have been named."

"I think it was mainly a matter of professional ethics," responded the Editor. "A psychiatrist could say something in general about the condition and categories of his patients, as long as he did not identify them. To give away his own identity might give clues to the identity of his patients."

"I suppose there would also be some branch of journalistic ethics concerned with justifying those opinion polls you did of Catholics concerning birth control, and of priests concerning their attitudes towards their Bishops?"

"I'm really sorry if you've taken exception to some of our stories, Bishop Bradley. But we've got our job to do, as you have yours. . ."

"Your job? Journalistic duties? Hoyle, this is lurid stuff, fit for confession magazines (and I mean the other type of 'confession')."

"We don't go out looking for the lurid and sensational, Bishop. Our goal is to publish the truth. If you've read our paper in the last few weeks, you may have noticed that we reported in a quite objective fashion on the Bishop of Tours' condemnation of the cult of the Red Virgin there, we gave front-page coverage to the conclusions of the last conference of American Bishops (although I must say I personally did not find them too exciting), and we faithfully reported on all the major arguments in the Pope's recent Encyclical condemning premarital sex. But if there are currents of opinion that depart from the official position, or are critical of the Church, we have to report that, too."

"Do you really think all this breast-beating and self-criticism is doing any good?" asked the Bishop. "Everyone thought that when the Second Council of the Vatican inaugurated all its reforms and encouraged a 'critical spirit' a few years ago, the revitalization of the Church was going to be the end result. And look what's happened. The people are leaving in droves. Is it your objective to help perpetuate this exodus? Do you want to wipe religion off the face of the earth?"

Hoyle became very firm and serious. "You wouldn't want us to falsify the facts, would you, Bishop?"

"Facts? Of course not. But you don't have to dig up every hidden fact that might possibly threaten the faith of ordinary people."

"Bishop Bradley, I'm not afraid of the truth. I tend to think Jesus was right when he said, 'the truth shall set you free.'"

"Is your objective truth or subscriptions?"

"We've been losing subscriptions lately."

"See--you've created satiation; your readers are jaded with the morbid and sensational."

Hoyle leaned back in his chair and sighed, then spoke with deliberation: "We can't judge our performance by subscriptions any more than you can judge the viability of religion by the number of churchgoers."

The Bishop apparently did not see the logic of this argument. "Before dismissing success as a goal,

you should ask your co-workers where they plan to work
as they are laid off because of diminishing sales. . ."
Bishop Bradley paused reflectively and then began
speaking in a calm and lower tone of voice. "Look. I
certainly am not against the truth. You might say that
my objective in coming to you is 'aesthetic.' There
are just certain bounds of propriety that should be met
in discussing religious subjects. If I don't see some
semblance of a higher level of tastefulness in your
pages during the coming months, I'm going to have to
condemn you from the pulpit, and on the pages of our
Archdiocesan newspaper."

"Your Excellency, are you threatening me?"

"Not at all. I'm just giving you advance notice
of what my probable moves will be, and of course I
hope I will not have to proceed this way."

"You're going to condemn us for 'aesthetic'
errors?"

"Remember my analogy of the 'confession' magazine.
Much of the stuff there may be true, but it's trash;
it's not worth knowing."

"Bishop, do you really think you are the one best
qualified to make these 'aesthetic' judgments?"

Bishop Bradley did not want to pursue the
discussion of aesthetics any further. "Mr. Hoyle, I
have a duty to foster certain standards of religious
excellence in the diocese under my jurisdiction, where
you happen to do your work. I'm not asking you to get
an imprimatur before you print anything, but simply to
be a little more cognizant of the sensibilities of your
fellow Catholics here and elsewhere, in deciding what
is 'news.' I can remember your insisting or implying
many times on your pages that the Church should
compromise on this or that issue. I hope you are not
above making some decent compromises yourself." The
Bishop rose to leave.

Hoyle arose from his chair slowly and faced the
Bishop.

"When I have the next Friday-morning session with
my staff, I'll bring up the subject of 'aesthetics,' as
you call it. But I can't promise you that we'll make
any radical changes in our news reporting style."

"Yes, I understand that. 'Newsmen first'. . ."

". . .'and Christians second'? No, I don't see
any incompatibility between the two."

"I hope not," said the Bishop.

As the Bishop made his departure, Dante turned to me and asked, "Did you notice any major difference between the editor here and the personages you observed earlier?"

I reflected for a moment. "There did seem to be a difference, but it's hard to put one's finger on it. . . There was a certain commitment and enthusiasm about this fellow, but I don't know if it was really that distinctive. Also, he was definitely intensely interested in religion, but so was the theologian we encountered earlier."

"And so was the Bishop," Dante reminded me.

"Yes, in his own way. I guess the chief thing that struck me, that could be called a 'difference,' was the self-confidence and optimism of the editor. He seemed to think he knew where he was going, and where the Church was going. He also seemed to be on the offensive more than the others, at the vanguard of some important action that was taking place, or that he thought was taking place."

"Yes, I think you could say that," said Dante. "And I think you'll find that the next two personages we observe will exemplify those qualities even more.

5. The revolutionary

Our next stop was in the middle of a barren and forbidding range of mountains. The terrain was totally unfamiliar to me.

Padre Ernesto Gonzales was tired and winded as he made his way along the last valley ridge to the outpost, where he gave the usual signal and password, and was given the go-ahead to enter the cave where the revolutionaries had their headquarters. As he made his way to the main caverns, there was not much in the way of spoken greetings, but handshakes, kisses, and hugs all around. He received an especially mighty hug from the leader, Juan Carlos. Juan Carlos sent for some cheese, bread, and wine, and many of the men and women present ceased from their duties for the moment and sat or stood around to chat with the priest. "What's happening down there?" they asked--offering him the opportunity to provide a full-scale news report.

The food was brought to Gonzales, and he took a sip of the wine after making a half-gesture toasting his audience. He wasn't the talkative sort, but knew the essentials of information they were after. "Manuel has finally collected the provisions and will be bringing them up tomorrow," he announced. "Dolores wasn't able to receive the arms shipment from Mexico because her middleman is under suspicion. She is going through alternates, but it will take a little longer than we expected to get the cargo here." Murmurs of disappointment greeted this report, and Gonzales made a gesture of helplessness. He then brought a rosary out of his pocket and pried open the large crucifix with a knife, taking out a slip of paper and handing it to Juan Carlos. ". . .and this is for you from agent 'R' in the 'downtown' area." Juan Carlos read the missive and slipped it into his shirt pocket. "Good news this time!" he announced. "We're winning many from the army and police over to our side." There was general pleasure at this announcement, and Juan Carlos' lieutenants began to talk in low voices among themselves. Padre Gonzales, in the meantime, alternated between eating and offering tidbits of information about relatives, friends, places and events to those around the table.

Finally there was a lull and someone asked, "How about you, Ernesto? When are you going to join us? Everytime you go back, we wonder if you'll return. Do your parishioners really think you are going mountain-climbing?"

Gonzales gestured as if to wave aside the implications of that question. "My parishioners are sympathetic to our cause," he assured them. "We have no landowners or industrialists or government officials in my parish. Even if they knew where I was going, they would say nothing to the authorities."

"But they like to gossip," someone suggested.

"Not about matters like this," the Padre insisted. Juan Carlos caught the prevailing mood. "Listen to us, Ernesto. Even Jesus had his Judas. Stick it out with us here. The government of the big-time generals will topple pretty soon. They can only absorb so much mutiny in the army and navy. They're getting desperate now and looking for sacrificial victims. You're going to be caught with your pants down. Look, we can get others less conspicuous than you to serve as our liasion. Stay here."

The priest laughed. "You don't seem to realize it, but I may just be the best possible errand boy you'll ever have. I've been doing this for six months now, and no one suspects. Someone else may not be as successful. And you've got to have this sort of input, if 'La Causa' is ever going to be anything more than a motto." Since no one argued with Gonzales, he took their silence as signifying tacit agreement. He continued, "And besides, I'm not afraid of death in any form, now. I have been witnessing the 'life' of my friends, the peasants, for all these years now. Could death be any worse?"

Some nihilist answered spontaneously, "Viva death!" A more sober voice chimed in with, "To hell with life under capitalist oppression!" And others shouted or grunted their concurrence.

But Gonzales still felt the need for clarifying his position. "One reason I'd rather not join you here is that I don't want to get involved in attacking and killing. I don't even carry a gun, you know. I never want to."

Juan Carlos sighed. "If only you hadn't been exposed to seminary training for all those years and built up these inhibitions. . . Ernesto, you spent years studying Marxism and planning with us, and now we scarcely see you. The time to strike is drawing near. If you expect us to win with rosaries, why are you supplying us with guns? If you expect us to use the guns, why should you have any qualms about using them yourself in the name of justice?" Juan Carlos softened his tone a bit. "We respect your decision, of course. We just have difficulty understanding. . ."

Gonzales deliberated briefly, then said, with downcast eyes, "Because you might be victorious."

"Of course we'll be victorious! What does that have to do with it?" Juan Carlos looked puzzled and a little irritated.

Padre Gonzales finally looked up. "You know what some of the other revolutionaries have done when they succeeded--mercilessly executing soldiers and

landowners and recalcitrant peasants and anyone who
appeared to be a 'suspect.' I'm afraid we might go
that route. Now that we're getting the smell of
victory just around the corner, I'm beginning to wonder
what this strange state called 'victory' might actually
be like."

"Ernesto, don't worry. We've suffered enough from
oppression. We're not going to continue the
oppression."

"Some of the others said that, too."

"But you know us, you can trust us. You know
that. And if you're afraid things might go awry, then
let us find someone else to be a liasion, and you join
us here in a leadership capacity. You can't very well
lead us from a rectory!"

There was general agreement about this. "He's
right," said someone. "Come on, Ernesto," urged
another comrade.

Gonzales fell silent and shook his head.

The girl sitting next to Juan Carlos spoke.
"Sure, you wanted to be a priest and it's hard to give
that up. But how can you go on kissing the ring of
that fat bourgeois bishop 'downtown' after all this?
You don't believe in that Church anymore. Join the
cause of justice--the religion of the future."

"The religion of the future is love," responded
Gonzales. "I feel the same repugnance you do for what
the bishop stands for, but I try to understand him, and
I must love him. Other revolutions have been spurred
on by one form or another of hate. Ours must be based
on love, even for our enemies."

This idea was greeted with a few spontaneous moans
and groans, but these were curtailed by the firm stares
of the majority. The priest was genuinely liked and no
one wanted to chastise him for "problems of
conscience." Finally, someone standing near the wall
made light of the situation and shouted out, "Viva the
impossible revolution, the revolution of love!" The
shout was shortened to "Viva love!" and the others
joined in.

When everyone had quieted down, Juan Carlos met
the eyes of Gonzales momentarily and said to him, "We
are for love--but only with equality. There must be
equality," he reiterated. "At any rate, think our
little suggestion over and let us know if you change
your mind."

"I will," said the priest.

Juan Carlos filled the cup of Padre Gonzales with wine and passed the jug around to everyone. The priest looked at his watch and said he had to leave shortly, in order to arrive back at his parish at dusk.

I turned to my guide with the question that was uppermost in my mind. "What do you think, Dante? Is the Christian message of love really compatible with violence and revolution?"

"That's a difficult question to answer," said Dante. "Another important question is: 'Can ordinary human beings really love those who oppress and subjugate them?' It seems that perhaps some sort of equalization is a prerequisite to genuine, normal and stable love."

"This seems to be a perennial dilemma."

"Yes, some very similar problems arose in my own lifetime, but they didn't refer to it then as 'the problem of revolution against oppression in a Christian culture.'"

I told Dante that I remembered reading something about the great political conflicts that took place in his time.

"The next person we are to visit thinks he has found a way out of your dilemma," said Dante, as we took our leave of the desolate mountains of South America.

6. The saint

"The next person you meet will not be unfamiliar to you," said Dante. My curiosity was aroused by this announcement. Like a tourist who has spent some time by himself in a foreign country, I was excited by the prospect of seeing a familiar face.

We passed through the heavily populated streets of a foreign city. From the color and features of the people I saw, I surmised this must be India. Beggars lined the street at almost evenly spaced distances in the late afternoon sun. Hawkers in open air markets

were trying to sell off a few more of their wares
before closing time. Slim and beautifully proportioned
women in saris were carrying goods on their heads with
exquisite grace, children were weaving in and out of
the crowds, bicycles were weaving in and out of
traffic.

Very soon all of this was behind us and we were
passing through the cool and dimly lit stone corridors
of a monastery. I could hear oriental-sounding songs
and chants coming from one end of the complex of
buildings. We proceeded further along several
corridors and the silence became progressively deepened
until we arrived at a cell, in which a man with western
features but Eastern monastic garb was seated in a
lotus posture, and apparently in a state of deep
concentration. His small cell was almost completely
bare except for the plain mattress on which he was
seated, and a table upon which some books were stacked
next to a basin and a pitcher of water.

The features of this monk arrested my attention,
and I suddenly realized I _knew_ this man. My mind went
back to the time when, as a teenager, I heard there was
a "saint" in the neighborhood, a Spanish priest who
could read minds and cure diseases and even, on
occasion, when his prayer or meditation became
particularly intense, levitate a few inches off the
ground. I had decided to see this man for myself, and
after an interesting but quite unspectacular first
meeting, began to visit him occasionally. I was sorely
disappointed in never seeing any of the "miraculous"
phenomena attributed to him, but felt strangely
attracted to him because he seemed to have an unusually
acute perception of my problems and aspirations, and
(as I see it from my present perspective) helped to
amplify my understanding of myself at a particular
stage in my development when I seemed to be an
impenetrable enigma to myself as well as to others. My
association with him was cut short, however, after a
year, when he returned from the United States to Spain.
There had been some occasional correspondence with him,
and an exchange of Christmas cards, after that. But I
gradually lost track of him... So here is where that
remnant of my past was now--in India!

Though Dante was my host, he suddenly looked like a guest who was at the door and just about to take his leave. He spoke briefly: "I have brought you to the outer limits of the Church I knew, the Church we have in common. This man will be your guide into the Church of the Future. Goodbye." He disappeared. I felt some regret at the suddenness of his departure, but this regret was allayed somewhat by my mixed curiosity, puzzlement and delight at suddenly being confronted with a friend out of my past.

"Hello, I've been waiting for you," he said.
"Fr. Aloysius, what are you doing in India? Have you left the Church? Have you left the Claretian Order?"

He laughed. "Not at all. Nothing like that." He excused himself and went out to fetch two chairs. After we were seated, he continued: "No, there's a little more to my story than a mere change of religion. After I returned from the States to Spain I took up the study of Hinduism and Yoga, and I began to realize how extraordinarily advanced the Indians were in asceticism and mysticism. They may be behind us in science and technology, but in techniques for actuating the consciousness they are far ahead of the West. In the few years that I have been practicing these 'foreign' techniques, I think I have advanced more in prayer and meditation than I had in a lifetime before--and with a certain degree of 'scientific' precision."

I told him that at the time I first met him, I had heard that he was very advanced in the "spiritual life." Was that a mistake?

"Yes, it was," he replied. "It was a case of 'mistaken identity.' I possessed some ESP powers and seemed to have the gift of healing, which is a form of psychokinesis. From the time I was very young, I was conscious of having these 'natural talents,' but, like most psychics, did not have them fully under my control, and employed them in a 'hit and miss' way. When I became a priest and a spiritual director, people who witnessed these 'paranormal' manifestations confused this with a high degree of spiritual perfection, and I'm afraid I was guilty at times of the same confusion. However, after I had embarked on the theoretical studies I just mentioned, I eventually

came into contact with an Indian swami who opened up
spiritual horizons that I had never been aware of.
Under his guidance, I began to make real progress. At
his suggestion I obtained permission to spend some time
at this monastery. Eventually I will return to Spain
again."

I thought back to certain books I had read on
mysticism. "It seems to me that religious experience
and mysticism are fundamentally the same in all
religious persuasions, although they may be interpreted
according to different dogmas or rubrics. But you seem
to think there is quite a difference at least between
Chrisian and Hindu religious experience."

"Yes, not just a difference in degree but even a
difference in kind. In the traditions of Western
mysticism, the peaks of spiritual experience are looked
upon as a kind of 'grace,' over which one can never
exert full control. In the Hindu yogic tradition there
are tried and true methods, by following which anyone
with a basic natural aptitude can arrive at perfection.
I still have a long ways to go to spiritual
'perfection,' but at least I see clearly now how far
I've come and in which direction I'm going."

I was interested in whether there was still that
old possibility of confusing psychic powers with
advanced spiritual perfection, and I asked him about
this.

"No, as one advances to the higher spiritual
states, the so-called 'psychic' powers appear more and
more trivial--one no longer attaches any great
importance to them. However, the proficient yogi, just
as he gains a mastery over his mind and body, also
gains control over the psychic powers which he, like
everyone else, possesses to some degree. In my own
case, I've noticed that my use of ESP or psychokinesis,
when it is called for, is no longer the haphazard and
unpredictable sort of operation it used to be."

I though of Padre Gonzales in South America and
wondered what he would say about all this. "Many would
say that what you call 'progress' in the spiritual life
is a form of escapism, that it withdraws man from
social concerns and the pursuit of justice. They would
point to the tremendous amount of suffering and misery
in India and in the world at large, and would insist
that it must be our primary concern to eliminate this."

Father Aloysius nodded his head emphatically. "I realize there is a problem here. But the problem is partly due to the failure of Western man to realize that spirit is something more than an excrescence on matter. It contains such a fantastic variety of positive riches that one is justified in pursuing spiritual goals in preference to, if not to the complete exclusion of, material goals. And besides, although the motives of those who pursue absolute social equality and justice are admirable, they are on an impossible 'mission.' The love-energy present in mankind now is hardly equal to the attainment of utopian dreams. What the world needs most of all is some pathfinders of the spirit, who will endure immense but hidden sufferings in intensifying their own consciousness and increasing their own love-energy and gradually raise the level of consciousness and love energy in mankind to the point where perfect justice and harmony is no longer utopian but. . . attainable."

"I don't understand," I said. "How can the intensification of consciousness and love-energy in a relatively few individuals cause a dramatic reactivation of consciousness throughout mankind?"

"We Westerners have deluded ourselves into thinking that each man is an island unto himself. The truth is that the more a man plumbs his own spiritual depths, the more he finds that he shares 'humanity' with others, not just as an abstraction in thought and discourse, but in reality. We are 'connected at the center', so to speak, with all other men. Any great riches which I amass at this deepest level, which is also our common center, become more easily accessible to all other interested and properly disposed men. It's like an opening which an individual makes in a dike or a dam for the purpose of irrigating his farm. In most cases in real life it would be impossible to direct this irrigation to only his own farm. When the deeper spiritual powers in man are unleashed, it is never possible to confine the benefits of this to one individual. To use another analogy--they tell us that at the present time a relatively few farmers feed the populations of the world, and that that number, because of technological advances and automation, is still decreasing. So also, a relatively few spiritual pathfinders could transform the consciousness of the world and make the dreams of the revolutionaries possible at last."

I found these references to a possible "transformation of consciousness" in mankind interesting, but rather vague. I asked Fr. Aloysius whether he thought the number and proficiency of individual "pathfinders" would ever be sufficient to bring about the wholesale transformations he envisaged; and, if so, how would the life of people differ from what it is now; and, in particular, what part the Church might play in bringing all this about.

"Come with me," he replied, "and we'll take a look."

C. Via Unitiva

7. The last Pope

The "journeys" which I now took differed somewhat from the journeys I had already taken. Under Dante's guidance, I seemed to be actually visiting various places and persons. But with Fr. Aloysius as guide the experience was more like watching television: one may be absorbed in what he is watching, but he is at least subliminally aware that he himself is situated elsewhere. My new guide simply concentrated, and asked me to do the same.

As I concentrated, I sensed that I was in the papal palace in Rome, and I saw a gaunt and graying man seated at a desk and reading the New Testament. A coat of arms on the wall above the table bore the inscription, "Petrus II."

Pope Peter seemed to be reading the same passage over and over again: "And when you see the Abomination of Desolation standing in the midst of the temple, you will know that the end has come." The Pope finally closed the Bible and buried his head in his arms. His body seemed to be rocking with sobs, but I heard no sounds. After some minutes he composed himself and picked up the telephone on his desk. "Is the Secretary of State in his office today?" he inquired. "Send him in, please."

The papal Secretary came in shortly, carrying a small bundle of documents. "I thought you might want to sign some of these while I'm here, Your Holiness."

"Monsignor Baldi, forget about those for now. I have something important to discuss with you. Sit down." The Monsignor sat in his usual chair at the side of the Pope's desk, and the Pope turned his chair to face his aide directly. He met the eye of the other and began to speak, but caught himself. There was a long silence in which the Pope seemed to be having difficulty formulating his words. Monsignor Baldi began to look confused and lowered his eyes in embarrassment. Finally the Pope announced, "Monsignor, I am the Abomination of Desolation!"

The Secretary of State crossed his legs and seemed to be thrown off balance momentarily. He caught the desk to keep himself from falling, started to smile, and then put on a very serious expression. "Your Holiness," he whispered, "don't say that so loud! Someone may hear you."

The Pope was adamant. "I don't care. Let them hear me. It's true. I must be the Abomination of Desolation. I lost my faith long ago, I can't formulate the vaguest conception of God anymore, my prayers are dry monologues and have never been answered. What am I doing here directing the spiritual lives of five hundred million people? What hypocrisy!"

By now Monsignor Baldi looked very disturbed. "Your Holiness, please try to relax. You've been under tremendous strain lately after that new Encyclical on celibacy, and the communist attempts to appropriate the Vatican. Try to avoid any rash conclusions. This is a trial, a temptation of the spirit. Who knows why God permits these doubts and anxieties? But even the saints get them, sooner or later, to some degree."

"No, Monsignor, this is no trial sent by God to perfect a pure and innocent soul. It's my own fault, the result of my own ambivalence and dissemblance. I've known for a long time what I should be doing, but kept from doing it out of respect for tradition and a vague commitment to 'gradualism.' But there are limits to how long you can live with a guilty conscience and call it 'fidelity to duty.' Monsignor, take out your notebook, so you can write this down."

The Secretary of State reached mechanically under his cassock and drew out his pen and notebook. His face was properly expressionless as he flipped a few pages and readied his pen for note-taking.

"First of all, have Cardinal Perini draft an Encyclical, infallible and ex cathedra, to the effect that the Pope from this time on is no longer infallible. . ."

Monsignor Baldi stopped writing and looked up to the picture of the Madonna on the wall, as if seeking inspiration.

"Monsignor, have you got that? Take that down, please."

"Your Holiness, if you don't mind my saying so, this is going to be extremely confusing to the simple faithful. . .and even to some of our more learned and sophisticated people. . . An infallible announcement about non-infallibility?"

"It's no more confusing than a non-infallible announcement of infallibility. Write it down."

Monsignor Baldi finished writing the sentence with great deliberation, but then had an afterthought. "Your Holiness, Cardinal Perini will never be able to write an Encyclical like this, I assure you. . ."

"If he can't do it, then get that German theologian, what's his name?. . ."

"Von Stuben."

"He'll do it, I'm sure. And send Perini back to his cathedral."

"Back to Milan?"

"Back to Milan, if he doesn't cooperate."

The Secretary of State wrote this down dutifully. The Pope continued. "Second announcement: I'm retiring."

"Your Holiness--if you don't mind--you're only 62, in good health. . . Don't overreact to these temporary administrative difficulties. Besides, no Pope has retired since the time of. . .of. . ."

". . .Celestine V, in the 13th century, to go to a hermitage. I'm thinking of going to a monastery, myself."

"They never allowed Celestine to remain there. Do you think things will be different with you?"

"That remains to be seen."

The Secretary of State sighed. "So be it. If that's the will of your Holiness, I trust that you would like us to arrange for a convocation of Cardinals to elect--"

"No. There will be no more election by Cardinals." Pope Peter set his jaw. "Instead of election by the College of Cardinals--write this down, too--nominations will first be sought from all the major ecclesiastical regions and provinces, the College of Cardinals will choose seven of these nominees, and primaries and elections will be held under the jurisdiction of the bishops throughout the world to narrow down the choice and finally select one candidate. The bishops will have to work out the details, to see that everything is done properly and above board."

The Secretary of State began to show an unwonted testiness instead of reluctant compliance. "Does the Bishop of Rome realize that as a result of such an

election, an African or Chinese or South American
Marxist could be our next Pope?"

"I realize that. But, by the way, there will be
no more 'Pope.' Give the papal throne to the Musaeo
Nationale Romano. And announce that the head of the
Church will hencefrorth be a 'General Pastor,' elected
every six years."

"'General Pastor'?"

"Yes. And it occurs to me--perhaps you'd better
make this announcement before that other announcement
about non-infallibility."

Monsignor Baldi, in spite of his obvious
opposition to these decsions, could not deny the
prudence of this last directive. "Yes, it's
unfortunate, but some might want to take advantage of
your 'fallibility.'"

"And--one thing more, Monsignor--we're going to
initiate a kind of 'equal opportunity' movement in the
ecclesiastical hierarchy. For the next six or seven
elections, stipulate that the General Pastor must be
not only a non-Italian but a non-European. And you'd
better announce that before the non-infallibility,
too."

"Yes, of course." The Secretary of State fell
silent for a moment, and then he spoke in a calm and
serious voice, as if the implications of this decision
had just begun to sink in. "Your Holiness, I don't
know how to say this but--you're courting danger. Yes,
the Italians are 60% communist now; but you know and I
know that they still want someone who understands the
peculiar nature and needs of the Italian Church in the
Vatican, if someone must be in charge there. They
won't like this at all. We may end up with some
super-efficient American adminstrator. The Italian
people won't stand for that!"

Pope Peter, seeing that his adjutant for so many
years was genuinely worried, tried to reassure him.
"Giuseppe. I appreciate your concern for the Roman
See. But these things had to be done sooner or later.
Why should I leave them to my successor? Call in my
advisors tomorrow so we can begin working out a
suitable timetable."

The papal Secretary of State knelt and kissed the
papal ring, then rose to full stature, paused as if to
make sure that the Pope really did want him to execute
these orders, and made his exit.

"Let's see what results from all this," said Fr. Aloysius. He made a sweeping gesture as if to dissolve the scene we had just witnessed, and closed his eyes again in deep meditation. I did likewise.

We were in the papal palace and began to hear a great din outside--angry shouts, windows breaking. It sounded like a riot. Monsignor Baldi and four cardinals were with the Pope at a conference table, completing transition arrangements. The worried Commander of the Swiss Guard, who was standing at the door, finally walked up to one of the cardinals and spoke to him in a low voice. The cardinal nodded, reached for a portable telephone on the table and pointed to a hookup near the entrance. The Commander installed the apparatus and dialed a number. "Communist Headquarters? This is Commander Talot of the Gendarmeria Pontifica. It's urgent that I speak to the mayor. Is he there? Thank you. . . Excellency, we have a very urgent situation here. You're watching it on TV? No, I didn't know that you hadn't been in contact with the Vatican for ten years. Really, excellency, I don't understand these political matters. We need help desperately. A helicopter? That would help him to an airport. Where to? Just a minute, please." The Commander set down the telephone and hurried over to confer with the cardinal with whom he had spoken previously, then returned. "Can you take him out of Italy? Cardinal Terini suggests that he be taken temporarily to his friend, the Lutheran bishop of Wittenberg. What's his name? Just a minute. I've got it right here. Sterner. Bishop Sterner. You'll make all the arrangements? Fine. We'll appreciate that. Thank you very much."

It was not long before a helicopter arrived at the balcony outside the conference room. But because rocks and other items were being thrown at the helicopter, the Commander motioned the helicopter onto the roof. The Commander, the Monsignor and the cardinals then escorted the last Pope onto the roof, and bade farewell to him as he flew to retirement in Wittenberg.

The vision ended, and I opened my eyes. "It looks like bad news," I said to Fr. Aloysius. "I was hoping that the future would be a time of peace."

"It's sad that it had to happen this way," he repiled, apparently not realizing that he was referring to these events as past rather than as future. "But the transition took place so suddenly that chaos was almost inevitable. The chaos will take a few decades to subside. But after that, things will stabilize somewhat, as you will see. . ."

8. Sister Superior, in the new dispensation

The next scene was a schoolyard, in which I saw a handful of younger children playing on geodesic monkey bars and sliding down surrealistic slides under the jurisdiction of two women. And, in another part of the yard, some older girls and boys were playing a spirited old-fashioned game of softball. At a corner near the school building were standing a slight, blondish woman with a small cross around her neck, and a heavy-set, hirsute man in something like a turtleneck, with a large crucifix suspended from his neck.

Fr. Aloysius explained. "This is a Sister Superior of the Trinitarian Order, speaking to her local bishop."

The woman was speaking. "So I have the dubious distinction of presiding over the demise of the last parochial school in the United States?"

"Yes, that's the way it appears. What is your community going to do now? Have you discussed this matter with the other sisters?"

"Yes, as a matter of fact we've been brainstorming that question for some time now. And we've settled on the real estate business for a start. But our ultimate objective is to get into the construction of condominiums geared to family living. And we're hoping to get your help for that."

The bishop did not seem very enthusiastic about either of these proposals. "Real estate and building? I'm not sure if there are sufficient grounds for a

religious order getting into these areas. I will help
you all I can, of course, but I'm hoping you can come
up with some alternative proposals."

Sister Superior did not have any alternatives in
mind. "Bishop, times have changed. Perhaps no orders
are engaged in these businesses now as their 'mission,'
but why shouldn't they be? When a two-bedroom home
averages $220,000, it's a real work of mercy to supply
shelter for people at reasonable prices."

"First of all," the bishop answered, "I want to
correct an apparent misunderstanding. The fact that
yours would be the first order in this business would
not be a major consideration. You should know that the
Church in this diocese has never been loathe to support
worthwhile projects just because they were innovative.
For instance, my predecessors in this diocese got the
Augustinian nuns started in the nonprofit motel
business, and without the Chancery's help that
restaurant chain of the Poor Clares would never be a
reality now. And I myself gave the green light to the
Daughters of Charity to establish minimum-security
prisons with the help of a government subsidy, and
encouraged your Franciscan counterparts to pioneer in
setting up their marital-compatibility testing bureaus
in this city (for which I received endless criticism
from both secular and ecclesiastical authorities). So
I have no particular prejudice against getting into
uncharted or unpopular areas of endeavor, when there is
good reason for doing so. But, especially with regard
to housing construction, I have my doubts whether the
religious sector of society can really do better than
the secular sector, and. . ."

"Bishop, I don't like to bring this up"--Sister
Superior said this in such a way that it was obvious
she had been waiting for a chance to bring it up for a
long time--"but I know that the Daughters of Charity
had to get help from the Jesuit caucus in the U.S.
Senate to extract permission from you for their prison
project; and the Franciscan nuns made no headway with
you whatsoever with their dating-bureau plans until
they got those Carmelite Fathers who specialize in
psychological counseling to intervene for them. Are
you sure you aren't prejudiced against us because we're
women?"

There, she had finally gotten it out, but the
Bishop was ready to defend himself. "In both of these
cases, I just wanted to make sure that the sisters had
the necessary expertise for--"
"Your Excellency," she interrupted, "we all know
that the construction industry has always been
dominated by men. Let me ask you something: if our
male counterparts in the Franciscans had decided to go
into construction instead of starting communes, or the
male Dominicans had decided on the construction
business instead of specializing in medicine and
law--would you have the same sort of 'doubts'?"
Bishop Ferrera was obviously taken aback at this
suggestion. "Sister, you're unduly sensitive. I judge
each case on its own merits. The cause for my state of
doubt in this case is not sexist considerations but
some very practical problems--like how do you get
investors and finance institutions to back you up when
you've aroused the ire of the whole construction
industry (as you will be doing)? This construction
project is a much more massive venture than starting a
motel or a restaurant. You would like me to sink what
would have to be a major part of diocesan funds into
your construction enterprise. But as far as I can see,
you'll never be able to get sufficient initial capital
behind you to justify support from the diocese. Also,
I must say honestly that I have some questions about
expertise. Do any of the seven sisters in your
community have a background in these areas?"
"A few of us majored in business, finance, or real
estate in college," responded Sister Carla. "But we
can acquire any further 'expertise' we need."
The bell rang to signal the end of the
second-to-last recess forever at Trinity Primary
School, and the bishop glanced at his watch. "I have a
suggestion for you, Sister. Before we get any further
into a discussion of this idea, why don't you test the
budding talents of your community to see if they can
find a buyer for this old school of yours. The income
from this sale should help finance the education of
your community in the ins and outs of real estate,
finance, etc., and to set up a nonprofit real estate
company of your own (which I hope you won't advertise
too vociferously). And then, eventually, if you can
get some 'fat cats' to come up with a major part of the

investment, and if the diocese's projected part in the enterprise is something it can afford, I'll back you up for your debut in the construction industry. However, I advise you to get this construction thing into readiness before my death or retirement, since I can't guarantee how my successor will react to the idea."

"May I ask how old you are now, Bishop?"

"Fifty-five."

"That should give us enough time."

"Provided I don't retire early," cautioned the Bishop. He hopped onto a bicycle which had been leaning next to the fence, and rolled up his pantlegs. As he rode off, Sister Superior said, "Bishop, I didn't mean to accuse you of sexism."

"Don't apologize," he said, "I'm wagering you'll never get sufficient capital to start condominuim-building anyway."

"You're wrong," she yelled after him. "Sister Daphne's father is a multimillionaire philanthropist."

The Bishop circled once on his bike as if to return and say something, but apparently decided to keep his silence, and headed down the street.

As the vision faded, I asked Fr. Aloysius what he thought his own order might be doing in the 21st century. He laughed. "I don't know. Perhaps we might do well as gurus!"

9. The Pentecostalist holdout

As I joined Fr. Aloysius in concentration once more, I saw a large group of men and women around a conference table. A meeting was going on, and some heated debates were apparently taking place.

"This is a meeting of the World Council of Christian Churches," explained Fr. Aloysius. "By this time" (he was speaking in the past tense again), "all the major Christian denominations, with the single exception of the Pentecostal Church, had affiliated with the central church."

"How on earth was this ever achieved?" I asked skeptically. "Was there some miracle you forgot to tell me about?"

"No 'miracle,' except for the extraordinary abdication of power and doctrinal supremacy by the papacy, which you witnessed. It appears that the papal claims had been the main stumbling block all along. As soon as this obstacle was removed, doctrinal and ritual differences began to disappear as if by magic. Certain essentials were finally agreed on--such as commitment to Baptism, celebration of the Lord's Supper, and belief in the divinity of Jesus in some sense--but on many other points compromises were hammered out and had remained viable at least to the time of this meeting."

I still suffered from incredulity. "I just don't believe that the Roman Catholic Church, even <u>sans</u> Pope, could work out satisfactory and stable compromises with such a multiplicity of Christian denominations."

"The Catholic Church had the essential apparatus for adapting itself to all these differences all along, but didn't realize it. This apparatus was the diversity of 'devotions' within the Church, which formerly expressed itself in the rich variety of cults that sprang up with regard to various aspects of Christ or the saints, or various concepts of religious perfection. As a result of the Second Council of the Vatican there was an attempt to diminish this variety and make it more manageable. This initially caused disillusionment and a loss of religious bearings, but in the end it predisposed Catholics to look on other Christian denominations as just different ways of interpreting Christ, religious beliefs, and ritual practices. Most Protestants responded very well to this new openness and flexibility, but the Pentecostals held out, and the present meeting is an attempt to iron out final differences with a noted Pentecostal preacher, the Rev. Floyd Barrington, who has become the representative of the various branches of Pentecostalism. The Pentecostals are not 'strong' on organization, so he is only a titular representative. But it is generally agreed that, if they could reach a meeting of minds with him, the others would follow."

We tuned in on the Reverend Barrington as he was speaking with animation and emotion and some table-thumping: "No, I guess I have never been a compromising type of individual. But I don't reckon that's necessarily a bad quality, especially when it

comes to standing up for the Word of the Lord. Look
what you liberals have done to the Bible with your
'scientific' methods and 'critical' spirit. The Bible
should be at the heart of Christian witness, and hardly
anybody knows what its place is in your churches
nowadays. You want me to join you when you hold almost
every word of the Bible in disrespect? There's no way
I could do that. I think we're wasting our time here."
     An Anglican representative with a very cultured
accent tried to reason with Barrington. "There's
really not that much of a problem, Reverend. It should
be emphasized that your function, perhaps your major
contribution to our organization, would be precisely to
help maintain the integrity of the literal sense of the
Bible. We welcome you to do this, like the Baptists.
It is well known that, for instance, at our last
scriptural conference, the Baptists formed a powerful
bloc with other fundamentalists in insisting on the
importance of returning to the literal meaning of the
Scripture in the original language, and also in
redefining 'literal.' You could join them in helping
to 'keep us on our toes,' so to speak, and preventing
us from getting lost in the wilds of interpretation."
The fundamentalist Baptist representatives nodded and
showed evident satisfaction at these latter remarks.
"Outside of our group," the Anglican continued, "you
are just one individual voice, but in concert with us
you can have a decisive and powerful influence on the
interpretation of Scripture in our times."
     Reverend Barrington seemed unconvinced by this
rhetoric. "Fellows, I'm not made to fight with the
likes of your Scripture scholars and modernist
theologians about the meanings of Greek and Hebrew
words and whether or not the Gospel writers really
wrote the Gospels and so forth. I'm a plain man, and
my religion says, 'keep away from all this stuff--it's
from the devil.' I surely think that if the Lord wanted
Scriptures to be interpreted your way, he would have
said so. But He didn't because He didn't want to
confuse plain folks."
     One of the Baptist ministers who was sitting next
to Barrington intervened in a quiet voice. "Floyd,
it's up to us to stay here and make sure the interests
of plain folks are represented. What have we got to

lose? Nobody's going to make us change our religion.
All we have to do is make sure we work along with other
Christians."

"--and think along with them, too," added the Rev.
Barrington.

A scholarly looking Presbyterian took out his
pocket New Testament and read the following excerpt
from Jesus' prayer at the Last Supper: "Father. . .I
pray that they may be one in us, that the world may
believe that you sent me." He closed his New Testament
and looked at Barrington significantly. "It seems to
me, Reverend, that the Word of the Lord itself is
telling you that this is a good idea."

But Barrington seemed intractable. "But unity
like this?--you fellows are arguing all the time,
taking notes, trying to come to agreement on
everything--you've watered the Lord's Gospel down so
much that you can't even say when someone's wrong
anymore."

The Presbyterian disagreed. "No, we've even had
cases where we had to censure members or expel
individuals because of doctrinal errors--"

"Pragmatic decisions!" said the Pentecostalist.
"The unity you've got now is all man's work, not God's.
You depend on organization and techniques and
negotiations like the politicians do, and you've built
up a tower of Babel just like them. The tower is
standing up now, and it's a nice model of 'unity,' but
the Lord didn't build it, and it could come tumbling
down at any minute. Don't you forget that. Maybe
this Christian unity is a good thing, but only the
Spirit of the Lord can bring it about. I mean, Jesus
will send his Spirit when the time is right, and unite
all Christians, if he wants to. But I don't think it's
time, yet. At least, the Spirit hasn't showed me that
this is to be done, or how to do it. So I just can't
go along with you."

The Reverend Floyd Barrington rose and made it
clear that he was going to leave, although some tried
in vain to get him to remain and reconsider. One
Methodist was heard to say, "Maybe he's right--we've
got one big headache here, trying to make a stew out of
incompatible vegetables." But an idealistic Catholic
universalist countered with "All vegetables are
compatible when properly mixed and proportioned"--a
statement which at least had the virtue of not

reproducing the Methodist's mixed metaphors. Barrington simply offered his apologies very politely and left.

Fr. Aloysius rose and put his hand on my shoulder. "We are near the end of our journey," he said. "You don't need me for the remainder. Concentrate as before. You have learned to follow the currents of the past into the future, and have built up a certain momentum. See now if you can visualize the conclusion of all these events. He began to walk to the door, then turned back and noticed that I was still looking at him. He motioned in a silent but firm way for me to begin concentration, and made his exit. I did as he said.

D. The Great Ecumenical Demonstration

For the last few days delegates from all the major religions in the world had poured into Jos, in the plateau regions of Northern Nigeria, and were walking this morning towards the great amphitheater where the assembly was to be held. It was just after sunrise, and, as they walked down the roads running among cliffs, crevices and valleys, devout Moslems were spreading out prayer mats towards Mecca and alternately raised their hands in supplication and bowed their heads in adoration, without seeming to notice passersby in the least.

This final assembly had originally been billed as a "prayer-meeting," but agnostic religions such as Buddhism objected that this designation as usually employed in Christian circles connoted the idea of a transcendent God, and the more deterministic members such as the Moslems and neo-Marxist Taoists objected to the Christian idea of prayer as implying that man can influence the deity by his petitions--so the delegates finally compromised in calling the meeting a "demonstration," in which the stated purpose was "to make more explicit the implicit unity of all men and to witness to the ability of man to surpass himself through meditation and/or prayer." The delegates had spent the last two days working on the statement of their common Creed, to which these purposes coresponded. The general feeling was that a consensus concerning belief was an indispensable foundation for religious unity. At times it seemed that they never would be able to agree on a statement, but they did finally produce a final formulation which received unanimous assent (although a few delegates were still arguing back and forth about the interpretation of various words and phrases in it).

Some time before the ceremonies were to begin, a large group of delegates gathered on the large center stage. In the midst of Indian yogis and orthodox Hebrews I noticed one gentleman who looked vaguely familiar. On reflection, I realized this was the Rev. Floyd Barrington, bearded now and much older than when I had last seen him. He was talking in a quiet and reserved way to one of the Jewish delegates sitting next to him. The ceremonies began with some massive gymnastic displays in which the gymnasts on the field used large cards of many colors and sizes to create designs simulating symbols or insignia of the world religions. This event was followed by some intra-cultural instrumental music, and chants which were sung alternately by a choir and the participants in the grandstands--all of which I found a little strange to my ears, yet interesting and uplifting. The central segment of the ceremonies was prefaced by the solemn reading of the Credal Statement, which read as follows:

"We believe in the untapped capacities of man to become divine, and the corresponding and mysteriously proportional power of mankind to become one in spirit through a general outpouring of love and compassion which has to the present only begun to flow. We believe this twofold goal, which is ultimately only one single goal, is the central content of all true religions, and that every religion can justify itself only to the extent that it facilitates the achievement of this goal.

"We also accept and ratify the following theological theses:

1) Life and death are not two separate states or conditions, but are inseparable realities and must be seen and experienced together.

2) The gulf between God and man can only be completely bridged when and if man becomes divinized.

3) The truth and distinctiveness of each religion can only appear as it loses its pretensions and mingles on a basis of equality with the other religions.

4) The true unity of God can only be expressed by a multiplicity of interpretations of the divinity.

5) The sins of men are caused by suffering and the most intense and intrinsic sufferings are caused by sin.

6) Sin and suffering are the greatest impediments to the union of man with God or Nature, and man with man; but are also remedied by these latter unions.

7) Only to the extent that a religion promotes social justice and compassion in this life will it render itself worthy of any afterlife.

8) The world and each event and incident in the world are sacraments which, when accepted with the proper dispositions, have the power to transform and divinize every individual man."

After the reading of the creed, there began a series of invocations, which were to be followed afterwards by sermons and elaborately worked-out ecumenical rituals which had been described by the committee which originated them as "combining and interrelating elements of sacrifice and sacrament, nature and transcendence."

A Hindu priest and an orthodox Jewish Rabbi, as representatives of the two oldest streams of major world religions, began the invocation by alternately and eloquently recounting man's struggles over the centuries to find ways to activate the best in himself, and to overcome the alienation of individuals from the natural world and from their fellow men. They went into the specific contributions of Hinduism and Judaism towards these ends, and elaborated on the ways in which these seminal contributions both stimulated and complemented the contributions of others.

As the Hindu delegate was coming to a conclusion, however, his speech began getting slower and slower, and finally trailed off and stopped. Everything was hushed and people began looking significantly at one another. The Rev. Floyd Barrington began embracing everyone around him, and others on the stage near the podium began to follow his lead with embraces and handclasps. The people in the grandstands began to be affected by a festive mood, and some ran down onto the field and began to dance or gesticulate spontaneously. Some were talking excitedly, others were quiet. Some had fallen to the ground, and looked like men trying in vain to regain consciousness. A Buddhist delegate ran onto the field and began greeting and shaking hands with those there, and others followed his lead. And soon it began to affect me, too: a feeling of intoxication, of being so brim-full of happiness that it was almost painful. I had never had anything like a mystical experience before, or what the Rev. Barrington might like to call the "baptism of the spirit," and I found myself unprepared for it, confused and even a little embarrassed at the fact that it was so completely uncaused, irrational and uncontrollable. I had some deep-rooted Freudian suspicions of such things, and I remember myself (I suppose a real mystic might be scandalized at this) "testing" the experience for erotic overtones, even going so far as to consciously conjure a few sexual images, but I found to my surprise that my whole being was so absorbed in this total ecstasy that erotic fantasies seemed dry and uninteresting in comparison. I soon left them behind, and the experience progressed and deepened until it seemed to me that I knew in an instant and with absolute certitude the unity of the human spirit as expressed in a rich diversity of religious modes, and the birth of "God" or the equivalent within the Bethlehem of human consciousness. All words and ritual formulations began to seem to be mere imperfect and halting instruments for expressing that fundamental insight and experience.

At the height of this happening, there was something like a thunderclap, and the attention of all of us became riveted on some words written above us in the sky: "The hour has come when you will worship neither on this mountain nor on any other, but you will worship the Father of all in spirit and in truth." These words were apparently visible to the forefront of everyone in this circular stadium, and the words seemed to be changing in neon-light fashion from one language to another. I remember wondering whether the Buddhist delegates might take exception to the words "Father of all," which could connote a transcendent and personal

God, but they were as engrossed as I was, and exhibited
no apparent reaction. I fixed my eyes on the writing
and continued to watch in a contemplative mood, as did
the others; but then, still feeling embarrassed and
exasperated that I couldn't figure out or
satisfactorily categorize what was going on in me and
apparently in the others, I began what (for want of a
better word) might be called "mental doodling" with the
words in the sky--I played with the words, arranged
them in different configurations, changing their colors
at will. As I went on doing this as a kind of nervous
reaction, I became starkly aware of the truth that I
was the agent behind the scenes creating all the images
that had been arresting my attention in this journey.

With this realization I returned with a kind of
dismal suddenness to "reality." I was back in the
parking lot, sitting in the early afternoon shade of
an apartment building next to the parking lot. People
were passing nearby, but no one seemed to be taking any
notice of me. I arose and looked around, beating some
of the dust off my pants. I spotted my own car a few
aisles away in the crowded lot and headed for it,
vacillating as to whether I should proceed to discuss
this "trip" with Walter, as I had originally planned to
do.

NOTES

1. Erwin Iserloh, in The Theses Were not Posted: Luther between Reform and Reformation, draws on the research of Volz, Aland, Honselmann and others to answer the question of the validity of the "legend" of the posting of the theses. According to Iserloh, Luther's repeated statements and all the evidence indicates that he did not post the Theses on October 31, 1517, but only mailed the Theses to Bishop Allbrecht of Mainz on that day; he also sent letters to three other bishops, and waited for their reactions (which were negative) before publicizing the Theses. This position, which goes against the majority opinion, presents a subdued, low-key depiction of Dr. Martin Luther: not the defiant monk, who is sounding a clarion-call for all decent and thinking Christians to forsake the corrupt Roman Catholic Church; but a conscientious effort by a professor at Wittenberg to call the attention of his superiors to some heresies and abuses prevalent in the 16th century Church, coupled with a vague intention to propose his tentative objections as a matter for public debate (a debate that, unfortunately, never took place).

2. See R.W. Hepburn, Christianity and Paradox (New York: Pegasus, 1966).

3. There was strong opposition in the Church to the teachings of Aristotle, culminating finally in the condemnation of many Thomistic-Aristotelian propositions in 1277.

4. In The Future of Man (New York, 1964)

5. See A Christian-Communist Dialogue (New York: Doubleday, 1968), p.40.

6. Cf. Jn. IV, 4 ff.

7. This sense of faith is also found in Protestantism--e.g. when a Protestant speaks about his belief in the Resurrection as an objective event. But in Catholicism this is the primary sense in which the term is used.

8. Here again, this is not to imply that only Protestants utilize the term in this sense. Catholics sometimes speak of their faith-as-trust, for example,

in the Apostle's Creed where they speak of "believing-in" God, and "believing-in" Jesus Christ and the Holy Spirit. To most Catholics this means more than a belief in the existence of the Trinity. Trust is implied.

9. Some of Kierkegaard's statements would apply to faith$_3$ as well as faith$_2$. For example, the faith of Abraham which is the subject of Kierkegaard's <u>Fear and Trembling</u> is faith$_3$ insofar as it is a direct and absolute trust in God, but also faith$_2$ insofar as it is based on Abraham's vision of a future state of blessedness, guaranteed by God's promises.

10. King tr. (New York: Avon, 1974), p.23.